Fine
WoodWorking

Best Finishing Techniques

From the **Editors of** *Fine Woodworking*

The Taunton Press

THE TAUNTON PRESS, INC.
63 South Main Street, PO Box 5506
Newtown, CT 06470-5506
e-mail: tp@taunton.com

EDITOR: Jessica DiDonato
COPY EDITOR: Diane Sinitsky
INDEXER: Jim Curtis
COVER AND INTERIOR DESIGN: Carol Singer
LAYOUT: Laura Lind Design

Fine Woodworking® is a trademark of The Taunton Press, Inc., registered in the U.S. Patent and Trademark Office.

The following names/manufacturers appearing in *Fine Woodworking's Best Finishing Techniques* are trademarks: Apollo Sprayers®; Behlen™; Benjamin Moore®'s Studio Finishes®; Binks®; Bondo®; Bounty®; Briwax®; Butcher's® Bowling Alley Wax; Chinex®; Earlex®; Elder & Jenks' Capital Ox®; Formby's®; Gemini®; Goddard's™; J. E. Moser®; Johnson® paste wax; Lie-Nielsen®; MagnaMax®; MagnaSand®; MAPA®; Minwax®; Mirka® Abralon®; Mirka Abranet®; Mirka Mirlon Total™; Mohawk® Blendal®; Norton® 3X™; Olympic®; Pore-O-Pac™; Pratt & Lambert®; Purdy®; Qualasole™; Rexson®; SATAjet® 3000; SATAminijet®; Sherwin-Williams®; Solar-Lux™; Stanley®; Syntox™; 3M™ Cubitron™; 3M™ Fre-Cut™ Gold; 3M™ Perfect-It™; 3M™ Regalite™; 3M™ SandBlaster™; 3M™ Scotch-Brite™; TransFast®; TransTint®; Turbinaire®; Tynex®; W. D. Lockwood®; Watco®; Waterlox®; Winsor & Newton™; Wizard Tints™; Wooster® Alpha™; Zar®; Zinsser® SealCoat™

Library of Congress Cataloging-in-Publication Data

Fine woodworking best finishing techniques.
    p. cm.
  ISBN 978-1-60085-366-1
  1. Wood finishing. I. Fine woodworking. II. Title: Best finishing techniques.
  TT325.F529 2011
  684'.08--dc23

Printed in the United States of America
10 9 8 7 6 5 4 3 2 1

ABOUT YOUR SAFETY: Working wood is inherently dangerous. Using hand or power tools improperly or ignoring safety practices can lead to permanent injury or even death. Don't try to perform operations you learn about here (or elsewhere) unless you're certain they are safe for you. If something about an operation doesn't feel right, don't do it. Look for another way. We want you to enjoy the craft, so please keep safety foremost in your mind whenever you're in the shop.

JANUARY 2012

ACKNOWLEDGMENTS

Special thanks to the authors, editors, art directors, copy editors, and other staff members of *Fine Woodworking* who contributed to the development of the articles in this book.

Contents

Introduction

I was attracted to woodworking because I like to build things. I'm guessing it is the same for you. If I loved applying paint or varnish, I would have taken up decorative painting or gone to work at an auto-body shop. That said, I wasn't woodworking very long before I realized that I needed to become a finisher, too.

After putting in months on my first big piece of furniture, a trestle table, I saw it all go south when I applied a coat of brown stain to the maple. I hadn't prepared the surface properly, and the color was a bad choice. Every sanding scratch and every bit of tearout became a dark-brown testament to my incompetence. Rather than try to sand away $1/8$ in. of wood to get the stain to disappear completely, I decided to live with it—for a while anyway. I eventually couldn't live with that table anymore and gave it to a friend!

But you can bet I started reading up on finishing, starting with my favorite magazine, *Fine Woodworking*. Pretty soon I had mastered a few go-to finishes that I could trust like old friends, and once I became an editor here, I learned a few more. Read on, and you'll do the same.

This collection from *Fine Woodworking* represents the best of the best, the most foolproof finishes, handpicked by our editors to create a trustworthy resource you will turn to again and again. You may never love finishing, but you don't have to fear it.

—Asa Christiana
Editor, *Fine Woodworking*

Choosing Sandpaper

SCOTT GIBSON

Few woodworking shops would get far without sandpaper. It's used for everything from flattening rough panels to polishing delicate finishes. Its versatility comes from the variety of available grits, coatings, and backings. Following is a primer on the combinations that work best for the types of sanding you are likely to do.

Manufacturers offer a variety of sophisticated abrasives, backing materials, and adhesives. Sandpaper is engineered for specific uses, depending on the material to be abraded and whether the paper is designed for hand- or machine-sanding.

Some of these new high-performance abrasives have migrated into woodworking from other industries. While they make sanding faster, they also cost more than the old standbys.

For woodworkers, striking a balance between cost and performance amounts to knowing what you are buying and understanding what the abrasive is designed to do. Manufacturers put a variety of abrasives into belts, disks, sheets, rolls, and sanding sponges, and these products come in several price ranges. There is a sandpaper for just about any purpose.

Printed on the back of most sandpaper is information about abrasive type and grit size (see "Pay attention to your grades" on p. 11). You also might find the weight of the backing and the type of glue. The information, however, isn't likely to be all that helpful.

For example, unless you know there are three conventions for grit size (in addition to the generic coarse, medium, and fine found on some inexpensive papers), you might not really know how coarse or fine the sandpaper is. Do you need an A-weight or a C-weight paper for sanding varnish between coats? Knowing the basics of abrasives, backings, and coatings can help you sort through the jumble of trade names and murky product codes.

Abrasives: the sand in sandpaper

Although manufacturers still use a few natural minerals, synthetic abrasives coat most of the sandpaper we buy. The most common abrasives—aluminum oxide, silicon carbide, and ceramics—are synthetic, while garnet and emery (used mostly in metalworking) are the only common abrasives that occur naturally.

Manufacturers have concentrated their research on aluminum oxide and newer ceramic abrasives, designing abrasive grains that are friable or semifriable, meaning they break down to expose fresh cutting edges as the sandpaper wears.

"Friability is an excellent thing," says Chris Minick, a former consulting editor to *Fine Woodworking*. "What it does is rejuvenate the points, so it extends the life of the sandpaper. Second, it gives you a much, much more consistent scratch pattern than you'd get with a nonfriable material."

The minerals make the difference

Abrasive performance is a balance of hardness, sharpness, durability, and friability. Friability is the highly desirable tendency to fracture with wear and expose new, sharp cutting edges. For general use, aluminum oxide seems to present the best compromise, although several other abrasives have specific uses that make them worth keeping in the shop.

ALUMINUM OXIDE: THE SHOP WORKHORSE

Aluminum oxide is the most common abrasive in woodworking sandpaper. It works well on a number of materials, including bare wood, painted surfaces, and metal. In its most basic form, this furnace-produced mineral does not fracture easily. It tends to wear down until it becomes too dull to cut efficiently. More expensive forms are friable or semifriable. A number of companies offer more than one grade of aluminum oxide in sandpaper. More expensive, heat-treated versions of the mineral tend to go into higher-priced product lines, such as Norton®'s 3X™ or 3M™'s SandBlaster™. Generic aluminum oxide, with its familiar brown and black flecks, is used in tandem with hide-glue adhesives on less expensive sandpaper.

SILICON CARBIDE: FOR LEVELING FINISHES

Also a synthetic, silicon carbide is sharper and harder than standard forms of aluminum oxide. It has needlelike grains that resemble shards of broken glass. These hard, sharp grains cut glass, plastic, and metal very well under light pressure, but silicon carbide is not a tough mineral. Its elongated shape shears off easily, making it too friable for bare-wood sanding because the abrasive wears down too quickly, according to manufacturers. It's an excellent choice for smoothing finish between coats and for rubbing out film finishes like lacquer and shellac because it cuts quickly and produces a uniform scratch pattern. Waterproof versions won't degrade when used with water or oil.

Most sandpaper for woodworking has an open coat, meaning that abrasive grains cover between 40% and 70% of the backing. The space between grains gives sawdust a place to go, so the paper doesn't clog as readily. On the other hand, closed-coat sandpaper produces a more uniform scratch pattern, making it a good choice for sanding finishes.

Coatings keep abrasives on and sawdust out

Stearates are no-load coatings that help to prevent clogging when sanding painted surfaces between finish coats or resinous wood like pine. Stearated paper costs more, and it's not really necessary when sanding dry hardwood.

Unlike some of their predecessors, modern stearates are engineered not to interfere with water-based finishes. However, there are

ALUMINA ZIRCONIA AND CERAMICS: THE TOUGH ONES

A tough alloy of aluminum oxide and zirconium oxide, alumina zirconia outlasts aluminum oxide but costs about 20% more. Because its greater durability is most evident under heavy loads, alumina zirconia is used mainly in products for power sanding.

Other high-performance abrasives include ceramic aluminum oxide from 3M (Cubitron™) and a similar mineral from Norton (SG). Ceramics are extremely tough, sharp, and long-wearing—and at least several times as expensive as anything else. They often are blended with other abrasives on premium belts and disks. Norton's 3X random-orbit disks, for example, combine its SG mineral and aluminum oxide. 3M makes disks and belts with both aluminum oxide and Cubitron (they're purple and called Regalite™).

GARNET: THE NATURAL

One of the natural minerals still on the shelves is garnet, a relatively soft substance with a characteristic orange color and without fancy trade names. Garnet is garnet. Although it won't last as long or cut as quickly as aluminum oxide or the ceramics, traditionalists think garnet produces a finer and softer scratch pattern for final sanding. You'll find it in sheets for hand-sanding or for use on an orbital block sander for fine finish work. Garnet is steadily being replaced by newer aluminum oxides—Norton sells less garnet every year, and Mirka® lists no garnet products.

anecdotal reports to the contrary. Jeff Jewitt, a frequent contributor of finishing articles to *Fine Woodworking,* claims good success using 3M's 216U Fre-Cut™ Gold and Mirka's Royal papers, as long as he wipes down the stearate-sanded wood with alcohol. Jewitt says this technique works best on close-grained woods. On open-grained woods such as oak, stray accumulations of stearate can remain in the pores.

Backings also affect performance. Backing paper comes in five common weights—A, C, D, E, and F. A-weight paper is the lightest, used for finer grits. E and F weights are found on disks for heavy grinding. Cloth backings are more durable but not quite as smooth as paper. Cloth comes in J weight, the most flexible, and X, Y, and Z.

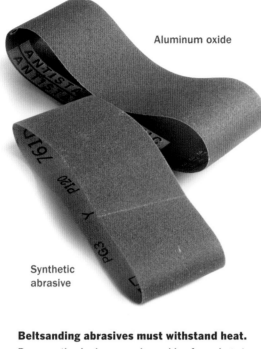

Aluminum oxide

Synthetic abrasive

Beltsanding: look for cloth backing and tough abrasives

Belts for stationary sanding machines come with either a cloth or paper backing. Belts for portable sanders are always cloth, typically X weight. Because of their short length, belts for portable sanders run hot; paper-backed belts wouldn't last long.

Some belts should run only one way

Tape-reinforced butt joints (left) allow belts to run either way, slightly extending their life. Older-style, lap-joined belts (right) run in only one direction.

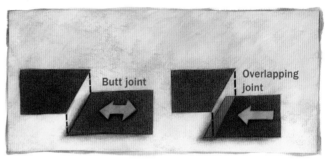

Butt joint

Overlapping joint

Beltsanding abrasives must withstand heat. Because they're heavy and capable of running at high speeds, belt sanders excel at rough sanding. The resulting heat and high pressure require that sanding belts be made from tough material, such as cloth backing, and tough grits like aluminum oxide (top) or the newer synthetic abrasives (bottom).

Turning abrasive grit into sandpaper

Paper or cloth, glue, and abrasive particles are combined to make durable and reliable sandpaper.

4. A pass through a second roller coats the paper with the second, or "size," coat of glue, followed by more baking, then the application of any special coatings or backings.

2. The backing passes between rollers, which apply measured amounts of hide glue, urea-formaldehyde, or phenolic resin as the first, or "make," coat.

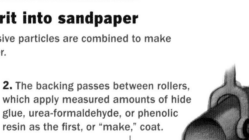

Abrasive

1. Sandpaper starts as a huge roll of cloth or paper backing. The thicker and stiffer the backing, the more aggressive the sandpaper.

3. A static charge of about 20,000 volts applied to the glued-up paper attracts a uniform coat of abrasive. A trip through an oven sets the adhesive.

5. In the final step before packaging, a large press die-cuts the paper to the shape you'll use in your shop.

The standard abrasive for portable-sander belts is aluminum oxide. Manufacturers also offer belts coated with alumina zirconia or ceramic aluminum oxide, which stand up to heat and pressure better than ordinary aluminum oxide.

Open-coat belts don't clog as readily, and belts with P-graded abrasives (see the sidebar "Pay attention to your grades" on p. 11) produce a more consistent finish. Butt-joined belts can run in either direction, so they are easier to put on the machine and last slightly longer.

Bargain hunters should think twice about stocking up on belts for their portable sanders. According to Lisa Beard of Klingspor, the adhesives used to join belts last for only about a year. Belts that have been sitting around too long can pop apart when they're put on the sander. Beard suggests buying no more than will be used in a year.

Holes allow dust collection. Five- and eight-hole disks are intended for specific sanders, while the universal type fits any machine of a matching diameter. A mesh alternative, Mirka's Abranet®, comes in grits from P120 to P600 and is intended for virtually dust-free sanding. It's said to work on hook-and-loop bases, but an adapter is also available.

Five- and eight-hole disks

Universal disks

Mesh disks

Random-orbit sanding: a variety of disks for the finishing touch

Random-orbit sanders can be fine finishing machines or nearly as aggressive as belt sanders. Consequently, disks for these sanders are available in almost the entire range of backing-paper weights, abrasive types, and coatings. Most are perforated for dust collection.

Most random-orbit disks have either five or eight holes that feed dust into the sander's collection system. Some disks come with slots instead of holes and so can fit any base with a matching diameter.

Disks can be had with paper, film, or cloth backings, although C-weight paper seems to be the most common. Cloth backings are more durable but not quite as smooth as paper. The edges of a cloth random-orbit disk don't crease or tear as readily when sanding into a corner, but for most applications, paper works fine. Flatter and more expensive than paper, film backing often is used in automotive finishing. It may be overkill for sanding wood.

Because random-orbit machines don't generate a lot of heat and pressure, they don't take advantage of the properties of premium alumina zirconia or ceramic abrasives to the same degree as do belt sanders. Manufacturers offer these abrasives on random-orbit disks nonetheless, promising longer disk life over standard aluminum-oxide products.

Are high-performance abrasives worth the cost?

Premium belts wear slowly and can be cleaned repeatedly to nearly new condition with a rubber cleaning stick. Likewise, the alumina-zirconia and ceramic random-orbit disks seem to cut faster and wear more slowly than conventional aluminum oxide.

Meaningful tests for abrasive life and efficiency require expensive testing equipment that wasn't used for this study. However, a lot of time was spent sanding wood, and while there is no scientific data, results show that high-performance belts and disks are worth the extra money.

High-performance abrasives really shine when used under high heat and pressure, like machine sanding. High-tech abrasives are not usually worth the money for hand-sanding, especially if most of the hand-sanding you do is limited to light finish work. It's worth paying extra, however, for a waxy coating called stearate. Stearated papers don't clog as quickly and often are used for sanding out finishes.

High-tech abrasives pay for themselves in time saved. Not only do they cut faster, but premium sanding belts and disks also last longer under the heat and pressure of power sanding than do traditional abrasives.

No-load coatings work great for sanding finishes. Shown in the photo at right, uncoated garnet sandpaper (left) clogs quickly, while stearated paper (right) remains clean and effective longer.

For sanding finishes, random-orbit disks are available with stearate coatings. Some even come in extremely fine grits: Mirka's Abralon® pads, useful for polishing high-gloss surfaces such as a rubbed-out finish, are available in grits up to P4000.

Disks are available with either pressure-sensitive-adhesive (PSA) or hook-and-loop backs. Hook-and-loop systems are worth the extra cost because they can be reused. PSA disks stick only once, so if you need to switch between different grits frequently, count on wasting a lot of paper.

Hand-sanding: rolls and sponges add versatility to the old standby, sheets

Power sanders help take the tedium out of sanding, but it's still sometimes less trouble to pick up a sanding block or a scrap of sandpaper and do the job by hand. A bit of sandpaper wrapped around the pad of your thumb quickly takes off milling marks from the inside curve of cove molding, and several suppliers sell detail-sanding blocks that match a range of profiles.

Hand-sanding offers outstanding control when sanding between coats, and a final hand-sanding with the grain can eliminate even a random-orbit sander's minor cross-grain scratches.

You can buy abrasives intended for hand-work in just about any form—sheets, rolls, sponges, and even thin cord on 50-ft. spools. Rolls come in a variety of widths, typically from 1 in. to 6 in., in lengths of 10 ft. and 25 ft., and they can be had with either hook-and-loop or PSA backing. A new class of abrasives, non-wovens, isn't sandpaper in the traditional sense at all. Nonwovens resemble nylon scrubbing pads used in the kitchen and are intended for contoured areas and for rubbing out finishes.

Standard sheets of sandpaper, which measure 9 in. by 11 in., can be found on the

Pay attention to your grades

Manufacturers grade the size of abrasive particles using the CAMI standard, the FEPA standard, and micron grading (identified by the Greek letter µ). The first two are the most common. CAMI is the old American standard. FEPA is the European standard but appears more and more often on products in the United States. It is sometimes identified with a "P" placed in front of the numbers that designate grit size. In both CAMI and FEPA scales, the higher the number, the finer the grit.

FEPA-graded abrasives are more uniform in size than CAMI abrasives and thus leave a more uniform scratch pattern, which is better for fine finishing. CAMI and FEPA grits are roughly the same until they get above 220. Above this grade, FEPA papers are significantly more abrasive than identically numbered CAMI papers.

The most accurate scale, micron grading, sometimes is found on finishing films, more common in auto-body work than in woodworking. Micron-graded papers in very fine grits aren't necessary for most woodworking.

The four major manufacturers whose products are available in the United States use the CAMI and FEPA scales as follows:

- 3M: Both CAMI and FEPA; FEPA papers all carry the P designation. CAMI abrasives are silicon carbide and garnet.
- Klingspor: All FEPA; some marked, some not.
- Mirka: All FEPA and marked.
- Norton: Most FEPA, but unmarked; silicon carbide is CAMI grade.

Hand-sanding requires a range of abrasives on a variety of backings. For hand-sanding as well as machine, aluminum oxide (above) is the first choice for rough work. Garnet (top right) is still loved by many for the last sanding of bare wood because of its soft scratch pattern. Silicon carbide (bottom right) cuts quickly with light pressure and so is great for wet-sanding finishes.

Backings come in many forms. Abrasive cords of varying diameters get into the nooks and crannies of intricate turnings. Sanding sponges conform to molded surfaces to remove machine marks. Abrasive-loaded plastic wool knocks down finishes. Flat paper comes in adhesive-backed rolls for quick sticking to sanding blocks.

shelves of every hardware store. These sheets are effective abrasives and are generally the least expensive option. They can be cut into four equal pieces to fit a sanding block. Sheet sandpaper also can be had with a lightweight cloth backing that's more flexible and more durable than paper. Look for a no-load coating when sanding resinous softwoods or finishes.

Sanding sponges, which combine flexible foam blocks and sandpaper in one, are available in different foam densities and thicknesses, so they can be matched to the application. Firm rectangular blocks get into corners more easily than a folded piece of sandpaper or a conventional sanding block.

Will you find the huge range of modern abrasives in your local hardware store? No, but you are likely to find most of what you use from day to day. And every product mentioned in this chapter is easily found in catalogs or online.

Sharpening and Using Card Scrapers

BRIAN BOGGS

I started using scrapers more than 20 years ago, and I'm still learning some of their nuances. But I'm convinced they are essential tools for woodworkers. Card scrapers are ideal for lightly cleaning up areas of torn or gnarly wood that no other tool can deal with. This is not to say that scrapers cut better than planes; they seldom do. On really difficult grain, though, a scraper can finish a surface where almost any smoothing plane will need follow-up work.

Scrapers range in thickness from 0.016 in. (0.4 mm) to 0.042 in. (1 mm). I prefer to use 0.032-in. (0.8-mm) scrapers. The 0.020-in. (0.5-mm) and thinner scrapers flex nicely to smooth out hollows, but they make it harder to maintain a flat surface. With thick scrapers, it is easy to gouge a groove in the wood with the corners, but for heavier work, their stiffness is a virtue.

How a card scraper works

Scrapers and planes both attempt to do the same thing: cut wood without tearing the surface (see the drawings on p. 14). Planes do this with the edge of a sharp blade and a separate part called a chipbreaker. Scrapers cut with a burr edge, and the face of the scraper acts as the chipbreaker.

As the shaving forms, it immediately encounters the near vertical face of the scraper. Before the shaving can lift off the workpiece, it is compressed between the uncut wood

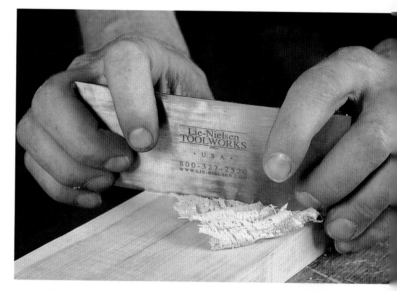

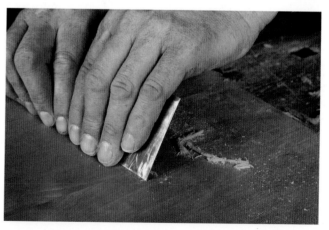

A well-tuned scraper. With polished edges and a small burr, it takes only a light push (top) to get clean shavings off almost any wood surface. To remove marks from the previous pass, pull the scraper with the blade angled toward you (bottom) to produce light shavings and, in turn, a flawless surface.

Scraper vs. plane

Both the scraper and the plane blade slice wood and then compress the shaving before it can lift and cause tearout. The scraper compresses the shaving while it is still short, so it is less prone to cause tearout on difficult woods.

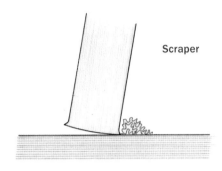

Scraper

The face of a scraper acts as the compression point and is just behind the burr's cutting point.

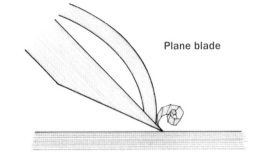

Plane blade

On a plane, the chipbreaker acts as the compression point, which is considerably farther from the cutting point than on a scraper.

ahead of the tool and the face of the scraper. The angle of the face of the scraper determines how compressive the force is. It also determines how deeply the burr will bite into the wood. Therefore, as the scraper is angled forward, it takes a more aggressive cut yet works extra hard to compress the larger shaving and minimize tearout. The downside is that the extra downward force actually crushes the pores as the scraper moves along, leaving a slightly fuzzy surface behind. The solution is to follow with a lighter cut, made with the scraper more upright, which will exert less downward force and leave a cleaner surface. A good way to maintain this higher angle and take a lighter cut is by pulling the scraper toward you.

The most common mistake when using a card scraper is to try to remove too much material. Beginners tend to create an enormous burr on the scraper and then angle the blade forward, hogging off vast shavings. Not surprisingly, their thumbs get hot from the friction, and they find it difficult to maintain the flat plane of the surface of the workpiece.

You can use all four edges of a card scraper, so as soon as you feel the blade getting warm, turn it over and use another edge. The burr will last longer if it is kept from overheating.

Preparing a scraper

Sharpening card scrapers is one of the tasks that frustrates even experienced woodworkers, but there are a couple of jigs that get rid of the guesswork.

Most if not all scrapers need a lot of honing when new. Cheaper scrapers need initial work on a medium (325-grit) stone, but a fine (600-grit) stone is good for better scrapers. Just put all of your fingers right over the edge and hone away until the sides and edges of the scraper are smooth and meet at 90°. Now it's time to form the four cutting burrs. Lay the scraper on a piece of wood about 1¾ in. from the edge. With an oiled burnishing rod resting on and at about a 45° angle to the edges of the scraper and the wood, stroke the scraper a couple of times. This stretches out the corner of the scraper so that a longer burr can be turned.

Hone the sides of the scraper. Polish the sides of the scraper on a fine diamond plate or sharpening stone.

Guide block for sharpening

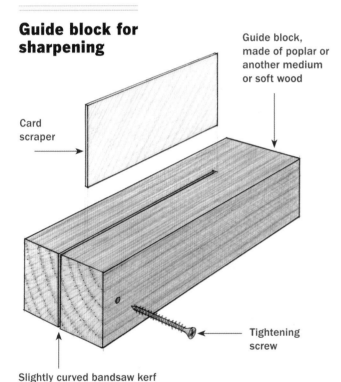

Card scraper

Guide block, made of poplar or another medium or soft wood

Tightening screw

Slightly curved bandsaw kerf

Hone the edges. A guide block helps hone the edges of the scraper 90° to the sides. The scraper should fit loosely enough that it can be pushed onto the sharpening stone.

The burr on a well-tuned scraper is so small that it's hard to tell what angle it actually is, but it appears to be less than the 5° normally recommended. To help create the perfect burr on a scraper, use a wooden guide block, which also is used for honing (see the right photo above). Place the scraper in the guide block so that the top edge protrudes between $\frac{1}{32}$ in. and $\frac{1}{16}$ in. (see the drawing on p. 16). With the guide block locked in a vise, slide the burnishing rod across an edge of the scraper with the rod angled forward so that it rolls the burr off the edge.

With a well-honed scraper edge, the weight of your hand and forearm should generate enough pressure to turn the burr. The rod has only a small area in contact with the scraper, which translates into a lot of pressure per square inch. The more passes

Creating a burr

1. Rest the rod on the corner of the scraper to maintain a consistent angle.

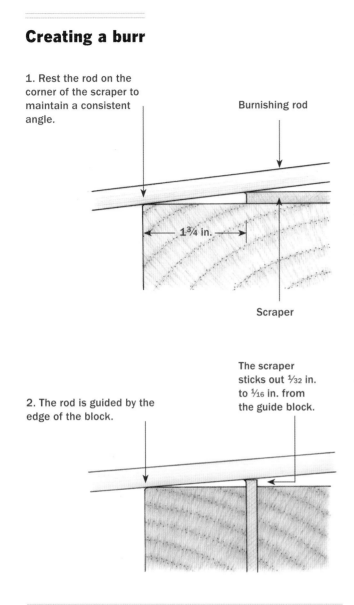

Burnishing rod

1¾ in.

Scraper

2. The rod is guided by the edge of the block.

The scraper sticks out ⅛₂ in. to ⅛₆ in. from the guide block.

Stretch the edge. Push the burnisher along the side of the scraper to draw out a burr.

Roll the burr. With the scraper in the guide block, slide the burnisher at a 45° angle to roll the burr off the edge. It should take only one or two passes.

you take, the more you will roll the burr, thus changing the cutting angle, so try to get the job done with one or two passes.

Renewing a scraper

You can repeat the stretching and rolling steps two to six times without rehoning, depending on the type of wood and the amount of material you are removing. Eventually, the edges of the scraper will become hardened from the burnisher, preventing a new burr from being rolled. Unlike a new scraper, before this used scraper can be rehoned, the work-hardened metal must be filed away. Lay a single-cut bastard file on the bench and stroke the blade over it, perpendicular to the file. You'll feel the file start to cut easily as soon as the work-hardened surface of the scraper is removed.

To remove the file marks and to square the edge, place the scraper in the wooden guide block. Apply even pressure on both the blade and the block to keep the scraper square to the diamond plate (see the top right photo on p. 15). As you do this, keep checking the edge until it develops a uniform shine. Remove the scraper from the block, and repeat the face honing with light pressure until the wire edge is removed. Now you can stretch and roll new burrs using the burnishing tool.

It may take you a few tries before mastering your card scrapers, but stay with it. You will be rewarded with greater efficiency and a more enjoyable finishing process on all your projects.

The burnishing tool is crucial

As important as anything else in scraper sharpening is the condition of the burnishing rod. It needs to be very hard steel that is polished and scratch-free. You can round the edges and polish an old triangular file, but Lee Valley makes a good teardrop-shaped burnishing rod. The slightest nick in the rod will tear off a burr instead of putting one on, so protect your burnisher and treat it as you would your best chisel.

You can also use the shank of a solid carbide router bit with good results. You can either use it with the guide block described at left or make a jig and insert the bit into the angled hole (see the photo below). Because the bit should be oiled when used as a burnisher, it is best to choose an old bit or remove all of the oil before using it in a router again.

An alternative jig for rolling a burr. A carbide router bit is placed in a hole angled down 2° to 5°. The scraper is pulled through a bandsawn kerf across the bit, creating a burr on the scraper.

The Best Brushes

MARK SCHOFIELD

Many woodworkers use only one finishing tool—a cloth. That is a shame because applying a finish with a brush has many advantages: You build up a protective finish much faster; you can use waterborne finishes, which are very hard to wipe; and you waste far less finish than with a spray gun and don't need a special spray booth.

One obstacle to getting started, though, is the vast amount of brushes for sale in hardware stores, home centers, and online. Brushes come in all sizes and shapes, at every point on the price scale, and with different types of bristles (some with no bristles at all). You want to apply a perfect finish to your just-completed project, but should you spend $50 on a brush or will a $10 one work just as well?

A brush is simply a tool for spreading finish on a surface. But like all tools, there are specialist versions for different products and situations, and to a great extent price does determine quality. I'll explain what to look for in a quality brush, why you will get better results using one, and how to keep your brushes working well for many years. I'll also tell you what brushes work best with different types of finish, and suggest a selection that won't break the budget. You'll be surprised at how easy brushing can be when you have the right brush.

Choosing your first brush

Start out finishing with a 2-in. brush. A brush of this size is small enough to learn on but large enough to finish most surfaces up to small tabletops. Because most brushes are designed to apply paint, they are stiffer than is ideal for applying most clear finishes. Look for a brush that feels relatively flexible

Practice and the right brush make perfect. A 2-in.-wide flat brush with a square end is a good place to start as it will let you develop your brushing skills (top). An angled-sash brush is designed to handle areas of different widths as well as corners and tight spots (center). Get a size between 1½ in. and 2½ in. Once you're comfortable brushing and you're ready to tackle a large surface, buy a round or oval brush (bottom). Their extra capacity means fewer trips to reload the brush.

Square end

Angled sash

Oval

Two ways to create a chisel profile

Brushes work better with a pointed end, but there is a good way and a bad way to form it.

Trimming the ends removes the flagging from the edges.

Shaping the bundle leaves the flagging intact.

Flat bottom
POOR QUALITY

Shaped bottom
GOOD QUALITY

TIP Buy quality, not quantity. A starter pack of brushes is usually a false economy. The quality will be so-so, and you'll probably use only one size regularly. Spend the same amount on one quality brush from a company that specializes in making them. Good choices include Elder & Jenks (www.elderandjenks .com), Purdy® (www.purdycorp.com), and Wooster® (www.woosterbrush.com).

Taklon is the exception to the brush-and-finish-matching rule

One synthetic filament, Taklon, works for both solvent- and water-based finishes. The filaments are extremely fine and leave virtually no brush marks, but their flexibility makes them suitable only for thinned finishes and they can't deliver as much finish per stroke. A good way to get a really smooth final coat for fast-drying finishes like lacquer or shellac is to thin them by at least 50% and use a Taklon brush to lay down a coat almost devoid of brush marks.

Water-based finishes also dry fast but can't be thinned as much as shellac and lacquer. To get around this problem, you can buy slightly stiffer Taklon brushes made especially for these finishes. Homestead Finishing Products (www.homesteadfinishingproducts.com) sells one for $25. Some Taklon brushes have a glue size applied that keeps the bristles stiff for packaging and transport. Before first use, submerge them in warm water or alcohol to remove the size.

Thicker version for water-based finishes. The double row of filaments can handle thicker water-based finishes.

Brushing the last coat. Taklon brushes are ideal for the last, thinned coat of finish. But there is a specially made Taklon brush (top right) for water-based finishes that can't be thinned as much.

Perfectly smooth final coat. Taklon does an incredible job laying down a thin, smooth coat of solvent-based finish.

and has filaments around ½ in. longer than the brush is wide. Shorter filaments don't have enough flexibility. Buy a natural-bristle brush for solvent-based finish, or a synthetic-filament brush for water-based finish.

Natural hair or bristle brush

Despite some manufacturers' claims, brushes with synthetic filaments can't match a natural-filament brush when applying a solvent-based finish. Most woodworkers refer to a brush's bristles rather than its filaments, but that is rather like calling all cheese Cheddar. Bristle refers only to hog bristle, also known as china bristle because that is where nearly all of it comes from. Sold to brush makers for $8 to $12 per pound, bristle is the work-horse among natural-filament brushes.

Split ends are good

Brush makers split, or flag, the tips of both natural and man-made filaments to combine stiffness with the ability to leave a smooth finish.

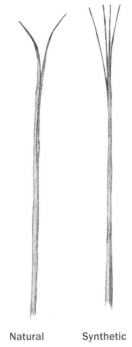

Natural   Synthetic

A good start. Your first brush should be made from hog (china) bristle. The black or beige color of the bristle makes no difference, and you can get a fine 2-in. brush for less than $15.

Top of the line. The Cadillac of solvent brushes is made from pure ox hair. Very fine and soft, it will lay down a coat of varnish with almost no brush marks but costs at least $40 for a 2-in. brush.

Nice compromise. An ox hair/bristle blend works very well. It can't quite match the surface left by pure ox hair, but this won't matter if you are rubbing out the finish. Expect to pay $20 to $25 for a 2-in. brush.

The other natural filament you're likely to find in brushes is European ox hair, which comes from these animals' ears. Slightly less stiff than hog bristle, it is also softer and, at $80 per pound, much more expensive. You can buy ox hair/bristle blend brushes such as Elder & Jenks' Capital Ox® (about $20, www.elderandjenks.com), or you can buy a pure ox-hair brush from Tools for Working Wood (about $40, www.toolsforworking-wood.com). Once you get the feel for brushing a finish, either type of brush is well worth buying if you are using solvent-based varnish.

Your grandfather may have sworn by his badger-hair brush, and some catalogs offer "badger-style" brushes. However, genuine badger hair costs around $400 per pound,

Go natural with these finishes. Natural-hair bristles work best when applying a solvent-based finish.

Synthetic filaments for water-based finishes. Brushes made from nylon, polyester, or a blend of the two work best with waterborne finishes.

Look for fine filaments. Two good choices are Purdy's Syntox™ brushes (top) and Wooster's Alpha™ line (bottom).

All-purpose? Not really. Most synthetic-filament brushes are designed to apply latex paint and are too stiff and coarse to be ideal for clear finishes.

so it is likely that the brush is really hog bristle with a black streak painted on the bristles to resemble badger hair. Read the fine print closely.

Synthetic-filament brushes

When hair and bristle hit water, they swell and go limp. This makes them unsuitable for water-based finishes.

When latex paints were introduced, brush manufacturers had to create suitable brushes, and now the majority of brushes in stores are designed for latex paint. They have synthetic filaments: nylon, polyester, or a blend of the two. Brand names include Chinex® and Tynex®, both nylon, and Orel, made from polyester. Polyester is the stiffer of the two filaments and is probably better just for paint, but even most nylon brushes are too coarse to be able to lay down an even coat of clear finish. Instead, focus on the thinness of the filaments.

Wet the brush first. Before dipping the brush in finish, wet the filaments in a solvent compatible with the finish. This will coat the filaments with solvent and make cleaning the brush easier after you've finished with it.

Dip a toe in. Only submerge about a third of the filaments in finish. If you go deeper, it is harder to apply an even coat. Also, finish will tend to pool in the bottom of the brush and then run down the ferrule when brushing vertical surfaces.

Clean in three steps. Give brushes used for lacquer and shellac a dip in lacquer thinner or denatured alcohol, a good shake, and time to dry.

Clean a new brush before you begin

So you're anxious to see how your new brush works. Before you dip it in the finish, though, there are a couple of steps to take. First, even the best brush may have one or two loose filaments (inexpensive brushes will have many), so rather than pick hairs out of a wet finish, bend the filaments back and forth with your hand a few times, pulling gently on them. Hold the tip up to the light, and remove any filaments protruding above the rest. Now dip the brush into a solvent that matches the finish you'll be using and then squeeze out the solvent onto a paper towel. This coats the filaments with solvent and makes cleaning the brush much easier when you've finished using it.

In use, don't overload the brush with finish. If you are brushing vertical surfaces, periodically squeeze out as much finish as possible back into the can. These steps will

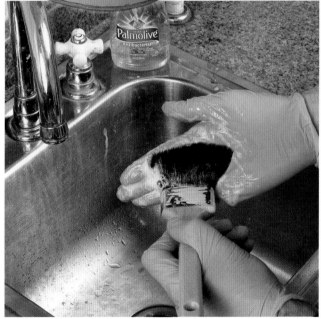

Easy cleanup. All you need is hot water and dish soap to remove water-based finishes from brushes.

Oil-based finishes are hardest to clean. Be prepared to spend a little time cleaning your brush after working with these finishes.

Let it soak between coats. If brushes are going to be reused within 24 hours, ones containing an oil-based finish can be suspended in mineral spirits. Use a kebab skewer through the handle to avoid bending the bristles.

prevent finish from pooling around the base of the filaments and flowing all over the ferrule or running down the handle.

Cleaning your brush after finishing

A 75¢ foam brush is disposable but a $40 ox-hair brush is not. Take time to clean a good brush thoroughly each time you are done with it, and you'll be rewarded with many years of flawless service.

Shellac, lacquer, and water-based finishes clean up easily

Brushes used for lacquer and shellac don't need to be cleaned thoroughly. Give the brush a swish in lacquer thinner or denatured alcohol, shake it out, and let it dry hard. When you need it again, just stand it in solvent. It will be soft and ready to use within 30 minutes.

Use hot water and dish soap to remove water-based finishes from brushes. Lather, rinse, and repeat two or three times.

Oil-based finishes are hardest to clean

You don't need to clean the brush if you plan to use it again within 24 hours. Instead, suspend it in mineral spirits that

Solvent, then soap. Rinse the brush two or three times in mineral spirits, then remove the solvent on newspaper before cleaning the brush with hot water and soap.

have previously been used for cleaning a brush. Keep the tips of the filaments off the bottom of the container so they don't get bent or contaminated with residue.

When you're done with the brush, rinse it a couple of times in used mineral spirits, then pure mineral spirits, removing the bulk of the solvent on newspaper each time. Next, rinse the brush in hot, soapy water several times before giving it a final cleaning using either citrus cleaner or household ammonia. If you can't smell any mineral spirits on the filaments, the brush is clean. Wrap it in paper and store.

Final cleaning. To remove any last traces of mineral spirits, rinse the brush in either a citrus cleaner or household ammonia.

Ready for next time. To let any moisture escape and at the same time keep out dust, wrap the brush in brown paper or the original cardboard wrapper.

TIP After you have cleaned a brush, pour the contaminated mineral spirits into a sealable container. After a few weeks, the residue will sink to the bottom of the container, and you can pour off clean mineral spirits for reuse.

Spray-Gun Choices

MITCHELL KOHANEK

When professional finishers talk about an "off-the-gun finish," they are describing a finish so smooth that it doesn't require sanding. Achieving this state of finishing perfection requires practice and knowledge of finishes, but, above all, the right equipment.

If you've been thinking about making the leap into spray finishing and have started to research equipment, it might seem that the choices are endless. In fact, the basic technologies are not that complicated, and they may be a lot easier to understand than some of those fancy dovetail jigs!

The two main types of spray guns are those powered by a turbine and those that run off an air compressor. I limited my search to guns that can get reasonable results when spraying a water-based finish, as most woodworkers don't own explosion-proof spray booths and thus are not set up to spray solvent-based finishes (see "Spraying water-based finishes safely" on p. 33). Also, water-based finishes are among the most difficult to atomize, so if your gun can spray them well, it should be able to handle most solvent finishes. This requirement ruled out the $100 hardware-store spray guns, but I discovered that furniture makers can get a beautiful finish for around $500—and spend far more for inferior results. This chapter will help you zero in on the system that is right for you.

Choose a low-pressure gun

High-volume, low-pressure (HVLP) spray guns use enough air to atomize the fluid into small, even-sized particles but not so much that the spray bounces off the target.

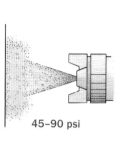

45–90 psi

10 psi

High-pressure guns have low efficiency. Old-fashioned high-pressure spray guns atomized the finish into a fine mist. This gave a good finish, but only about 25% of the liquid ended up on the workpiece.

Low-pressure guns are highly effective. Sophisticated HVLP guns also give good atomization, but their lower pressure means that far more of the finish ends up on the workpiece.

What happens when you mix air and finish

To understand spraying, you need to grasp two conflicting concepts: atomization and transfer efficiency. Atomization is forcing a liquid to become small, round particles; the smaller the particle, the better the look of the coating. Large particles can produce an effect known as "orange peel." There are many reasons for this pebbly look, but poor atomization is one of the most common.

Early spray guns used air at high pressure (45 to 90 pounds per square inch, or psi) at the tip of the gun to blast the liquid finish into a fine mist of tiny particles. This produced a beautiful, smooth finish, but only about 25% of the liquid ended up on the object being sprayed. The rest missed the target or bounced off because of the high air pressure. To improve on this 25% transfer efficiency, high-volume, low-pressure

TIP Steer clear of budget-priced HVLP spray guns. They cannot properly atomize heavy water-based finishes and spray a stream of large droplets, leaving a rough finish.

(HVLP) guns were developed. HVLP technology reduces to a maximum of 10 psi the amount of air needed to atomize liquid. This increases the transfer efficiency to between 65% and 90%, but it comes at a price: You spray more slowly and the quality of atomization varies among the various systems.

This conflict between optimum atomization and maximum transfer efficiency is particularly acute with water-based finishes, which are generally thicker and harder to atomize than traditional solvent-based ones. That's why budget-priced HVLP guns generally cannot achieve the atomization needed for a smooth water-based finish. However, water-based finishes continue to be improved to make them easier to spray.

Turbine guns

Turbines are rated by their number of fans (or stages), ranging from two to five. The higher the number, the greater the volume and the pressure of air they can pump out. All turbines are considered HVLP because they don't shoot more than 10 psi at the tip of the gun. A good-quality three-stage turbine with around 6 psi will spray the majority of water-based finishes; a four-stage model with 8 psi gives you the flexibility to spray thicker water-based finishes and paints, and to spray faster, but it costs more.

A newcomer in the turbine market is the two-stage Earlex® HVLP spray station. Reasonably priced, it comes as a handy little unit, and had no trouble spraying water-based finishes, allowing them to flow out into a smooth coating.

Turbine technology demands larger, heavier guns and hoses than compressed-air guns, so consider the ergonomics of each type

Ideal for a small shop. Compact and inexpensive, the Earlex spray station is a good alternative to brushes and rags.

A compressor-powered spray system

A midsize compressor is enough for many HVLP spray guns, but you also will need a hose, a filter, and a pressure gauge.

FILTER

Compressed air leaving the tank contains small amounts of water, oil, and other contaminants. If allowed to pass through your gun, they create unpleasant finishing defects. You need to invest in some kind of filter. Disposable filters attached between the gun and the air hose are worthwhile if you only spray occasionally (www.pacificaircompressors.com). The crystals inside turn from blue to mauve as they become saturated (below). If you intend to spray regularly, invest in a coalescing filter (right) made up of a series of filters you change every six to 12 months depending on the amount of use.

CHECK THE PRESSURE AT THE GUN

Long or small hoses cause the air pressure to drop between compressor and gun. To measure the exact air pressure at the gun, attach a pressure gauge or regulator.

before you buy. The main advantage of turbines is that they come as complete spray systems—air source, hoses, and gun—so their instructions are far more comprehensive than stand-alone compressed-air guns.

I tested three- and four-stage turbines from Apollo Sprayers® and Turbinaire®, two leading manufacturers in this category, and could see little difference between the finishes. All the sample boards had slight orange peel and needed a light sanding before the next coat.

Compressed-air guns

If you already have compressed air in your shop, you probably will opt for a compressor-driven gun. The capacity of the compressor, in terms of how much air it can deliver in cubic feet per minute (cfm) at what psi, will determine which gun is compatible. A 2- to 5-hp, 20- to 25-gal. midsize model is adequate for many guns, and I even used a SATAminijet® successfully with a portable 1.6-hp, 4.5-gal. compressor. The compressor ran continuously, but

it never affected the spray pattern. An advantage of compressor-driven guns is that they generally have a greater maximum pressure at the tip than a turbine gun. This means you can increase the psi to achieve better atomization of thicker finishes but at the cost of lower transfer efficiency. Using a midsize compressor, I've had good results from HVLP guns made by Binks®, Kremlin, Rexson®, and SATA®, among others.

Compressed-air guns also come in an LVLP (low-volume, low-pressure) category. Because they use less air, you can get by with a smaller compressor, but you generally pay the price in slower speeds. Better guns are constantly being developed, however. In the spray test, all the compressed-air guns received an A grade for producing excellent off-the-gun finishes.

You'll need the right supply hose to connect the compressor to the gun. The smaller the internal diameter (ID) of the hose and the greater its length, the more the pressure will drop between the compressor and the gun. It is recommended that an air hose with

Three containers for holding finish

Whether you choose a turbine or compressed-air system, you have a choice of where the finish is contained before it enters the gun.

SUCTION-CUP GUN

The most common type of spray gun has the finish in a cup underneath. The fluid can be sucked into the gun or, as in this case, the cup can be pressurized by a plastic tube from the gun. This type tends to spit finish when it runs out.

The tube pressurizes the container with air.

GRAVITY-FEED GUN

With the container above the gun, the finish flows into the gun by gravity alone. The gun can feel top-heavy but will stop cleanly when the cup is empty.

Gravity causes finish to flow into the gun.

Easy cleanup. 3M makes gravity-feed containers that have a disposable lining.

PRESSURE POT

Without a cup of fluid attached to it, a spray gun is much more maneuverable and can access tight spaces. Small pressure pots can be carried or hung from a belt.

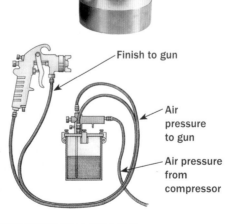

Finish to gun

Air pressure to gun

Air pressure from compressor

Pressurize the can. When using a pressure pot, the finish can either be poured into the pot, or the can of finish can be placed in the pressure pot, which reduces cleanup.

a $\frac{5}{16}$-in. ID be limited to no more than 20 ft., a $\frac{3}{8}$-in. ID hose to 50 ft., and a $\frac{1}{2}$-in. ID hose to 100 ft. On many occasions the wrong hose size is to blame for a poor finish, not the gun or the coating. A good way to make sure that you have sufficient pressure is to attach a pressure gauge at the base of the gun. Alternatively, some guns such as the SATAjet® 3000 come with a built-in digital readout in the handle.

Different ways to contain the finish

With either a turbine or compressed-air system, the most common container used to hold finish before it enters the gun is a cup located underneath it (see the sidebar on p. 31). However, when the fluid level gets low, the gun starts to spit the finish.

If you have the cup on top of the gun (gravity feed), the gun simply stops spraying when the fluid runs out. One way around this is to adapt a disposable 3M cup system that comes in three sizes. Called PPS (paint preparation system), these cups are quickly interchangeable, so you can shoot your dye, sealer, and topcoat from different cups with minimal cleaning (www.homesteadfinish-ingproducts.com; www.jamestowndistribu-tors.com). The system allows you to use the gun in any position, even upside down.

Better still is to remove the cup entirely and have a hose leading back to a pressurized container (pressure pot). No longer will the cup on your gun bump into the project as you try to spray the inside of cabinets. Pressure pots also allow you to spray larger amounts of coatings without stopping to refill. A 1- or 2-qt. pot is common, while many of the cups hold a pint or less. Smaller pots can hang from your belt, while larger ones are on wheels.

A nice feature of some pots is that you can place the can of finish directly in the pot.

When you are done spraying, remove the pressure in the pot and open the lid; place a rag over the gun's air cap, squeeze the trigger, and force the air back down through the fluid tube. Known as back flushing, this will push the finish out of the fluid hose and into the pressure pot.

Not much additional air power is needed as pressure pots normally operate at 2 to 5 psi, but by increasing the pressure you can atomize heavier finishes such as water-based types. You certainly should be able to supply a pressure pot and an LVLP gun using a midsize compressor. Turbines are not designed to divert their air via a pressure pot, so a separate source of compressed air is needed.

Making sense of this information

The first step is to decide if turbines or compressed-air guns are right for you. You may decide it's worth paying for a turbine system to get the simplicity of a whole system designed to work together. I recommend you save money and only go for a three-stage turbine. In my testing, I didn't see better results with a four-stager.

If you have a compressor, check its capacity and then have a retailer match it to a suitable gun. If you intend to spray only small projects, or a large piece in sections, you can team a small compressor with a low-air-consumption HVLP or LVLP gun such as the SATAminijet IV or Kremlin's M22 HTIG LVLP gun. If large tabletops are on your list of things to spray, use at least a midsize compressor and invest in a pressure pot. Whatever gun you choose, practice spraying on $\frac{1}{4}$-in.-thick plywood. Sooner than you think, you, too, will achieve an off-the-gun finish. Good luck and have fun.

Spraying water-based finishes safely

Assuming that most of your spraying will be done in the garage, you'll want to set up a temporary spray booth. A good design is shown here. Wherever you decide to spray, you will need a method of drawing in fresh air and directing the fumes and overspray outside. Some novice sprayers assume that just because a water-based finish can be sprayed without the risk of an explosion, it is safe to breathe. Even though some solvents have been taken out and replaced with water, these finishes still contain serious chemicals and solids—and you need to protect yourself. Always wear a cartridge-style respirator rated for organic vapors whenever you are spraying.

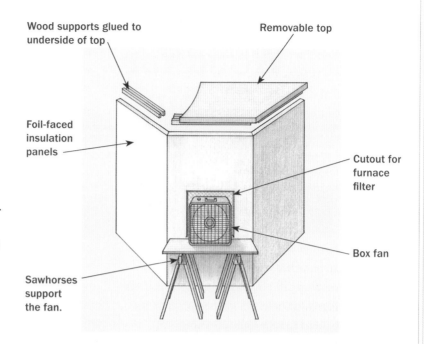

Wood supports glued to underside of top

Removable top

Foil-faced insulation panels

Cutout for furnace filter

Box fan

Sawhorses support the fan.

This spray booth is made from three foil-faced rigid-foam insulation panels joined with duct tape. A removable top made from rigid-foam insulation helps keep the booth stable. A box fan draws air from the booth through a hole in the central panel. The hole is covered with a furnace filter.

TOP VIEW OF A SPRAY BOOTH SET UP INSIDE A GARAGE

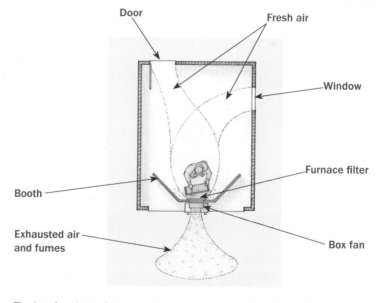

Door

Fresh air

Window

Booth

Furnace filter

Exhausted air and fumes

Box fan

The box fan draws fumes and overspray outside. To achieve this, there must be a source of fresh air such as a door or window behind the operator.

Preparing Wood for Finishing

ARI TUCKMAN

Perhaps more than most woodworking topics, debates on surface preparation elicit strong opinions. No doubt handplaning takes more finesse and practice than sanding, and pushing out fluffy shavings with a card scraper takes practice. But which method produces the best surface for applying a finish?

When I started woodworking, I took a class on surface preparation. I remember the awe I felt as the instructor, with a few swipes of a well-worn Stanley® No. 4 handplane, revealed the fire inside a piece of cherry—a staggering contrast to the slightly chalky, sanded surfaces I was used to. I was sold and quickly bought a used No. 6—in retrospect, a bit overenthusiastic for a starter plane.

Since then, I've added some better-quality handplanes and card scrapers. I have worked at mastering these techniques and learned how

Three ways to prep the surface. Few woodworkers enjoy the noise and dust of power-sanding, but it takes little skill to get boards that are uniformly smooth (top left). It takes practice to properly tune and use a card scraper so that it produces thin curls of wood and little dust (bottom left). Handplaning is traditionally viewed as the best method of surface preparation, but few woodworkers can achieve a flawless surface this way (right).

to sharpen well, if not quickly. Thinking that I had discovered the secret to surface preparation, I was perplexed to see well-known woodworkers who sanded their work after handplaning and scraping and still produced pieces that looked great after a finish was applied. Curious, I decided to test the three surfacing methods as objectively as I could.

A disclaimer is relevant at this point. I am a pretty good woodworker, but I am far from a master. This is not a test of each technique under laboratory conditions but rather under conditions found in a typical home shop where a balance is struck between quality of work and speed.

Does wood species determine the finishing method?

To test whether the type of wood made a difference, I used cherry as a sample of a close-grained wood and a particularly open-grained piece of mahogany. To minimize variation, I cut each board into three sections, one per method. Each board was jointed flat for a uniform starting position, using fresh jointer knives to minimize tearout and the pounding that dull blades can cause.

For the sanding test, I used a random-orbit sander starting with P120 grit followed by P150, P180, and P220 grits, vacuuming the surface after each. I then hand-sanded the board with the grain, using P220 grit. Finally, using a paintbrush to loosen as much dust as possible, I vacuumed the surface again.

I moved on to the scraper for the next board, choosing a 0.4-mm card scraper from Lee Valley, rounding the corners with a file to prevent damage to sharpening stones and fingers. I polished the flat faces and long edges of the card with a pair of 220/1,000-grit and 4,000/8,000-grit combination waterstones, finishing with a green buffing compound. I used a block of wood to hold the card vertical when working the bottom edge, moving it around the stones to prevent it from gouging. Finally, I put a small hook onto the scraper with a burnisher.

The surface left by a well-tuned handplane is one of the reasons I enjoy woodworking. On the third board, I used a Lie-Nielsen® No. 4 smoothing plane with the standard 45° frog, flattening the sole on a diamond plate. I touched up the back of the blade and used a honing guide on a 4,000/8,000-grit stone to sharpen the bevel. I also eased the corners of the blade, putting a gentle crown on it so that the corners wouldn't leave tracks on the board. I adjusted the frog to get the smallest mouth possible without binding the shaving, and then set the blade so that it just protruded.

Once the boards had been surfaced, they were marked A, B, and C and sent to the *Fine Woodworking* staff for a blind judging before I applied finish. While it was easy to spot the two sanded boards because of their duller appearance, the scraped and handplaned cherry boards could be distinguished only when held up to a bright light. The scraped surface was slightly more irregular, while the planed board had one or two narrow streaks with a higher sheen caused when the plane's sole burnished the high points. On the mahogany boards, the planed and scraped samples were hard to tell apart.

The finish is the true test

Most woodworkers don't leave their projects bare, so the real test of surface preparation takes place after finishing. I selected the three most popular types of finish—pure oil, an oil/varnish mixture, and shellac—to test whether any of these finishes would be more sensitive to the way the wood was surfaced. When the editors returned the boards to me, I used blue masking tape to divide each board into four sections, one for each finish and one left unfinished.

I applied Parks boiled linseed oil with a cloth, allowed it to soak in for several minutes, and then wiped the surface with a clean cloth, wiping again after 10 minutes. I let the surface dry for 24 hours, then smoothed it with a gray abrasive pad. I repeated this procedure twice.

I used the gloss version of Watco® Wipe-On Poly, because a gloss finish provides greater clarity of the underlying wood than a lower-luster finish and therefore gives a more rigorous test of surface preparation. Following the manufacturer's instructions, I applied three coats with a rag, scuff-sanding the first and second coats with P220-grit sandpaper after they were dry.

I used Zinsser® SealCoat™, a clear dewaxed shellac, in a 2-lb. cut. Several coats were brushed on until the surface started to become tacky. After letting it dry overnight, I smoothed the surface with a gray abrasive pad and repeated the process. Three applications were made with the last coat left untouched.

Can you tell the difference?

The editors and I examined the samples and concluded that there is little difference between the three methods after finish has been applied. This was a real surprise, given the clear differences between the unfinished boards.

However, these results may not apply across all circumstances. Highly figured grain may be tamed only with a scraper, while some softer woods become fuzzy when scraped. I also did not test how the samples would react to stains and dyes.

Even so, I find the results liberating. Now I can choose a surface-preparation method based on the wood without concern for the final finish. Because I still get great satisfaction from watching shavings unfurl from a handplane, I'll hang on to my planes and scrapers. But I won't feel like I'm cutting corners and sacrificing results when I pull out the random-orbit sander.

The finished results

Each sanded, scraped, or planed cherry and mahogany board was divided into four parts (below). The first section was left unfinished, the second finished with boiled linseed oil, the third with shellac, and the last with an oil/varnish mixture. With all three finishes on all six boards, it was hard to tell how the surface had been prepared.

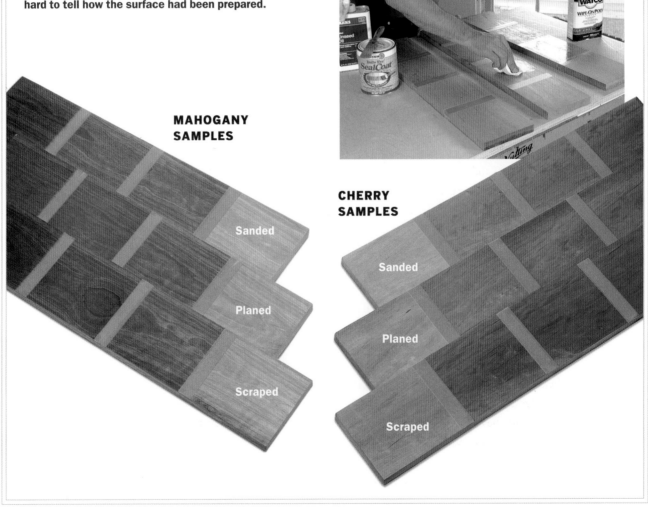

MAHOGANY SAMPLES

Sanded

Planed

Scraped

CHERRY SAMPLES

Sanded

Planed

Scraped

Combine Power- and Hand-Sanding for Good Results

DAVID SORG

The course of true love never did run smooth, according to Shakespeare, and smoothing wood true rarely causes love to course, it would seem. Boredom and fear are more common feelings among woodworkers when sanding their projects. But proper sanding is a crucial part of woodworking, so please read on for some tips and techniques that will turn your boredom into serenity and your fear into fun.

I'll stick my neck out and state that no project should be finished without first being sanded. Even if you are a hero with the handplane or skilled with the scraper, you won't be able to get a surface to be uniformly smooth and with an even sheen without sanding. Inevitably, there will be tiny depth changes from adjoining passes of the blade, while the sole of the plane can burnish strips of wood that may show up after a stain or a clear finish has been applied.

Those who rely solely on power tools will inevitably be left with planer- and jointer-knife marks and fibers crushed by the feed rollers. Router tables can leave gouges and scratches, and assembly often produces some errant glue splotches. All of these blemishes should be removed before a finish is applied, and sanding is the best way to achieve this. The most efficient way to sand a surface is with a combination of power-sanding and hand-sanding.

Power-sanding comes first

Of course, you could do all of your sanding by hand, but why? Even if you use power sanders wherever practical, there will be enough hand-sanding on almost any project to give you plenty of hand-done satisfaction. Power sanders deliver results with much greater speed, and with minimal practice they'll also deliver a flatter surface than sanding by hand alone.

The good news is that unlike much of your other shop equipment, quality sanding tools will not cost you much. I strongly suggest you get a random-orbit sander. A pad sander also is useful, and I'll explain why a detail sander is optional. Don't forget a dust mask and hearing protection.

Random-orbit sanders

Random-orbit sanders are wonderful machines. The pad has dual motion: It spins in a circle as well as in an eccentric orbit. These sanders are great for rapidly smoothing and leveling raw wood. The 5-in.-dia., palm-held models are most common, but you also can buy 6-in.-dia., two-handed versions.

Most random-orbit sanders have holes in the pad (and, of course, in the sandpaper) for dust extraction. The sanding disks are backed with either pressure-sensitive adhesive (PSA), which is inexpensive, or reusable hook-and-loop systems.

Older sanders need to be switched on when already resting on the surface of the wood, or they will spin too fast and gouge the wood when you try to bring them in for a landing. Most new models have electronic speed control, which allows you to lift the sander to apply it to an adjacent surface without having to turn it off and restart it each time.

Random-orbit sanders will do a speedy job on large surfaces and bring two pieces of wood into the same plane. However, at the edges of a workpiece, keep the majority of

Random-orbit sanders. For removing large amounts of wood from large surfaces, random-orbit sanders can't be beat. They are less suitable for small areas, and their shape prevents them from reaching into inside corners.

Pad sanders. Less aggressive than random-orbit sanders, pad sanders are easier to control, which makes them suitable for narrower and more confined areas such as table legs and the insides of cabinets.

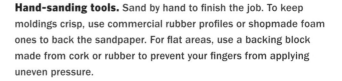

Hand-sanding tools. Sand by hand to finish the job. To keep moldings crisp, use commercial rubber profiles or shopmade foam ones to back the sandpaper. For flat areas, use a backing block made from cork or rubber to prevent your fingers from applying uneven pressure.

Large panels. With their wide contact surfaces, random-orbit sanders are naturally at home on large, flat panels.

Wide, flat parts. Again, a random-orbit sander does well here. Note: It is easier to sand parts such as table aprons before assembly.

TIP When using a random-orbit sander, orient your project, if you can, so that you're working horizontally (see the photo on p. 38). By letting the weight of the sander work for you, you'll gain more control with less fatigue. Also, sand subassemblies before glue-up. It's much easier to sand a frame-and-panel, table aprons, or drawer parts before they're assembled.

Narrow parts. On smaller, flat pieces such as the parts for a frame, a pad sander gives more control than a random-orbit sander.

the pad on the wood, or you'll risk dishing or rounding over the edge. By the same token, keep these sanders moving; don't concentrate on one spot, or you could create a little bowl.

Pad sanders

Pad sanders, also called palm sanders or finish sanders, use a simple orbital pattern, and the pad does not rotate, giving a much slower sanding action but greater control. The square pad allows the tool to get fairly close to inside corners (but beware of getting it too close, where it quickly can chew up the adjacent surface). This type of sander works well on small surfaces like the edges of shelves or table legs, as well as on the insides of cabinets and in other confined spaces.

How do you know when you're finished power-sanding?

Wipe some mineral spirits on the surface, and sight across the wood toward a strong light. Pay no attention to the beautiful color that appears; instead, look at the surface for telltale scratches, especially the ugly orbital kind. You would like to see a uniform appearance with no rough areas or single outstanding scratches. Sometimes it's easiest to see this right at the moment of evaporation, when the ruts of the scratches will still be shiny with fluid while the top surface is dull with dryness. If you take this step, you'll avoid the agony that many experience when they apply a stain only to see the scratches jump out.

Use the right grit from start to finish

With either type of sander, I'd rather start with 150-grit than 120-grit paper on most pieces, even though it may take longer to remove some milling marks. For wood that is already in good shape, especially with thin-veneered sheet goods, I start with 180-grit paper.

Note: The grits I refer to here are based on the Federation of European Producers of Abrasives (FEPA) scale, which uses the prefix P, rather than the alternate Coated Abrasives Manufacturers Institute (CAMI), or C, scale. In the 150 to 220 range, the grits are nearly equivalent, but it's best to work with the paper from one scale.

Don't continue using a piece of sandpaper until the sand is all gone and there isn't anything left but the paper. That's a false economy if you're charging for your time; if you're woodworking for fun, well, you're taking away a bunch of it. Move to a fresh section of sandpaper as soon as you feel it stop cutting or start to clog, or when it requires you to exert more pressure.

It's important to vacuum and/or blow off the entire piece between grits. I do both, then wipe it with a tack cloth. One piece of 150 grit being swirled around on your 220-grit pad will make you curse when you see the results.

Tips for efficient sanding

- With a cabinet, begin sanding on the inside: If you start with the inside while you're fresh, you'll take a few extra minutes to do it right instead of skimping on it at the end.
- For veneered plywood, you can start and stop with 180-grit paper if the inside will be minimally seen or used. Use a hand-sanding block on the corners and on any more visible areas such as solid-wood edging.
- Devote more time to visible areas and those likely to be touched. Ending with 180-grit paper is fine for softwoods, but go to 220 grit for hardwoods. On end grain, go one grade finer so that it doesn't absorb the stain or clear finish as deeply.

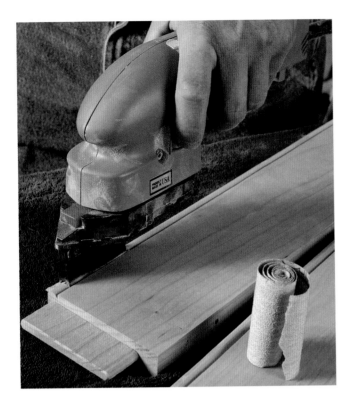

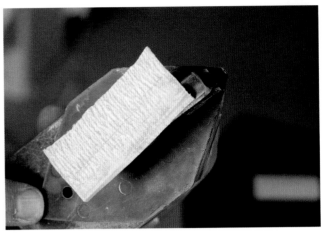

A quicker way to sand moldings. Detail sanders come with an assortment of different pads designed to fit most molding profiles. The radius on this pad matches the bead of the apron (left). One disadvantage of detail sanders is that the adhesive-backed sandpaper frequently comes away from the pad (above).

How to sand details and molding

After sanding the wide-open areas, how should you sand profiled areas? Manufacturers advertise detail sanders as the answer to sanding any shape and any confined space. These sanders come with a variety of pads designed to fit different profiles. Although I own a couple of detail sanders, I could live without them, mostly because it's too much trouble to constantly change the paper on them; by their nature, they put their sanding action into a small area of sandpaper that wears quickly.

Most of the time, I think it's quicker to do moldings, interior corners, and other small areas by hand. To keep the moldings crisp, use commercial rubber profiles that cover most convex and concave shapes, or you can make your own profile blocks from pieces of foam-insulation panel.

The end grain on raised panels requires a special sanding sequence to tone it into the rest of the panel. Start by sanding across the grain with 150- or 180-grit paper to deal with the rough texture. Then sand the entire profile on all four sides of the panel with 180- or 220-grit paper. Last, sand just the end grain with 320-grit paper, going with the grain in short strokes to eliminate any cross-grain scratches and to lessen the end grain's ability to absorb finish.

Final hand-sanding is a must-do

No matter how much you are able to use machines for the initial stages of sanding, you'll want to give each surface some final sanding by hand. Primarily, this is to get rid of the small orbital scratches left by the machines, replacing them with smaller, finer scratches that are all parallel to the grain of the wood and hence less noticeable.

You should back up the sandpaper with a sanding block or insulation foam cut to fit your panel's profile wherever possible to main-

Flat areas. To maintain a flat surface, you should always use a backing block when sanding large areas.

Rubber profiles. Using a rubber pad that fits the molding helps keep the edges of the profile sharp.

Edges. Break the edges on a project not only to reduce future damage but also to prevent finish from forming a mound at the edges.

End grain. To lessen end grain's darker appearance when the workpiece is finished, burnish the wood and fill the pores by sanding end grain up to 320-grit paper.

Sanding curves by hand. Contour the paper to fit curves in the wood.

tain a flat surface. I find the palm-sized rubber blocks most convenient because they also can be used for wet-sanding between coats of finish. Other choices include cork blocks or wood blocks faced with a sheet of cork (see the bottom photo on p. 39).

If you plan to use a water-based stain or clear finish, there are a couple of extra steps you should take. After the final hand-sanding, wipe down the piece with a damp sponge. After the wood dries, very lightly sand with the same-grade paper you finished with, but be careful to remove only the raised grain. Watch out for sandpaper coated with

stearates: Although they do a better job at preventing clogging, allowing the sandpaper to last longer and sand more smoothly, stearates are waxy and interfere with many water-based finishes, causing fisheyes on the surface. If you're planning to use a water-based finish, check with the manufacturer to see whether the finish is compatible with stearated sandpaper. Last, as I recommend for all finishing methods, test each sanding step on a sample board.

Sanding after glue-up

No matter how thoroughly you sand parts prior to assembly, there still will be small areas to touch up by hand-sanding with 220- or 320-grit paper. Areas where glue was removed with a damp cloth may need smoothing (top), or there may be two pieces that don't join in a perfect plane (bottom). To avoid cross-sanding where grain intersects, mask off one of the pieces.

Sandpaper backing for curves. Insulation foam shaped to match the panel's profile makes a good backing for sandpaper (top). The end grain may need to be sanded with paper that is one grade coarser than that used on the rest of the panel, in this case, 150 grit (center). Then sand the entire panel with 220 grit before removing any cross-grain scratches on the end-grain sides using 320-grit paper with the grain (bottom).

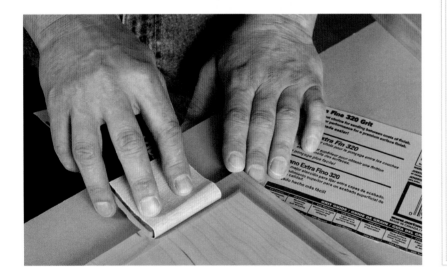

Sand between Coats for a Flawless Finish

JEFF JEWITT

Whether you spray, brush, or wipe, one of the keys to a great finish is learning to sand between coats. When I began finishing in the 1970s, there weren't many choices when it came to sanding a finish: Steel wool shed tiny hairs that got embedded in the finish; regular sandpaper (if you could find it above 240 grit) clogged quickly when sanding shellac or lacquer; and if you wanted to flatten defects between coats of finish, you used wet-or-dry paper, which was messy and made it hard to gauge your progress.

Today, not only are there much better choices among consumer-oriented abrasives, but the Internet also has given everyone

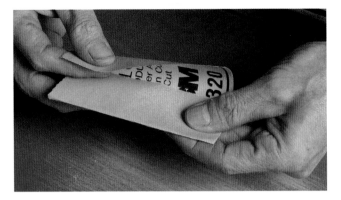

Fold sandpaper into thirds for tight spots. Fold a quarter sheet of sandpaper into thirds. All of the paper can still be used, but there is no grit-on-grit contact.

Sand inside corners. Folding the sheet into thirds allows you to work your way into tight spots.

Stearated sandpaper: no more clogging

The biggest advance in sanding between coats of finish has been the increasing availability and improving quality of stearated sandpaper. A waxy-feeling powder, zinc or calcium stearate (or a mixture), is incorporated into either aluminum-oxide or silicon-carbide sandpaper. The stearate prevents the dry finish residue from sticking and forming clumps, or corns, or clogging the spaces between the abrasive particles.

Dry-sanding between finish coats is better than wet-sanding because it allows you to see what you're doing much more clearly. If a surface is wet with lubricant, you could be sanding right through the sealer or finish because the lubricant creates an illusion of finish on the wood.

access to industrial abrasives. I'll narrow down what to use with film-forming finishes like lacquer, varnish, and shellac (in-the-wood 100% oil finishes and thin applications of oil/varnish mixes typically don't require sanding). I'll describe new products to use for dry-sanding between coats, and I'll cover the better use of wet-or-dry paper for sanding the final coat in preparation for the rubbing-out process.

Fine grits and a light touch

Going from sanding bare wood to sanding a finish involves a change of gears. Instead of power-sanding using grits mostly P220 or coarser, you typically hand-sand using grits P320 and finer.

The first coat of finish, whether a purpose-made sealer or just a thinned coat of the final finish, generally leaves a rough surface with raised grain embedded in the finish. At this stage, you aren't flattening the surface, just smoothing it, so there is no need to use a sanding block. Using P320-grit stearated paper, you can make a pad by folding a quarter sheet into thirds (as shown in the top left photo). This pad works best if you have to get into corners and other tight areas. Otherwise, you can just grip a quarter sheet of paper by wrapping one corner around your

Hand sander. For sanding flat surfaces, just wrap a corner of the sheet around your little finger and grip the opposite corner between your index finger and thumb.

Handy pad. You can hand-sand using disks designed for random-orbit sanders by attaching them to a pad backed with hook-and-loop tape.

pinkie and pinching the other corner between your thumb and index finger (as shown in the top left photo). An alternative is pressure-sensitive adhesive (PSA) paper in the same grit (P320) that comes in 2¾-in.-wide rolls. You can tear off only what you need and temporarily stick it to your fingers.

Another option, which costs a bit more, is hook-and-loop pads that allow you to hand-sand using disks designed for random-orbit sanders (as shown in the top right photo). If the sandpaper starts to load up with debris or corns, swipe the grit side of the paper against a piece of thick carpet (Berber is best). You also can swipe it on a gray abrasive pad.

It's important to remove the residue after each sanding, or it will cause problems with the next coat of finish. If your finish is oil-based, solvent lacquer, or shellac, dampen a clean cotton or microfiber cloth with naphtha or mineral spirits and wipe away the debris. I prefer naphtha because it evaporates faster and leaves a little less oily residue. For waterborne finishes, I make a mixture of 5% denatured alcohol in tap water (roughly 1 oz. denatured alcohol to 16 oz. water). It's OK to follow the solvent wipe with a tack cloth, but most tack rags can leave a residue that will interfere with the adhesion of waterborne finishes. One waterborne-friendly tack cloth is 3M's all-purpose tack cloth, item no. 03192.

TIP Unlike power sanders with onboard dust extraction, hand-sanding can clog the paper quickly. Wiping the pad on a carpet remnant gets it clean again.

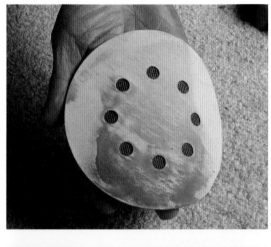

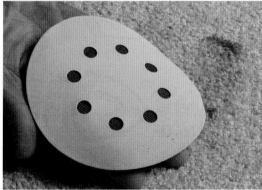

Myth-buster: new paper works with water-based finishes, too

Does stearated sandpaper cause adhesion problems with waterborne finishes? After finding little hard evidence to prove it does, several consumer and industrial sandpapers were tested with a variety of waterborne finishes.

One coat of each finish was applied to a separate sample board. When it was dry, the board was divided into sections and this coat was sanded smooth with a variety of P320-grit stearated sandpapers. After the sanding residue was removed, another coat of finish was applied; then after 72 hours, the surface was evaluated for flow-out and adhesion.

There were no compatibility issues with any of the sandpapers and waterborne finishes. If you use a premium stearated paper, you'll have no problems as long as you remove the residue after sanding.

Tough test reveals the truth. Eight waterborne finishes were applied to a sample board and then sections were sanded with different stearated sandpapers before a final coat of each finish was added.

Deep scratches. A special tool was used to scratch a pattern in the cured finish.

Perfect adhesion. No finish from the scratched area stuck to the tape when it was pulled away.

Higher grits for subsequent coats

After you have smoothed the sealer coat and applied the first real coat of finish, you should generally use P400- or P600-grit paper to sand; otherwise, you might see tiny sanding scratches in finishes that don't melt into each other, such as oil-based products and most waterborne ones.

You can use a power sander on large, flat surfaces once you have built up enough finish thickness (at least four to six coats). Use caution when sanding, staying away from the edges and using P400-grit paper or higher. For better visibility, always do this with dust extraction. The better papers out there have holes punched to match the ports on the sanding pad, or are made up of a mesh like Mirka Abranet. An industrial product called Clean Sanding by 3M is disk paper with a spiral progression of small holes for dust extraction.

TIP It's important to remove all sanding residue before applying the next coat of finish. For solvent-based finishes, dampen a cloth with naphtha or mineral spirits. The former dries faster (but is harder to spell).

Power-sanding comes later. Once you have applied five or six coats of finish, you can safely use a random-orbit sander equipped with P400-grit disks.

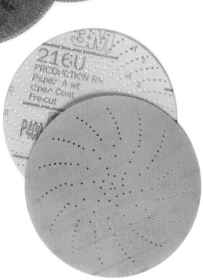

New disks, better dust extraction. Through-the-pad dust extraction has been one of the great innovations in wood finishing. The latest disks work even better and fit all sander models regardless of their hole configuration. Mirka's Abranet is an abrasive-coated mesh (above), while 3M's Clean Sanding disks have spirals of small holes (right).

Abrasive pads. These pads come in a variety of grits and are thin enough to get into carvings.

Sticky paper. Adhesive-backed sandpaper is useful for sanding narrow surfaces. Simply stick it to a finger.

Sanding sponges. Less flexible than the other products, sanding sponges are good for gentle curves and can be washed out when finished.

Special products for moldings, carvings, and turnings

Although you can use sheet sandpaper with shopmade or commercial profiled sanding blocks on gentle profiles, this won't work on sharp curves and other extreme profiles. For these areas, use ultra-flexible sanding sponges or a synthetic steel-wool substitute. Neither of these products has stearates because the face is more open and clogging isn't an issue. After use, most of them can be cleaned with soapy water and reused. I like ultra-thin synthetic steel wool, which more easily conforms to profiles and turnings. Choices include Mirka's Mirlon Total™ and 3M's Multi-Flex, both of which are available in a convenient roll, but look for 3M's SandBlaster flexible pads, which last a bit longer and are easier to find at most home centers and hardware stores.

On thin, flat areas like the inside edge of a picture frame or door, hold the pad with your thumb on top and the rest of your fingers underneath. This keeps it level. Or just use a small piece of the PSA paper mentioned earlier.

Wet-or-dry paper still the best for final flattening

Unlike stearated sandpaper, wet-or-dry sandpaper can be either FEPA (P) or CAMI graded. Make sure you know what you're using, because a P600 is equivalent to just under a CAMI 400. All FEPA-graded sandpaper should have a P before the grit number; if there is no P, assume it's CAMI grade unless otherwise specified. One feature of wet-or-dry paper is that you can get it in grits up to 2,000 and sometimes higher. If you have any trouble finding it, try an automotive parts supplier.

TIP Almost all stearated paper is FEPA (P) graded, but wet-or-dry papers can be either P or CAMI graded. The difference is significant in the higher grits, so make sure you know what you're using.

Foam mesh. 3M's SandBlaster is a drawer-liner type of foam mesh coated with abrasive. It can be folded over to reach into tight corners (top) or wrapped around curves (above).

Flat surfaces. Wet-or-dry sandpaper is the best way to smooth the surface prior to rubbing out the finish. Use soapy water as a lubricant, and wipe away the slurry to check your progress.

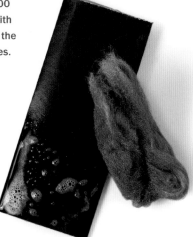

Tight curves. Use 0000 steel wool lubricated with soapy water to remove the gloss on curved surfaces.

Wet-or-dry sandpaper is a sharp and fast-cutting abrasive and works best for removing final defects and flattening the finish prior to rubbing out (where you polish the flattened surface to the desired sheen). You can use mineral spirits, a light mineral oil called paraffin or rubbing oil, or soapy water as a lubricant. Of the three, soapy water is the least messy, though it seems not to cut as fast or as well as the other two. Add a capful of dishwashing liquid for every pint (16 oz.) of tap water, and then apply the mixture using a plant mister.

Start with a quarter sheet of P600-grit paper wrapped around a cork, or a cork-faced, block. Spray some lubricant on the surface, and begin sanding with the grain if possible (as shown in the top photo). On a top, rub the outside 3 in. first so you can focus on keeping the block flat and not tipping it off an edge (that can happen naturally with arm motion if you're taking a long sweep from one end to the other). Once you've gone around a few times, come back and do the center. Wipe away the slurry and examine

Finish up with wax. Apply some paste wax with Liberon's 0000 steel wool, then buff the surface with a cotton cloth for a smooth, satin finish.

the surface. You're done when the surface looks about 80% to 90% dull. Don't try to make the entire surface perfectly dull because you'll probably sand through the finish.

After using the wet-or-dry sandpaper, you can follow up with paste wax applied with 0000 steel wool for a satin finish. An alternative to steel wool is a very fine abrasive foam pad such as Mirka's Abralon. The 1,000,

2,000, and 4,000 grits can be used for sheens ranging from dull to satin. You don't need compounds or polishes with these products. For a gloss finish, follow the steps in "High-Gloss Finish Made Simple" on p. 128.

When to Stop Sanding

ARI TUCKMAN

S anding is most woodworkers' least-favorite activity. It's dusty, boring, and time-consuming—the sooner done, the better. But what is the right stopping point? When does moving to a finer grit no longer yield appreciable improvements in the finished surface? To find out, I did a semi-scientific study. I took boards of cherry, white oak, and tiger maple as test woods, not only because they are familiar furniture woods but also to see if tight or open grain and figure would influence the best final grit. I cut each into six pieces and sanded them to six different grits. I then divided each piece into thirds and applied a different finish to each section because what really matters is not how the bare boards look but their appearance with a finish. The results were both interesting and reassuring.

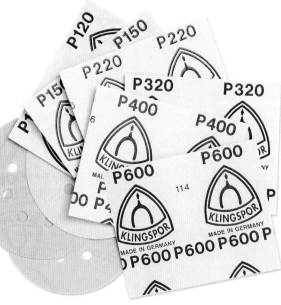

White oak

Cherry

Tiger maple

Six grits tested on three woods

I chose aluminum-oxide sandpaper graded to the FEPA scale (recognizable by the P prefix to the number) because it is the standard abrasive for sanding bare wood. I tested P120, P150, P220, P320, P400, and P600 grits because most of the sanding I had previously done was with either P220 grit or P320 grit. I wanted to see if coarser or finer grits would make a noticeable change in the finished appearance of the wood. Would the open-grained pattern on white oak conceal the scratches left by coarser grits? Would cherry, a blotch-prone wood, respond best to finer-grit sanding? Would the stripes of tiger maple be enhanced by a coarse final grit, or would they be left blotchy?

I used a random-orbit sander for the majority of the sanding, progressing through the grits. This was followed by hand-sanding with a sanding block, with the grain, at the same final grit. I changed the disks when they began to wear out, but I used fresh paper on each board's final grit for both the random-orbit and the hand-sanding. I chose these three woods to see if wood grain or figure would make any difference. I cut one long board of each species into six 17½-in. by 8-in.

sections and machine-planed them flat. Once the 18 sections were sanded to the appropriate final grit, I removed the dust using a clean paintbrush and a vacuum.

Three types of finish applied on each wood

After sanding, I used masking tape to separate each board into three sections. This allowed me to apply three different finishes to see if some are more sensitive to the final grit than others. I chose Danish oil for a minimal-build, in-the-wood finish; shellac rubbed out with steel wool and then waxed for a medium-luster, thin-film finish; and an oil-based polyurethane to give a more protective, high-gloss finish.

I used natural Watco Danish oil, wiping on the first coat with a cotton cloth, then wiping off the surplus. When dry, I applied a second coat and wet-sanded using P400-grit wet/dry sandpaper and a sanding block. Then I wiped it dry to remove the surplus sawdust and oil. The next day, I applied a final coat in the same way as the first.

On the next section, I rubbed on Zinsser SealCoat shellac with a cotton cloth. I applied eight coats over two days, sanded lightly with P320-grit sandpaper on a sanding block, and then added two more coats. When dry, I rubbed the surface with 0000 steel wool and applied a thin coat of paste wax, polishing with a cotton cloth.

I brushed three coats of Zar® oil-based, high-gloss, interior polyurethane on the final section, sanding between coats with P320-grit paper. The third coat was left untouched.

Results: 220 or less in most cases

This test set out to answer the question of how much sanding is too much. Based on these results, I can feel confident putting the

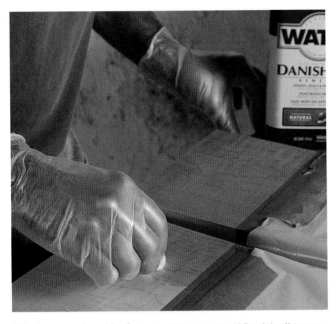

Oil gives a natural look. I wiped three coats of Danish oil on one end of each sample board to give a lower-luster, in-the-wood finish.

sandpaper down after using P150 grit if I'm using a film finish, P220 grit for an oil finish on nonblotchy wood, and probably P400 grit on blotch-prone boards.

I used clear finishes only. If you regularly stain your wood, you may want to do your own test. In general, wood sanded with higher grits tends to absorb less stain than wood sanded to a coarser grit. I also didn't test softwoods or hard tropical woods, but most furniture woods fall in the hardness range of my three test species.

You also should sand correctly, even if you stop at a lower grit. When using the coarsest grit, make sure to remove all the telltale ripple marks left by the jointer and the planer. After power-sanding at final grit, make sure that you remove any swirls left by the random-orbit sander by thoroughly hand-sanding with the grain.

I am thrilled by the results; as a weekend warrior, I already spend too little time in the shop. I have better things to do with that time than listen to my sander.

Shellac and wax supply a medium-luster finish. After building up a thin film of shellac, I dulled the surface with 0000 steel wool and then polished it with paste wax.

Varnish provides high-gloss protection. Three coats of oil-based polyurethane left a high-gloss film finish typical of a kitchen tabletop.

Results

Each sample board was sanded and had three finishes applied. The difference, or lack thereof, between the highest and lowest sanded grits is depicted in the photos at right.

WHITE OAK

The oak boards showed the least difference over the range of grits. Under the shellac and polyurethane finishes, all six boards were identical. The Danish-oiled panels were slightly lower in luster with the coarsest two grades of grit than with the finest two grits.

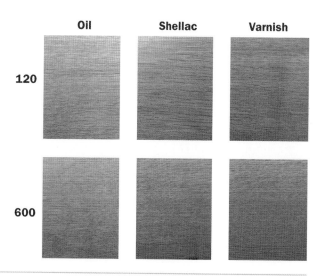

CHERRY

There was a slightly lower luster on the oil-finished P120-grit board compared with the P400- and P600-grit boards. I had expected to see some blotchy cherry, but the sample board behaved fairly well. However, based on previous experience, I would still sand cherry up to at least P400 grit if I were going to use an oil finish.

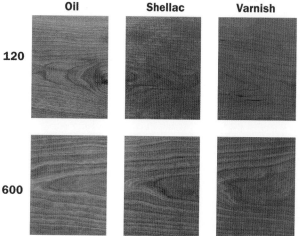

TIGER MAPLE

The coarser grits were expected to leave the stripes more porous, resulting in more finish penetration and more pronounced figure. Instead, the degree of figure was equal on the extremes of grit with all three finishes. As with the other woods, higher grits brought out a higher luster under an oil finish.

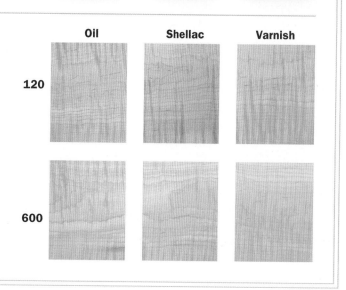

Finish While You Build

CHARLES NEIL

For most woodworkers, finishing is a chore to be put off as long as possible. So they wait until after a piece is assembled to figure it out. Instead, finishing should be one of the first things on your agenda; if it isn't, you will work yourself into a corner—literally.

At age 13, I ran across a guy who painted cars. I really enjoyed watching him work, and later I learned to do painting and finishing myself. I worked for years in that industry, and along the way I learned a lesson that has become invaluable in my woodworking: Look at each piece as a collection of parts. Just as a vehicle breaks down into the hood, the trunk lid, the doors, etc., a piece of furniture can be broken down into components.

This step-back cupboard, for example, consists of the doors, the face frame, the shelves, the crown molding, and other distinct parts. Not only is it much easier to sand and prefinish these parts before they are assembled, but I also have a number of ways to modify the design of the components slightly to simplify finishing.

On this cupboard, the upper cabinet interior is spray-painted and the rest of the piece is finished with Waterlox® wiping varnish, but you can use my techniques with any type of finish.

Think finish before you cut and glue

Few woodworkers are handy enough with dyes to be able to harmonize boards of

Sand before you assemble. Scrape or sand boards while they can be laid flat. Once a piece is glued together, it is much harder to reach into corners either by hand or with a machine.

different colors. Therefore, spend some time at the lumberyard sorting through the boards for matching color and grain.

Once you get the wood home and begin to lay out the parts on the boards, it often pays to alter the dimensions of your piece slightly. Unless you're building an exact replica, the design usually has a little flexibility. Say you have two beautifully matched boards that are ideal for the tabletop but are ¼ in. narrower

Mask off glue surfaces. Clear finish or paint will interfere with glue's ability to bond wood, so use masking tape to seal off surfaces that will be glued.

Temporary handles. Screw blocks of scrapwood to each end of the shelves. You'll be able to handle the shelves cleanly while finishing them, the glue surfaces are protected, and both sides can dry at once.

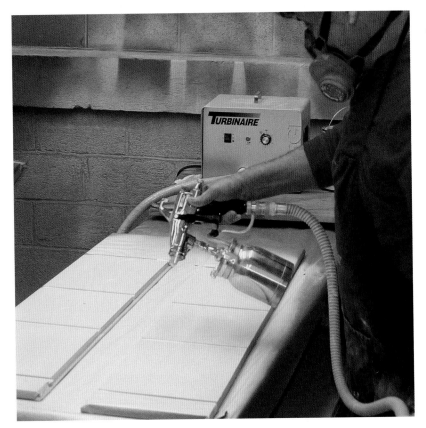

Finish the inside. Whether you use a brush or spray gun, it is much easier to finish the interior of the upper cabinet before the cabinet is assembled.

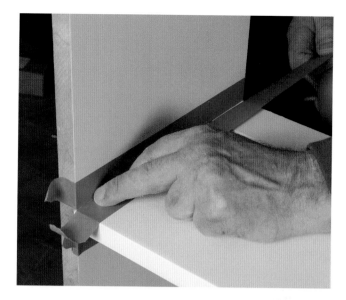

Tape and peel. When you dry-assemble the piece, place masking tape adjacent to glue surfaces (above). Disassemble and apply the glue (right). When the parts are glued up, any squeeze-out goes onto the tape and is easily peeled away (below).

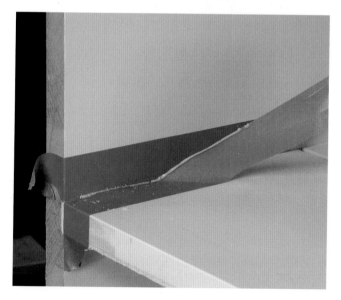

than your planned width. It is much better to compromise on the design and use the best matching boards for the premier surface. No amount of skilled wood coloring will make up for an ill-matched top.

Pre-finish the interiors and anticipate squeeze-out

After finding the best match between the boards and the individual parts of the project but before you do any assembly, think about the finish. For example, on this step-back cupboard, if you assemble the top case and glue in the shelves, sanding or scraping and finishing will be difficult where the parts meet at 90°. Instead, finish the entire interior of both upper and lower cases now. You may have some touch-up to do later, but finishing these panels while you can lay them flat is much easier than wrestling with the whole case. You also will get much better results.

Mask off areas that will be glued. On shelves that are finished on both sides, screw on end caps sized to cover the entire area on the shelf ends that will fit into the dado in the cabinet sides. In this way, you can turn over the shelves without marring the finish, both sides can dry at once, and the area to receive glue remains unfinished. I find that ⅛-in.-deep dadoes give ample shear strength, are easy and clean to cut, and leave plenty of material in the shelf sides for adding the screws and antique-looking square plugs I used in this piece (see "A novel way to hide screw holes" on p. 62).

After applying the finish, remove the masking tape from the glue surfaces and dry-fit everything. Now apply masking tape to the areas adjacent to glue surfaces. When you glue the cabinet together, any squeeze-out will collect on the tape and be easy to remove. The alternative is trying to remove squeeze-out in hard-to-reach areas that are already finished.

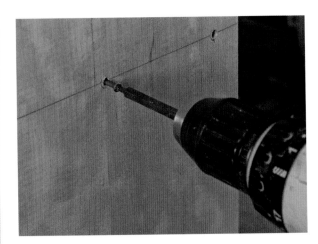

Drive the screws. As well as the hole for the shaft, drill ¼-in.-dia. holes to receive the head.

A novel way to hide screw holes

Neil reinforces shelf-to-side panel joints with screws, but matching filler to the finished wood is problematic. Sink trim-head screws ¼ in. below the surface. Tap in a square peg with diagonals slightly greater than the hole's diameter. Once dry, saw and sand the peg flush, apply a finish, and it will resemble an antique square peg.

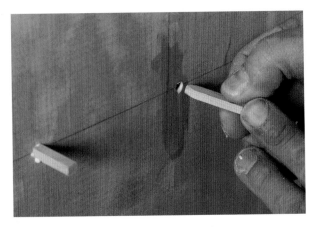

Square peg, round hole. Taper the tip of a square peg, then glue and tap it into the screw hole.

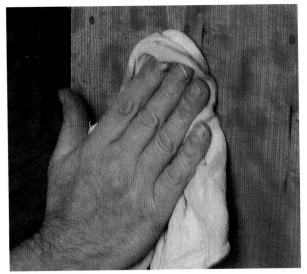

Meant to show. When finish is applied, the square pegs stand out.

Make and install the face frames

Here again, some pre-finishing and masking tape can spare you a lot of agony. Apply finish to the inside edges of the face frame. Before gluing the face frame to the carcase, place tape on the adjacent surface of the carcase to protect it from squeeze-out.

Don't worry about the exterior because those surfaces will remain accessible and you'll be scraping or sanding them after the piece is assembled. No matter how particular you are, you may still get some glue on the wood. Don't try to wipe it off with a damp cloth; instead, let the glue set until it's semi-firm like chewing gum, then use a chisel or scraper to peel it off the surface. Now clean the wood with acetone; it removes the glue better than water and works with polyvinyl acetate (PVA), polyurethane, epoxy, and hide glues.

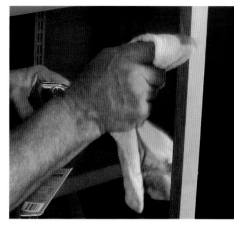

Prefinish adjacent parts. The face frame will be next to the already painted shelves, so prefinish the edge before attaching it.

Tape the cabinet edges. Apply tape to the interior cabinet adjacent to the face frame (above) to make removing excess glue much easier (below).

TIP If you get surplus glue on the wood while the glue is curing, remove any residue with acetone.

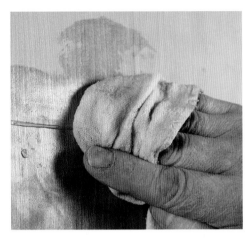

Pre-assemble the moldings

With the two carcases glued up, it's time to focus on the smaller parts, starting with the base and crown moldings. Any time you have a cross-grain application, such as where these moldings contact the sides of the cabinet, two issues come into play. First, the expansion and contraction issue prevents gluing on the pieces all the way across—an inch or two at the front is as far as you dare go. Second, there is risk of cross-grain sanding scratches.

However, there's a nice, simple trick that solves both problems at once. For the base molding, rather than using a narrow strip of wood that must be nailed to the cabinet with the subsequent nail holes to fill, make the molding a couple of inches wider and then notch it to fit under the lower case. This allows the base to be screwed to the underside of the cabinet using slotted holes in the sides of the molding that allow for movement.

Notched molding. The base molding fits under the cabinet instead of being nailed to the front and sides. This means it can be pre-assembled and screwed on.

Drill a hole. Use a Forstner bit just smaller than the corner area to drill a little more than halfway through the wood. Keep the point just to one side of the joint to avoid splitting it.

Shopmade circle. On a piece of wood slightly thinner than the depth of the hole in the miter joint, just start to drill a hole with the same bit and then cut out the circle on the bandsaw.

A stiffer joint. Glue the circle into the hole with its grain perpendicular to the line of the joint.

The horizontal top section of crown molding is attached to the top in the same way using slotted screw holes. The base and the crown can now be prepped and finished independently of the rest of the cabinet. The sides of the cabinet can be worked unobstructed, removing the risk of cross-grain scratches.

I have a novel way to reinforce the relatively weak miter joint at the front corners of the molding. After the miter is glued and dried, take as large a Forstner bit as will fit into the notched section of the molding and drill halfway through. Now bandsaw a piece of wood slightly smaller than the diameter and depth of the hole. Glue the circle into the hole with the grain running perpendicular to the miter joint.

Divide and conquer. It is much easier to prep and finish the molding and the case sides before joining them.

Finer grits for end grain. To prevent the end grain on a raised panel from absorbing too much finish and turning dark, sand it successively with P320-, P400-, and P600-grit paper.

Don't forget the frame. Sand the inside edges of the frame parts before the panel is inserted and the frame is glued together.

Prep and finish a frame and panel before assembly

Solid-wood panels are designed to move within the frame. While this is a neat solution to the problem of wood movement from a woodworker's perspective, it presents a number of problems to a finisher. When the frame and panel are finished after glue-up, an unfinished area that sits in the grooves becomes exposed if the panel contracts later. On the other hand, if finish "glues" the panel into the frame, either the panel will split as it tries to contract, or it will break the frame as it tries to expand.

Second, it is nearly impossible to scrape or sand the sides or back of a raised panel and the inner edges of the frame after the frame has been glued together. It is much easier to prep these areas while they are still individual parts.

On a raised panel, the end-grain beveled area will absorb more finish and appear darker than the rest of the panel. To avoid this, it is necessary to sand this area with much finer sandpaper or use some other form of absorption control. You can either finish just the profiled part of the panel or, if you prefer, the entire surface. With the components done, check to see if any finish needs touching up before assembling the cabinet. Screw on the moldings and feet, nail or screw on the prefinished backs, and attach the doors. By taking the time and making the effort to plan ahead, you'll be rewarded with a finish worthy of your masterpiece and a lot less hassle.

Finish the parts. Apply finish to the panel (above) and the inside edges of the frame (right) before glue-up.

Protect the finish. After the frame has been glued together, you probably will need to flush-sand the joints. To avoid damage from the sander, tape off the nearby sections of panel.

Home stretch. Finishing individual parts separately and controlling glue squeeze-out ensures a flawless finish.

Dyes Can Do It All

TERI MASASCHI

Coloring wood strikes terror in the hearts of most woodworkers. After spending six months building a piece, potentially ruining it in an hour is a definite cause for anxiety. Much of this caution stems from bad experiences applying typical hardware-store wood stains to bare wood. These mostly pigmented stains can cause results that are too dark, blotchy, and muddy. Far from enhancing the wood, the effect is to ruin the appearance.

Rather than throw out the baby with the bathwater and forswear ever coloring wood, switch to dyes. Like pigments, dyes also are called stains, but instead of lying on top of the wood like a pigment stain, they penetrate the wood. This ability enhances wood by offering figure-revealing transparency. Dyes come in a range of colors from subtle wood tones to brilliant primaries, and they can be applied to bare wood, combined with clear coats, or used as touch-ups. Dyes come in powdered form, concentrates, and ready-to-use liquids. The trick is to know where and how to use each type.

Dye bare wood for the boldest results

Whether you are seeking the rich tones of antique cherry or vibrant color on a more contemporary piece, you'll get the most impact by applying a dye to unfinished wood. However, this is something of a high-risk, high-reward situation.

Dye Comparison

TYPE OF DYE	SAMPLE BRANDS	BEST USES	LESS THAN IDEAL USE	TOPCOAT COMPATIBILITY	COMMENTS
Waterborne dye powder	W. D. Lockwood®, J. E. Moser®, TransFast®	Applied to bare wood	Tinting other dyes or clear finishes	All finishes. Seal with shellac before a waterborne finish.	Widest range of colors; cheapest dye
Oil-based dye powder	W. D. Lockwood, J. E. Moser	Tinting oil-based finishes	Dyeing bare wood	Will color-lift. Seal with shellac.	Best for tinting oil-based products
Alcohol-based dye powder	W. D. Lockwood, J. E. Moser	Touching up color	Dyeing bare wood	Will color-lift. Seal with shellac.	Use concentrates for tinting shellac.
Non-grain-raising dyes	Solar-Lux™, Mohawk® Ultra Penetrating Stain	Dyeing bare wood	Tinting other dyes or clear finishes	All finishes. If shellac, spray first coat (gun or aerosol).	Add retarder for large surfaces; add reducer for lighter tones.
Dye concentrates	TransTint®, Wizard Tints™, Sherwin-Williams®	Tinting all clear finishes	Staining bare wood (must be mixed)	All finishes. If shellac, spray first coat (gun or aerosol).	Expensive but goes a long way

Water-soluble dyes are your first choice

The most commonly available dyes are powders dissolved in water. Often termed aniline dyes (although no longer made from this product), water-soluble dyes provide great flexibility in how they can be mixed and also how they can be used.

Water-soluble dyes can be brushed, ragged, or sponged on, or sprayed with a spray gun or a plant mister. Their slow drying time means they can be manipulated with a damp cloth to correct uneven color, which makes them suitable for applying to large areas such as tabletops. They come in a greater range of colors than any other type of dye, and if you can't find the perfect color, you can blend two or more dissolved colors. Unlike many finishing products, dye powders have an almost infinite shelf life if kept in the dark.

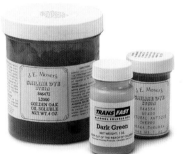

Powdered dye

Dye concentrate

Choosing a dye. Dyes come in three main groups: as powders to be mixed with water, alcohol, or mineral spirits; in ready-to-use form as a non-grain-raising liquid; or as concentrates to be added to clear finishes. Each group has different uses and characteristics.

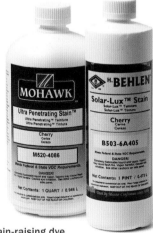

Non-grain-raising dye

The main disadvantage of water-soluble dyes is their tendency to raise the grain: Any water, whether clear or dyed, will raise the grain when applied to bare wood. To get around this problem, raise the grain before applying dye. First, dampen the sanded surface with a cloth moistened with distilled water. Avoid tap water, as any minerals may react with tannin in the wood. Allow the wood to dry, then de-whisker the surface by lightly hand-sanding with the grain using P220-grit sandpaper. If you raise the grain and then smooth the surface, the dye will not raise the grain as much.

The typical mix suggested by the supplier is 1 oz. of powder to 1 qt. of hot (not boiling) distilled water. Because you are unlikely to need a quart of dye, the easiest way to measure fractions of an ounce is to use the plastic measuring cup that comes with liquid cough medicine (also available at pharmacies). These cups measure volume, not weight; to account for this, fill slightly

Pick a color, any color. While most woodworkers reach for a wood tone to give their pieces a more distinguished or aged appearance, brighter colors play an important role. Walnut and mahogany are often dyed yellow before adding a shade of brown to bring out the color contrasts in the wood. Contemporary furniture makers use bright colors as accents or to make the whole piece stand out.

Raise the grain. Before applying a waterborne dye, the wood grain must be raised. Wipe the surface with a cloth dampened with distilled water. After the wood is dry, lightly sand the surface with P220-grit sandpaper.

beyond the desired level when pouring in the dye powder.

Allow the mix to cool, then strain it through a fine paint filter, or a plastic funnel lined with cotton cloth or a coffee filter.

If you add way too much powder to the water, eventually no more will dissolve and you will end up with sludge at the bottom of the container rather like a pigment stain. If a dye this concentrated is applied to the wood, it will leave a powdery residue. Remove this residue with a cloth after it dries, or you may have a problem when finishing over it.

Non-grain-raising dyes resist fading

Another type of dye suitable for bare wood is classified as a metallized or premetallized dye. Commonly known as non-grain-raising (NGR) stains, their biggest benefit is superior lightfastness compared with waterborne dyes. Away from intense light, waterborne dyes work fine, but NGRs are better near a sunny window. A second advantage is that there is no need to raise the grain before applying an NGR dye.

NGRs come ready to use in a blend of ethanol, methanol, and retarder. Common brand names are Solar-Lux, Mohawk Ultra Penetrating Stain, and Gemini® Super Penetrating NGR stains. This same dye is also available as a concentrate under brand names TransTint, Wizard Tints, and Sherwin-Williams Dye Concentrate. You can use these to tweak the color of the nonconcentrated NGRs to augment their rather limited range of colors. To dilute NGRs, it is best to use a purpose-made extender.

The easiest way to apply NGRs for even color tone is with a spray gun. Applied by hand, they are more troublesome because of their rapid evaporation. On a large project, it is difficult to work fast enough to maintain a wet edge and avoid streaking and at the same time achieve an even color density. To deal with streaking, you can add 10% of a

Dissolve and strain the dye. Waterborne dyes should be dissolved in hot distilled water in the ratio of 1 oz. of dye to 1 qt. of water. The easiest way to measure smaller amounts of dye is using a plastic medicine cup (above left). After the mixture has cooled, pour the liquid through a fine paint filter to remove any grains of undissolved dye (above right). Waterborne dyes can be applied with a cloth, sponge, paintbrush, spray gun, or plant mister (right).

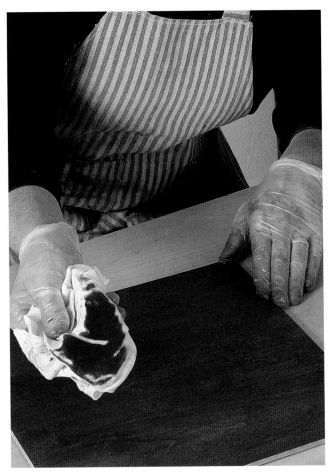

Apply fast-evaporating dyes quickly. Non-grain-raising (NGR) dyes need to be applied fast to avoid overlapping streak marks (above). However, you can blend away uneven NGR color by wiping the surface with a damp cloth (right).

Spray NGR dye for best results. With the gun set up to apply a fine spray, you can apply thin layers of color until you achieve the look you want in an even density.

purpose-made retarder to slow down the drying time, and while the stain is still damp, to some extent you can even out the color with a water-dampened cloth.

Tint a clear finish for added flexibility

So far we have covered dyeing bare wood only, but you also can add dye to a clear finish. You'll save a little time by applying the dye and finish in one step, but the main advantage is a more subtle shift in color. The result is comparable to the filters placed in front of lights in theaters, casting a delicate hue over the whole set.

A wonderful use for tinted oil finishes is on highly figured woods. Most people use oil to pop the stripes in tiger maple, for example, but if you apply a tinted oil, it will make the

For subtle color, tint the finish

Dyes are often used to bring out the best in figured woods, but what if you don't want to alter the overall color of the piece? The board on the left had an alcohol-based dye applied to the bare wood and was then clear coated. While the figure is enhanced, the overall tone has darkened considerably. The board on the right was finished with Danish oil tinted with an oil-based dye dissolved in mineral spirits. The figure pops, but the overall color is almost the same.

Dye applied to bare wood   Dye added to clear finish

stripes much more pronounced without coloring the whole board as much. To tint an oil-based finish, it's best to use an oil-based dye powder, although somewhat confusingly the powder must be dissolved in mineral spirits and not oil before being added to the clear finish. This mixture will thin the finish, so use as little mineral spirits as possible.

The best tinting agents for shellac, lacquer, and waterborne finishes are the concentrated NGRs. Drop by drop, these bottles of powerful color can transform a tone rapidly (see the top photos on p. 74). From clear shellac, you can make buttonlac, garnet, orange, or even green shellac.

Other benefits from tinting a clear coat include correcting the overall tone of a project, or, in combination with a base dye, creating a deep, rich color on woods like maple that are normally difficult to darken.

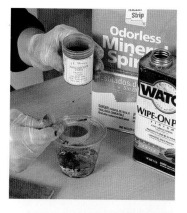

Dissolve oil-based dyes in mineral spirits first. After the powder dissolves, add the mixture to the clear oil finish of your choice (below).

Add dye straight to the finish. A drop or two of concentrated dye can alter a clear shellac, lacquer, or waterborne finish to almost any color you want.

A homemade garnet shellac. A few drops of medium walnut and a drop of Bordeaux added to clear shellac (left) will produce a color similar to that of garnet shellac (right).

Finishes may lift the dye

Keep the dye out of the finish. If you brush on a waterborne finish over a waterborne dye, you are liable to dissolve some of the latter. The solution is to apply a coat of shellac between the two.

How to seal an alcohol-based dye. Brushing shellac over an NGR dye is liable to dissolve some of the dye. The solution is to spray on a light coat of shellac with either a spray gun or an aerosol.

A special dye for touch-up work

Occasionally while leveling a clear coat, you might sand through some dye to the uncolored wood below. If you restore old furniture, you will come across areas of missing color. In both cases, a third type of dye powder excels at covering up mistakes and blemishes. Dip the end of an artist's brush into a 1-lb. cut of shellac and immediately pick up a bit of alcohol-soluble dye powder. Mix the two on an impermeable surface such as a plate or a piece of glass to create your touch-up "paint" to fix areas of color loss.

Don't be afraid of dyes

The message to first-time users: Definitely try dye. As with all new products and techniques, there is a learning curve, so try them out on sample boards before attempting the final project.

When you've mastered the art of applying dye to your work, whether as a base color, a tinted clear coat, or just a touch-up, you will know that you have joined the ranks of professional finishers.

A dye for perfect touch-ups. With a piece of glass as a palette, use an artist's brush to blend a dab of shellac and an alcohol-soluble dye powder (above). Apply the dyed shellac to the blemished area for an invisible repair (below).

Combining Dyes and Stains

PAUL SNYDER

You may think that the only reason to dye or stain a piece of furniture is to change its color, but many more subtle changes are possible. With dyes and stains, you can pop the curl in curly maple, enhance the rays of quartersawn white oak, and give fresh-cut, pallid cherry the deep glow of an 18th-century antique. More often than not, the secret to using these products is knowing that coloring wood is not a single process but a multistep technique that combines a dye with a stain.

The difference between dyes and stains

Dyes are made up of molecular-size particles that attach themselves to wood fibers. Because dye particles are microscopic, they are essentially transparent and can add a lot of color without loss of grain definition. Dyes are available in liquid form or as powders to be dissolved in a solvent such as water, alcohol, or oil. Unlike pigments in stains, dye molecules stay in solution and don't settle to the bottom of the container.

Stains consist of colored pigments combined with a binder that glues them to the wood. The binder can be oil, varnish, or acrylic (water-based), in liquid or gel form. Dyes and stains affect wood in different ways.

Dyes display figure

Because dyes are transparent, they enhance the figure and make wood shimmer (an

Dye only. Dye adds a uniform color change to the whole surface of the wood. The translucent color in dye will highlight a wood's figure without obscuring it.

Stain only. The pigments in stain lodge in open-pored woods, emphasizing the grain structure. Because they add less color to tight-grained areas, stains do not add color evenly to a board.

Dye followed by stain. A combination of dye and stain enhances both the curl and the grain, while the bright dye shining through the darker stain gives the wood a look of greater depth.

effect known as chatoyance). On highly figured woods like curly maple, dye produces a dramatic, three-dimensional look. But dyes do have limitations: They can cause bad blotching on woods such as pine and cherry and can leave open-pored species like oak looking off-white.

Stains enhance grain

Unlike dyes, which penetrate the wood, the pigments in stains color the wood by lodging in the grain and pore structure. This makes them a good choice for open-pored woods such as ash and oak. On tight-grained woods such as maple, the pigments find very little structure to lodge in, so most of the color is removed when the excess is wiped off, and the result is uninspiring.

Dye vs. stain

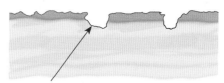

Dyes add tone but may not penetrate pores.

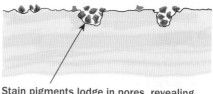

Stain pigments lodge in pores, revealing the grain.

Recipes for dyes and stains

INSTANT ANTIQUE CHERRY

Apply the following blend of Solar-Lux dyes: 3 parts golden fruitwood, 1½ parts American walnut, 12 parts denatured alcohol. After the dye has dried, seal the board with a washcoat of shellac. When dry, wipe on a coat of General Finishes black cherry water-based stain. Used as a glaze, the stain brings out the grain and imparts a darker tone but won't blotch the wood.

A DEEPER, DARKER MAHOGANY

Apply a coat of TransTint honey amber dye at standard strength to give the wood a warmer undertone. Then wipe on and wipe off Minwax®'s red mahogany oil-based stain. Used on bare wood, the stain gives a dark but shallow appearance. Used in combination, the overall look is darker, but the brighter dye shows through, giving greater depth.

AN ARTS AND CRAFTS FINISH FOR WHITE OAK

Here is a way to maximize the impact of quartersawn white oak. Dye the board with TransTint golden brown at standard strength. Next, apply a washcoat of shellac. Then wipe on and off a coat of Zar oil-based walnut stain. The combination gives the wood a rich tone, highlights the grain structure, and pops the ray flecks.

LIVEN UP KILN-DRIED WALNUT

Most commercial walnut is steamed during the kiln-drying process, which neutralizes the sapwood but leaves the whole board with a gray, pallid appearance. Use TransTint medium brown dye to improve the color. Next, use Bartley's dark brown mahogany gel stain as a glaze to deepen the color without hiding the figure.

Begin with a dye. Alter the underlying color of the wood and bring out any figure by applying a dye to the bare wood.

A washcoat is optional. A thin coat of finish, known as a washcoat, can be used at this point to seal the wood and control the stain's penetration. Dewaxed shellac is ideal for this step.

Wipe on a stain. After working the stain into the grain, wipe off the surplus. When a thick-bodied stain is applied over a washcoat, it is known as a glaze.

Although stains accentuate the grain and pore structure in the wood, the figure (shimmer) is not highlighted nearly as well as with a dye. Pay careful attention to surface preparation because stains will lodge in any scratches, tearout, or gouges that you may have overlooked.

Multiple coats of stain become more like paint, and because the binder usually isn't strong, multiple coats become a weak link in the finish.

Combine dyes and stains for custom looks

Some manufacturers tout combination dyes and stains as one-step solutions to coloring wood, but applying these elements separately will give you greater latitude over the final appearance.

The color of the dye will have a big impact on the look of the finish. Brighter colors, such as golden brown, red, yellow, amber, and orange, create highlights that will transmit through a wide variety of stains, increasing the depth and visual appeal of the wood. A stain applied over the dye adds color, either by contrasting or harmonizing with the dye, and defines the grain and pore structure. Examples are dyeing walnut or mahogany yellow and then applying a dark stain, or using a red dye to enhance that tone in mahogany.

Dyeing and staining can also enhance the natural look of a wood. Use colors that occur naturally in wood as it ages to give your piece an antique appearance. Use a dye as the underlying color of the antique to bring out the figure and the chatoyance. Then use a stain to tweak the color, to enhance the grain, and to add depth.

TIP Blotch-prone woods such as alder, aspen, birch, cherry, and pine may appear mottled or splotchy when a dye or stain is applied to bare wood. This is especially true for darker colors. The solution is to apply a diluted dye to the bare wood to pop the figure, then seal the wood and apply a dark glaze to add more color without blotching.

Test the strength of your dye

Before using a dye, you should test it in various dilutions on a color-step sample board. Dyes in small containers (for example, 2 oz.) are very concentrated and are designed to be diluted to a "standard" concentration of 1 oz. dye per quart of solvent. To use less dye, start with ½ oz. dye and 16 oz. solvent. After testing the standard concentrate, thin it with equal parts solvent, then 2 parts solvent to 1 part dye, then 4:1, and possibly 8:1, applying each dilution to the board. If the standard dilution is too weak, add more of the undiluted dye, but measure precisely and record the amount.

Dyes in larger bottles usually aren't as concentrated. With these, make a step board starting with dye straight from the bottle and thin from there. Keep the step boards for future reference.

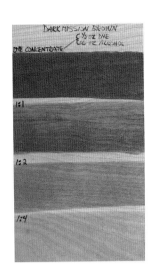

This two-step method can also be used to replicate dark woods, meaning you can create a deep, dark color such as ebony or dark mahogany from a different wood species. Often a dye or stain alone won't produce these deep shades, but using a dye and a stain in the same color range will make the final color much darker.

Glaze wood for subtle color changes

Until now I've talked about applying stain directly to dyed wood, which significantly alters its look. When a stain is applied over a coat of clear finish, it is known as a glaze. You can buy purpose-made glazes, or you can use a heavy-bodied stain such as a gel stain.

Apply a washcoat to seal the wood and prevent stain from penetrating it (possibly causing blotching). On wood with a prominent grain structure, a washcoat will allow glaze to accentuate the grain (see the photos on p. 79), without unduly coloring the whole board. Therefore, don't lay the washcoat on so thick that you fill the pores (unless you don't want to accentuate the grain patterns).

Dewaxed shellac works well as a washcoat because it can be thinned while still provid-ing a continuous seal. Thin the shellac to a ½-lb. cut or a 1-lb. cut. Use a ½-lb. cut on woods with a fine pore and grain structure in combination with a thick oil-based glaze. For a water-based or thin oil-based glaze, a 1-lb. cut helps prevent blotching. Also use a 1-lb. cut for wood with larger pores, perhaps applying a second coat to further limit how much color the glaze will add. If you use Zinsser's SealCoat, dilute it with denatured alcohol in a 1:1 ratio for a 1-lb. cut or 2:1 ratio for a ½-lb. cut. If you make shellac from flakes, a 1-lb. cut is about 10% flakes by volume. For example, to make 8 oz. of shellac, pour 7.2 oz. of alcohol into a measuring container and add flakes until the level reaches 8 oz.

After you seal the surface of the wood, applying the glaze adds only a small amount of color. The effect is rather like looking at the wood through colored sunglasses. Just as some sunglasses improve the contrast of everything you see, a glaze should have the same kind of effect on the wood.

Foolproof Dye and Gel-Stain Recipes

PETER GEDRYS

Gel stains have grown in popularity in recent years. Their viscosity and wipe-on/wipe-off application method make them easy to master, and compared with penetrating oil stains, they cause far less blotching on certain woods. However, using them on bare wood is often not the best method. Because of the pigment in gel stains, multiple coats tend to obscure the wood grain. And they come in a limited range of colors.

A better way to use them is in conjunction with dyes. You can apply gel directly over a dye to emphasize the grain and pore structure, or you can seal the dyed surface first and then apply the gel stain. Known as glazing, this is one of the most versatile and forgiving steps in the finisher's arsenal because it's so easy to change or even remove the glaze before it dries. I'll demonstrate how this works by highlighting my favorite finishes for three popular woods—a fumed oak finish for white oak, an antique finish for pine, and a high-shine finish for mahogany. I'll also provide the finishing recipes for each.

Three winning looks

Dye powders come in a huge range of colors, and their clarity doesn't obscure the wood. Used on top of the dye, gel stains allow you to tweak the color and highlight the grain.

White oak

Pine

Mahogany

A faux fumed look for white oak

White oak is one of my favorite woods because it takes colors and finishes in a predictable fashion. On this table, I'll show you how to create a deep, rich brown reminiscent of fumed oak, the signature finish of so many Arts and Crafts pieces.

The process starts with a water-based dye, which is used to lighten up or subdue the base or background color of the wood. Water-based dyes are economical and come in a huge range of colors. My choice for this table was W. D. Lockwood's English Brown Oak, a cool, deep brown. Dissolve ½ oz. of powder in 8 oz. of warm distilled water, let it cool, and then filter it.

After sanding the table to P180 grit, blow the dust out of the pores, wipe the surface clean with a dry cloth, and apply the dye with a small pad. Use a brush to help dab the dye into corners. Be generous applying the

dye, but wipe off the excess. Once the dye is dry, wipe on a coat of gel stain directly over it, and wipe off the surplus after a couple of minutes. This helps make the grain and pore structure more pronounced, while leaving the ray-fleck pattern pale. I used General Finishes Brown Mahogany, a deep, warm brown. This dye-and-stain combination results in a deep, aged brown like you'll find on many antiques.

Allow the gel to dry completely (about 24 to 36 hours) before applying a topcoat. If you're not sure it's dry, do the smell test: If there is a strong, discernible smell of oil, wait. I applied three coats of an oil-based varnish to give the table decent protection. If you want to use a water-based finish, seal the gel stain first with a coat of dewaxed shellac. Zinsser's SealCoat works very well and can be used at its regular 2-lb. cut.

 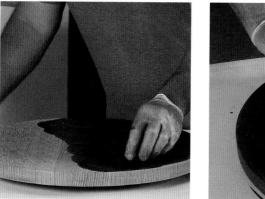 

Filter first. Before using the dye, pour it through a fine paint filter to remove any lumps of powder.

Apply dye liberally. Use a folded piece of cloth or paper towel to dye the wood (left). After a minute or two, wipe off the surplus with a clean cloth (right).

Wipe on, wipe off. Applied straight to the dyed wood, the gel stain packs the pores and emphasizes the grain pattern of the white oak.

Mission oak

Transform pale white oak into the rich, deep brown reminiscent of fumed oak without using hazardous concentrated ammonia.

THE RECIPE
- **W. D. Lockwood #871 English Brown Oak water-soluble dye**
- **General Finishes Brown Mahogany gel stain**
- **Oil-based varnish**

Antique pine

Sealing the surface is the secret to an even color on this notoriously blotch-prone wood.

THE RECIPE
- W. D. Lockwood #142 Early American Maple Medium Yellow water-soluble dye
- General Finishes Prairie Wheat gel stain
- Blond shellac

Sealing is the solution. This pine needed only a thin, 1-lb. cut of shellac. Wipe it on, let it dry, and then apply the dye.

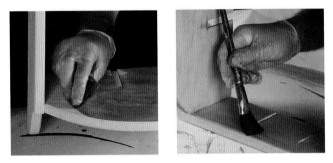

Yellow adds depth. Wipe the sealed pine with the yellow dye (left). Apply a 2-lb. cut of dewaxed shellac (right) to seal the dye before using the gel stain as a glaze.

An antique look for pine

If white oak is predictable when finishing, pine is anything but. A softwood, it can take dye stain in an uneven way and leave dark blotches. If the dyed sample boards indicate blotching, apply one or two washcoats of a 1-lb. cut of SealCoat shellac (three parts shellac with two parts denatured alcohol). When the shellac is dry, sand it with P220-grit paper and clean off the dust.

For this shelf, I used Early American Maple Medium Yellow dye. I mixed roughly ¼ oz. of powder in 8 oz. of water so that it would have just enough color to give the pale pine a little boost. When dry, apply a coat of undiluted SealCoat, and when this is dry,

sand it with P320-grit paper to flatten the surface.

Now that the surface is sealed, the gel becomes a glaze. Instead of quickly soaking into the wood, it sits on the surface and you can move it around. You can leave it denser in corners to simulate aging, or even remove it altogether if you don't like the appearance. When using any stain in this way, you need to dilute it by about 10% with mineral spirits to extend the working time. Don't overthin, or the gel will become watery and you'll lose the color strength. Instead of mineral spirits, you can add a little colorless glaze base such as Benjamin Moore®'s Studio Finishes® Glaze to get even more working time and control

over the color. The gel-stain glaze can be applied with a pad or brush, but if you choose a pad, use a dry China-bristle brush to feather out any application lines. Let the glaze dry prior to topcoating.

Because the shelf won't see as much wear and tear as the table, I used SealCoat shellac as a topcoat (three coats). When brushing on the first coat, use as few brush strokes as you can. If you work the shellac too much, it could pull the pigment and leave a patchy appearance. When the third coat of shellac is dry, lightly sand the surface with P320- or P400-grit paper. A coat of wax is an optional final finish, but it gives the piece a soft look and a nice feel.

A fiery finish for mahogany

Instead of the normal mahogany brown, let's have a little fun with this mahogany jewelry box (www.bartleycollection.com). Start with a Bismark Brown, but don't be fooled by the name; this alcohol-soluble dye is a deep, fiery red.

With an open-pored wood like mahogany, sealing is optional. If you want to emphasize

Reversible color. When applied to a sealed surface, the gel stain becomes a glaze and can be wiped on and off until the appearance is just the way you want it.

Glowing mahogany

A vibrant dye brings the wood to life while a layer of dark gel stain adds depth to the appearance.

THE RECIPE
- W. D. Lockwood #350 Bismark Brown alcohol-soluble dye
- Bartley Espresso gel stain
- Solvent-based lacquer

A brighter option. Powders dissolved with denatured alcohol are more vibrant.

Seal by spraying. When sealing an alcohol-based dye with shellac, spray it on. Brushing or wiping could pull the dye and leave a blotchy appearance. SealCoat is available in an aerosol can.

the pore structure, skip this step. Just be aware that the gel will be darker on raw wood. In this case, the grain pattern was nothing special, so I sprayed on a single coat of SealCoat shellac. For the glaze (gel stain), I used Bartley Espresso. I added a second coat of glaze to the bracket feet to deepen them. After applying the glaze coats, let the piece sit for a few days to dry completely and then seal it with shellac.

You now have a choice. For a high-gloss, rubbed-out finish, spray on two or three coats of solvent lacquer. If you don't have a spray outfit, aerosol cans are fine for a small project like this. Once the solvent lacquer has cured, you can refine it by rubbing it out. For a higher sheen, lightly abrade the surface with some 600-grit (CAMI) wet-and-dry sandpaper lubricated with water. Then rub the surface with a fine-cut automotive rubbing compound, and finally, apply some paste wax. For a softer sheen, smooth the finish with 1,000-grit CAMI-grade wet-or-dry sandpaper or a 1,000-grit Abralon pad, then rub it down with 0000 steel wool and wax.

Another shot of color. Wiped on over the shellac, the Espresso gel stain becomes a glaze. Use a dry brush to remove pad marks.

Altering the Colors of Dyes and Stains

PETER GEDRYS

All colors are not created equal. How many times have you bought a stain or a dye and been surprised or unhappy with the results? Each manufacturer presents us with its version of a particular color, such as cherry, and the versions can be as different as night and day.

However, with a little knowledge of color theory and how to "read" colors in different ways, you'll soon be controlling the color and not the other way around.

Learn to read a color

Before you can adjust the color of a dye or stain, you need to discover what its true color is by applying it on a white background. Oil-based colors can be tested on paper, but because water- or alcohol-based dyes are absorbed quickly by paper, they are best tested on plastic plates. Dab on a small amount of color, then drag some of it out into a thin line. Do the same with a color you think will blend well, and then with the two colors mixed together. When using any pigmented color, be sure to stir the can until all of the pigment is in suspension; otherwise, you will get an incorrect reading.

Test the color on sample boards

Once you have created a blend that looks good on a plate, it is time to test it on a sample board. Use a piece at least 4 in. wide and 6 in. long for each sample, and be sure to

Always make a sample board. When mixing colors, it is important to test them on scrapwood before applying them to the workpiece.

A color wheel helps dial in colors

The colors on a color wheel are divided into categories: primary, secondary, and tertiary. Primary colors —red, yellow, and blue—combine to create secondary colors—green, violet, and orange. Tertiary colors combine one primary and one secondary color. Colors opposite each other on the wheel are complementary colors. Mixing a color with its complement neutralizes (reduces the intensity of) the color. For example, if a stain is too red, add small amounts of green and watch the red change to a cooler brown.

Using a color wheel, first identify the main color of a stain. Then select stains containing colors adjacent to or opposite the main color on the wheel. Use these additional stains to mix the exact color you want. For a quick preview, you can pick a color on the rim of the wheel and rotate the inner circle to see the results of adding different colors.

The warm cherry and the cool walnut result in a deeper, cooler brown.

The golden oak combines with the cherry to give a brighter tone.

Cherry

Walnut
A color with "walnut" in the name often will contain a cooler pigment, such as violet or blue.

Golden oak
To add yellow tones to a stain, golden oak is a good choice.

Adding a color from the opposite side of the wheel will tone down the stain.

keep notes on what went into each color mix and how many coats you applied.

Alcohol- or water-based colors dry so quickly that you won't have the wet finished look you get with an oil-based color. So add a couple coats of clear finish to develop the final look of the piece.

Adjusting dyes and stains

To help explain the process of adjusting color, I made a few sample boards, using a variety of cherry stains and dyes. The goal was not to produce four identical shades of cherry but to show how each original color can be changed.

Oil-based stain

Many penetrating oil stains are a blend of dyes and pigments, but Minwax cherry stain is almost all dye with a small amount of pigment. The Minwax product had a weak, almost neutral tan color, with very little reddish tone, or warmth, to it. For a deeper, warmer shade, I added to the cherry stain 25% of Minwax's special walnut stain. If you want a brighter shade, add 25% of Minwax's golden oak to the cherry stain.

Gel stain

In general, because of the density of their pigment-based color, gel stains are best used over wood that has been sealed already. However, in this case I wanted to emphasize the color, so I applied Bartley cherry stain to bare wood.

The stain had a pronounced purplish hue that I wanted to tone down. Bartley's fruitwood gel stain is a greenish brown that resembles raw umber. I combined the cherry and fruitwood stains in a 50:50 mixture, which produced a pleasing, warm brown color. For a neutral, medium-brown color, I blended Bartley's country maple stain, which resembles burnt sienna (orange-brown), with the cherry stain in a 50:50 mixture.

Water-based dye

For clarity of color, powdered dyes are the most versatile because you can mix them yourself, which allows you to control the concentration. When handling dye powders, make sure you wear a dust mask.

I selected the W. D. Lockwood early American cherry, which produced an orange-brown color. To create a deeper brown, I added a few drops of violet, the complementary color to orange.

Non-grain-raising stain

Non-grain-raising (NGR) stains, such as Solar-Lux, are a mixture of water-soluble dyes and solvents that don't include water. They work well as a background color. Some start out unrealistically bright and in strong light fade faster than a campaign promise.

The Solar-Lux cherry is a warm, reddish brown. To bring out the red tones, I added about 25% of medium-red mahogany. If you want to neutralize a color but don't have its complementary color, try adding black in small quantities, say 2% or 3%.

Color, like food, is a subjective taste. The examples I have shown are a starting point. Don't be afraid to experiment, and don't get stuck using a color you don't like.

More recipes for cherry

Bartley, W. D. Lockwood, and Solar-Lux each has a different idea of what the color cherry should look like. Using the techniques described, read the color to get a better idea of where it falls on the color wheel. Then, using the wheel, add complementary or adjacent colors to manipulate the original color until you are satisfied with the shade. It is safest to use stains or dyes from the same manufacturer in your recipe.

Bartley gel stain

The Pennsylvania cherry stain (left) has a strong purple hue. Mixing it with Bartley's greenish fruitwood stain in a 50:50 ratio produces a warm brown (center). Substitute Bartley's orange-brown country maple for the fruitwood, and you get a medium brown (right).

W. D. Lockwood water-based dye

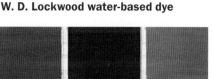

The early American cherry (left) is an orange-brown color. To neutralize the orange, add a small amount of its complementary color, violet, for a deeper brown (center). To create a more golden color (right), add about 20% of W. D. Lockwood's light golden oak to the cherry dye.

Solar-Lux non-grain-raising stain

The original cherry (left) is reddish-brown. Adding 25% of medium-red mahogany deepens the tone (center). If you don't have the complementary color to neutralize red or orange, add black to produce a dark brown (right).

How to Match a Finish

JEFF JEWITT

Sooner or later, most woodworkers will likely face the challenge posed by a client or a spouse: "Well, I know it's pretty wood and all, but can you make it match the rest of the furniture?" The first time I heard those words my heart sank. I had made two matching nightstands for my wife using the most stunning figured ash I'd ever seen. The last thing I wanted to do was stain them, but I had to admit that pearly white wood didn't exactly fit in with our decorating scheme.

Many factory finishing operations involve specialized stains (such as sap stains, equalizing stains, and pad stains) applied to the furniture in as many as six separate coloring steps. But it doesn't have to be that complicated. If you understand how stains work on wood and apply some basic color principles, the job can go a lot smoother. You don't need dozens of different stain colors. Armed with a few dyes and pigment stains in wood-tone colors—plus red, yellow, green, and black—you should be able to match just about anything by following a systematic process of staining, glazing, and clear coating.

Before we get into the process of matching one finished piece to another, it will help to keep in mind the following:

- Matching a finish requires the correct lighting conditions. Incandescent and some fluorescent lighting will distort the color. It's best to work in diffused natural daylight or under full-spectrum, color-corrected fluorescent lights.

- Work from light to dark gradually. You can always darken a color, but it's difficult to lighten wood tones under a transparent finish that are already too dark.

- It's easiest to match colors when the finish has high-gloss sheen. Most colors shift slightly when the finish over them is satin or flat. If the sample you want to match does not have a glossy sheen, wet the surface with some mineral spirits to simulate the effect of gloss.

Build color in different ways

Wood stains can be grouped into two distinct types—pigments and dyes. Manufacturers sometimes mix the two together, but I find it easier to work with one at a time when matching color.

Pigments

Pigment stains use an inert, finely ground colored powder as the colorant. This powder is suspended in a mixture of resin and thinner. When applied to wood and wiped, the small pigment particles lodge in the surface texture of the wood. When the thinner evaporates, the resin dries and binds the color in place. Soft woods with a spongy texture (such as pine and poplar) have plenty of minute cavities for the pigment to lodge in, so it's possible to make the wood very dark. Hard, dense woods (such as cherry and maple) have fewer cavities, so pigment stains won't work as well if your goal is a dark color.

Glazes are just modified pigment stains. Commercial versions are thicker, have a lower binder content, and they're slower drying because they're sometimes manipulated after application to produce special effects. Add mineral spirits to a pigmented gel stain, and you'll get pretty much the same thing as a store-bought glaze.

Paste wood fillers are pigment stains that contain a fine quartz-silica additive to bulk up the pores of open-grained woods to attain a glass-smooth finish. Oil-based versions are easier to apply and control.

Dyes

Dye stains are colored solutions in which microscopic dye particles are mixed with either water or alcohol. When applied to wood, the color is distributed evenly and deeply, so you can stain all types of wood more effectively. The result is a more transparent color than what you get with pigment stains because dyes don't muddy the surface. And because dyes penetrate deeper and contain no binder that would inhibit absorption, it's easy to shift a color that's slightly off the mark by using another dye.

A stain board guides the way

To help in the finishing process, make a stain board (see the photo on the facing page). Take a scrap cutoff from the piece you're working on, and divide it into several sections to give yourself some leeway to tinker with colors until you get a match. You can test colors on the stain board before applying them to your project.

For a basic color kit, start with an assortment of four dyes in wood tones: a honey-colored dye for undertones (especially the yellow undertones on antiques), a medium nut-brown color, a reddish-brown cherry color, and a dark brown. Add red, yellow, and green dyes to modify these wood-tone colors. For pigment stains, you should have comparable colors to those mentioned above plus concentrated versions of red, green, black, and white—sold as Japan colors for oil-based finishes and universal tinting colors (UTCs) for oil- and water-based finishes.

Match a finish in four basic steps

To match a finish, start with the undertone color of the wood (using dye stains). Over that you often need to change the color using a second dye stain or a pigment stain. When the color is close, add a coat of sealer to lock it in. To tweak the color even more, use a paste wood filler (on porous open grain) or a glaze (on tight grain). And finally, you need to match the sheen of the original finish (with a gloss, satin, or flat finish). Using the unfinished cherry side table in the photos to illustrate the process, let's go through each step.

Step one: match the undertone first

When matching old furniture or woods that change color easily, this step establishes an underlying golden-colored patina, which evens out different colors in lumber and veneer and helps blend sapwood to heartwood. The undertone is the hardest color to see, but it often is the lightest background color in the wood. It's best to use a dye stain and try it first on a stain board (see "A stain board guides the way" on p. 91). Also, if you're not sure about the color of the undertone, it's safer to go with a color that is a hair lighter.

Step two: adjust the color, and seal it in

Adjust the undertone with a second color of stain, if necessary. This step is more often required with tight-grained woods (such as the cherry shown in these photos) and darker colors. On open-grained woods (such as oak or mahogany), the color of the pores has a dramatic impact on the overall color and appearance of the finish. An oil-based paste wood filler or a glaze will vary that visual impact effectively. Before continuing, you can maintain more control in matching a finish if you first lock in the color with a sealer coat of shellac or lacquer.

Step three: fine-tune the overall color with a glaze

Once the wood has been sealed and the basic color established, you should need to make only small adjustments to the final color. You can sneak up on it by using a glaze of thinned, concentrated colors. They're easy to apply and, if you get the color wrong, easy to wipe off before they set up. Start with a glaze of wood-tone colors and mix in pure Japan colors such as red or green to adjust the final hue. Check the color of the glaze by smearing some on a piece of glass. When you have the color right, check it on a stain board. To darken a color, use dark brown rather than black, which makes the overall color "cooler," or less red. Swab the glaze on liberally, then wipe it off. A glaze should dry overnight before being covered with a topcoat.

Toning is another good way to produce darker color and tonal shifts, but you'll need to do this with a spray gun by mixing pigment stain or dye stain into the finish.

Step four: match the sheen with a topcoat

The color will deepen and go to a shade slightly darker once a clear finish has been applied. Avoid using dark or strongly colored finishes (such as exterior varnishes and orange shellacs) because they will change the final color. If you use a varnish or polyurethane with a glossy sheen, you can rub out the finish to any sheen you wish after the topcoats cure. To determine the sheen of an existing finish, place the sample under a fluorescent light. If the reflection of the tube is distinct, the finish is gloss; if it's slightly fuzzy, the sheen is satin; and if the reflection isn't discernible, the finish has a flat sheen. Gloss topcoats deepen the color the most, and satin and flat sheens lighten up the color slightly or add a frosted look.

Learn to mix your own. Store-bought, oil-based glazes can be tinted with concentrated Japan colors to get the exact shade you want.

Glaze refines the process. Liberally coat the workpiece with glaze, then wipe it off.

To match a color, always apply a gloss finish. After it dries, you can rub out the surface with fine sandpaper or steel wool to achieve the desired sheen, or you can use a satin or flat finish on the last coat.

All about Thinning Finishes

JEFF JEWITT

It's a rare woodworker who is not intimidated by the cans of solvents lining the shelves in a hardware store. The multisyllabic names are reminders of less-than-productive school chemistry classes, while the dire health warnings are equally off-putting. The temptation is to grab something vaguely familiar, hope that it is compatible with the finish you are using, and leave as fast as possible.

But it need not be like this. I will guide you through the world of solvents—the good, the bad, and the unpronounceable. I will show you which solvents are appropriate for water- or oil-based finishes, shellacs, or solvent lacquers, whether you are spraying, brushing, or wiping on the finish.

A quick word about chemistry

Almost all finishing materials contain liquids that are volatile, meaning they evaporate during the drying and curing of the finish. These liquids, called solvents and thinners, make the finishing material less viscous for easier application.

Chemists distinguish between solvents and thinners: Solvents dissolve or break up finishing resins and reduce viscosity, while thinners merely reduce the viscosity. Dissolving shellac flakes with denatured alcohol is the only occasion a woodworker is likely to use a solvent as such. Here, I use the terms solvent and thinner interchangeably, as many woodworkers do.

Thinning water-based finishes takes more than water

The widespread use of water-based finishes is rather new, and in many cases the chemistry behind it is still being fine-tuned. Many woodworkers are aware of water-based versions of lacquer and polyurethane, but water-based varieties of varnish, gel stain, and Danish-oil finishes are also available. While the novice might assume they would be the easiest finishes to thin because they are made up mostly of water, their chemical complexity makes them the least-forgiving finishes to tamper with.

You can get into serious problems if you add too much water. Usually 5% to 10% is fine for viscosity adjustments (to make it spray or brush better), but more than that can disrupt the chemical makeup of the finish, which will have a negative effect on how the finish forms a film.

For a finish that dries too fast, a better alternative is to use a retarder. A retarder is typically used in hot, dry conditions. It helps you avoid orange peel by giving the finish more time to flow out and achieve a level surface. Be sure to use a retarder recommended by the finish manufacturer. The wrong retarder can upset the chemical balance of the finish.

When spraying a water-based finish, before adding water or a retarder, try to compensate for viscosity by changing to a larger needle/nozzle and making adjustments to your finishing environment or technique. Spray thinner coats when it's hot and humid, and arrange fans so that air blows gently across the finish as it dries.

Shellac is compatible with more than alcohol

Shellac is one of the oldest finishes in woodworking. No other finish can match the depth and clarity it brings to wood, but

Adjusting water-based finishes. Among the finishing families, the evaporation rate of water-based finishes is the most difficult to adjust. They typically require a specific retarder, while plain water should only be added sparingly.

How much time do you need?

One of the reasons for adding solvents is to control the rate at which the finish dries. This control is desirable for any method of application. When spraying a vertical surface, too slow a drying time may cause the finish to run, whereas a finish that evaporates too fast may leave an orange-peel appearance. When brushing, the right solvent can maintain a wet edge yet not attract dust by taking forever to dry. See the chart on pp. 100–101 to find finishes and their drying times.

The slow and the fast. Mineral spirits and naphtha were simultaneously brushed onto a board. Three minutes later, the naphtha had almost evaporated, while the mineral spirits was still wet.

A brushed finish should go down without leaving lap marks. If you have trouble keeping a wet edge because the finish dries too quickly, which may happen in warm, dry weather, add a small amount of retarder to a water-based finish.

Thinning shellac. Most woodworkers use only denatured alcohol to thin shellac, but several other solvents offer slower evaporation rates for brushing shellac or spraying it on a hot and dry day.

its lack of durability makes it unsuitable for surfaces subject to heavy use.

Shellac is available in dried flakes that are dissolved in alcohol or in ready-to-use liquid form. For both premixed shellac and shellac flakes, the best all-around thinner is denatured alcohol.

As shellac is sprayed, the solvents evaporate, cooling the surface of the workpiece. If the temperature falls below the dew point, moisture condenses on the surface, causing a cloudy appearance in the finish known as blushing. If you are spraying shellac in hot, humid weather, you need to slow down the drying rate to avoid blushing. Suitable retarders include butanol or isopropanol, the latter being found at auto-parts stores as a gas-line antifreeze. Do not use rubbing alcohol; even though the active ingredient is isopropanol, the other 30% to 50% is water, which will not improve your finish. Glycol ether such as lacquer retarder also slows the drying time of shellac, but the finish may remain soft and be more easily damaged.

A retarder is also useful when you are brushing shellac on a large surface, such as a tabletop. If the shellac dries too quickly, you risk applying the finish to an area adjacent to

More brushing, less rushing. The addition of turpentine slows the drying time of shellac, allowing you to keep a wet edge while brushing a large surface. You can even go back and tip off the surface.

The right glove for each solven

When using solvents, many woodworkers protect their hands with disposable latex or vinyl gloves. Inevitably a particular solvent seems to eat through the glove as if it wasn't there, resulting in chapped skin or even chemical burns.

Shown here are disposable and reusable gloves made of latex, nitrile, vinyl, and neoprene. Less important than what th glove is made of is to remember that disposable gloves should be used only for splash protection, such as when blending a finish or brushing one on. For more sustained contact, such as when using a solvent to clean a spray gun or wiping on a finish, use heavy-duty gloves. Unfortunately, no one glove is suitable for all solvents.

Specific information on how different glove materials stand up to various solvents can be found at Mapa® 's Web site (www mapaglove.com) as well as other manufacturers' sites.

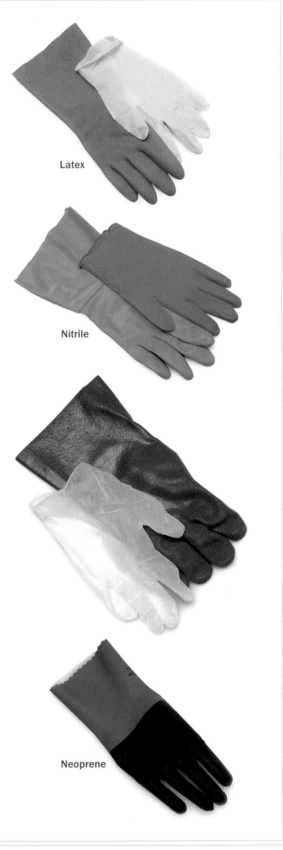

Latex

Nitrile

Neoprene

LATEX

Latex gloves are used primarily for mixing dye powders and applying water-based dyes. The main advantage of disposable latex gloves is their flexibility and feel, which make them good for doing detailed work. Neither type of glove shown will stand up to oils or hydrocarbon derivatives (mineral spirits, naphtha, paint thinner, or kerosene).

NITRILE

Nitrile gloves offer protection from almost any solvent a woodworker is likely to use. The only exception is a solvent that contains a ketone such as acetone. The disposable version offers more protection than the other two types of disposable gloves, but they are harder to find and are more expensive.

VINYL

These are okay for powdered dyes and dyes in a water solution. Disposable vinyl gloves are the cheapest protection available, but they tear more easily than disposable latex ones. Avoid contact with ketones and aromatic solvents. The thicker gloves offer good protection but at the expense of a clumsy feel.

NEOPRENE

This is another excellent choice for regular contact with most solvents, except lacquer thinner, in which case nitrile is a better choice.

one where the finish has already started to set up, preventing the edges of the brush strokes from blending together. Adding a teaspoon of pure gum spirit turpentine to approximately 4 oz. of liquid shellac acts as a retarder. With a retarder added, the first line of finish will remain wet until the second line can be brushed on and the two can blend together.

Hydrocarbon solvents and oil-based finishes offer the most choices

Linseed, tung, and Danish oils; oil-based varnishes and polyurethanes; and oil paint and waxes make up the largest family of finishes and are the products most woodworkers think of when it comes to finishing. These finishes are thinned with two groups of solvents: hydrocarbons and terpenes.

Hydrocarbons (kerosene, mineral spirits, naphtha, paint thinner, toluene, and xylene) are derived from petroleum oil.

Terpenes (turpentine, d-limonene) are derived from plants, with turpentine coming from pine trees and d-limonene from citrus trees. These two solvents are nearly always interchangeable with hydrocarbons. D-limonene has a pretty distinctive citrus smell that makes it more pleasant to work with, but it's hard to find. Its toxicity and flammability are about equal to mineral spirits, but the evaporation rate is slower.

Because of the high cost of extracting turpentine, this classic thinner has all but been replaced with mineral spirits. A drawback to using turpentine is the rosin content, which can vary depending on what trees were processed in each particular batch. If the rosin content is high in the can you are using, the finish will remain soft; however, you will not find a measurement on the side of the can.

The two best thinners to use are mineral spirits and naphtha. Mineral spirits is best for maintaining a wet edge when brushing,

Oil-based finishes aren't thin on thinners. The petroleum industry has produced a large range of solvents compatible with oil-based finishes. These range from slow-evaporating kerosene to fast-evaporating ketone.

To thin or not to thin. Some finishes, particularly oil-based ones, come with a warning not to thin the contents. In finishes advertised as having a "clean-air formula," any addition of solvent would place the finish above the emissions limit agreed with the government.

More than one drying speed for lacquer thinners. Besides the generic medium-speed lacquer thinner, slow and fast formulations are also available. The evaporation of lacquer can be slowed by adding a retarder or accelerated by adding acetone.

while naphtha is better for spraying or wiping. Kerosene can be added in small amounts (6 to 12 drops per pint) to oil-based stains to slow them down for easier application on large surfaces.

The right retarder makes lacquers easier to use

Solvent-based lacquer finishes have traditionally been the mainstays of commercial furniture makers and professional finishers. They are not as popular with hobbyists because of their reputation for needing expensive spraying facilities.

Solvent-based lacquer is thinned with lacquer thinner, a blend of ketones, alcohol, and hydrocarbons. By adjusting the ratio of these components, manufacturers can tailor a thinner to be fast, medium, or slow evaporating. Most woodworking finish suppliers stock only medium-speed thinner. The best place to find fast- and slow-evaporating lacquer thinners is an auto-finishing store. Fast-evaporating thinner prevents sagging on vertical surfaces, but if you can't find it,

use acetone. Unless you are spraying in very low humidity, however, an acetone-thinned finish is susceptible to blushing because of its fast evaporation rate.

Slow-evaporating thinners allow the finish to flow out and level better on horizontal surfaces. For this reason, slow-evaporating thinner is sometimes called "warm-weather" thinner. An alternative to slow-evaporating thinner is to add lacquer retarder (glycol ether) to a standard lacquer thinner, then add the mix to a finish.

For more information on the dangers of a particular solvent and to find out what type of respirator to use, check its material safety data sheet (MSDS) by entering the manufacturer's name for the solvent and MSDS (i.e., Sunnyside Denatured Alcohol MSDS) into an online search engine. Another useful source of information is the National Institute for Occupational Safety and Health (NIOSH), available at www.cdc.gov/niosh.

Adjust your lacquer for every occasion. When spraying a vertical surface, it is important that the finish dries before it has a chance to sag and run.

See how it runs. The top bar of black lacquer had fast-evaporating acetone added. The lower bar was thinned with slow-evaporating lacquer thinner, giving the finish time to run before it could dry.

Finishes and Their Compatible Thinners

In this chart, the finishes are divided into four families, roughly in order of the toxicity of their solvents: water-based, shellac, oil-based, and solvent-based lacquer. For each family, you'll find the range of compatible thinners and the points to consider when choosing one.

One point of particular note is drying time, as it may affect the look of your finish. The drying time of a solvent is rated as slow if it acts as a retarder (slows down the drying time). A rating of medium means that the solvent doesn't significantly change the drying properties of a finish, although the drying time of any thinned finish will speed up somewhat. And fast solvents do just that: speed up the drying time. The actual speed will vary based on application methods and environmental conditions.

TYPE OF FINISH	THINNER	DRYING TIME	COMMENTS
Water-based	Retarder (water glycol ether and additives)	Medium	Used to combat lap marks when brushing or orange peel when spraying. Follow the advice of the finish manufacturer carefully and use only the recommended retarder; otherwise, the chemical balance may be upset, rendering the product useless.
	Water	Fast	To avoid upsetting the chemical balance, never add more than 10% water. If the product is too thick to atomize properly for spraying or if it streaks when brushing or wiping, thinning may be required. If the humidity is 90% or more, don't add water because it will act as a retarder and lead to excessive drying time.
Shellac	Pure gum spirit turpentine	Slow	For an effective retarder, add a teaspoon to about 4 oz. of liquid shellac.
	Isobutanol	Medium/slow	Acts as a retarder but is difficult to find and has a very strong odor.
	Isopropanol	Medium/slow	A suitable retarder when brushing shellac. Auto-parts stores sell it as gas-line antifreeze. Check the label to make sure that isopropanol is the only component. An alternative source for 99% pure isopropanol is www.chemistrystore.com.
	Denatured alcohol	Medium/fast	Will slightly speed up drying time and improve the flow and atomization of heavy (3-lb. cut) shellac. It is the main solvent and thinner for shellac. Specific-brand formulas with different additives are available.
	Methanol	Very fast	Although no longer available to the consumer market, professional finishers can still obtain the product. Speeds up drying times considerably.
Oil-based	Kerosene	Slow	Used in small amounts, kerosene is effective as a retarder when brushing on an oil finish in dry weather.
	Odorless mineral spirits	Slow	Mineral spirits becomes odorless mineral spirits by removing the aromatics. This product is commonly available at art-supply stores as well as hardware stores. Acts as a retarder.
	Mineral spirits/ paint thinner	Medium	Use to change the viscosity without impacting the drying time significantly. Good for adding to a finish that will be brushed. Can also be used to thin gel varnishes that dry too fast and streak.
	Pure gum spirit turpentine	Medium	No longer used much in commercial finishing due to the variable quality. The rosin content is not reported on the can, but a batch with high rosin may leave a soft finish. The high price relative to paint thinner is another drawback.
	Xylene	Medium/fast	Best used for thinning conversion varnishes.
	VM&P naphtha	Fast	Varnish maker's and painter's (VM&P) naphtha is the best solvent for fast evaporation. Use it when spraying in cold weather, on vertical surfaces, or when using varnish or polyurethane as a wipe-on finish.
	Toluene	Fast	Dries slightly faster than VM&P naphtha but has a very strong odor. For consumers, naphtha is a better choice.

TYPE OF FINISH	THINNER	DRYING TIME	COMMENTS
Oil-based (continued)	Acetone (ketone)	Fast	Add to a thick varnish when spraying a single heavy coat to avoid runs and sags. When applied over a previous coat, may cause wrinkling of the finish.
Lacquer	Lacquer retarder	Slow	It's best not to mix retarder directly with a brushing lacquer. Instead, add 1 oz. to 2 oz. of retarder to 1 qt. standard (medium) lacquer thinner, then add small amounts of the mix to a finish.
	Slow lacquer thinner	Medium/slow	Most lacquer thinner available in hardware or woodworking stores has a medium-speed evaporation rate. The best place to find slow- or fast-evaporating lacquer thinner is at an auto-finishing supply store. If in doubt about their suitability, an alternative is to add lacquer retarder to a medium-speed thinner. This will produce a slow-evaporating thinner needed on hot days to avoid blushing and when spraying a horizontal surface to improve flow-out. Fast-evaporating thinner is recommended for cool weather and when spraying vertical surfaces. This can be made by adding acetone to a medium-speed lacquer thinner.
	Medium lacquer thinner	Medium	
	Fast lacquer thinner	Fast	
	Acetone	Very fast	Acetone evaporates so fast that it is prone to leave a finish blushed unless the humidity is very low. Woodworkers in the Southwest spraying during the summer may get away with using it.

A Traditional French Polish

SEAN CLARKE

I became hooked on French polishing at age 15, when I apprenticed with a large firm of period furniture makers in London. I instantly wanted to pursue this incredible art form, and for the following three years I learned all aspects of the craft by studying under master French polishers.

The aim of this technique, developed in France around 1820, is to use as little material as possible to gain the most effect. It's a traditional hand-finish that involves working several coats of shellac deep into the wood fibers, and the effect is one of exceptional depth and clarity. Because it is of moderate durability, a French-polished surface is best suited for display rather than hard use. But in my mind, no other finish can compare when it comes to illuminating the natural beauty inherent in wood.

As you would expect with a finish technique that is nearly 200 years old, there are many variations in the recipe, with each claiming to be the true French polish. This version has served me well for the past 18 years.

Before you polish, prepare the surface

Because French polishing magnifies imperfections, good surface preparation is imperative. Begin by sanding all surfaces up to 320-grit paper. Clean off the dust, then evaluate what the finished color of the piece will be by wiping the surfaces with a cloth

The language of French polishing

It is perhaps appropriate that many of the English terms for the different stages of French polishing are double entendres, a legacy perhaps of generations of master polishers embellishing the process with a mystique it doesn't deserve.

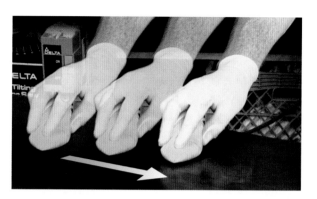

Floating. Floating is the process of applying shellac with the rubber in straight strokes with the grain. The purpose is to achieve a firm base on which to build the body of the finish.

Rubber. The term has nothing to do with latex but is derived from the method of using this tool to rub on thin layers of shellac. The exterior, known as the linen, can either be made from this fabric or more commonly from a 100% cotton bedsheet. The interior can be any kind of absorbent material, which also gives this tool its other name of tampon.

Bodying up. The stage where the bulk of the shellac is applied to the piece is called bodying up. The rubber can either be used in a padding motion to avoid pulling away a previous layer of stain or in a swirling or figure-eight pattern. Raw linseed oil is used to lubricate the rubber and prevent it from sticking to the shellac.

Spiriting off. The actual polishing stage of French polishing is called spiriting off. The oil used to body up is removed by rinsing the linen of the rubber in alcohol and then lightly floating the rubber across the surface. The alcohol not only removes the oil, but it also melts the top layer of shellac, creating a smooth, high-gloss surface.

Surface preparation is crucial

Don't skimp on surface preparation. French polishing leaves a high-gloss finish, and it will magnify any and all flaws in your piece.

1. Brush on a coat of boiled linseed oil, let it soak in for an hour, then wipe off any surplus. The oil takes at least five days to dry.

2. Using a large-capacity badger-hair mop, apply superblond shellac in the direction of the grain.

3. Use an old brush to apply a pore-filler/glaze mixture. Because the mixture sets up fast, work on small sections at a time.

4. Work quickly before the filler dries to produce a smooth surface.

soaked in denatured alcohol. The Georgian-style side table shown on p. 102 was built using Honduras mahogany for the legs and frame, but the drawer, with its highly figured Cuban mahogany veneer, and the single-piece mahogany top were both salvaged from antiques beyond repair. The alcohol revealed that the legs had a pinkish hue, but the top was more orange, and the drawer front was a dark brown.

To pull the colors together, I used a mixture of water-based powdered aniline dyes: red mahogany and golden-amber maple. I applied the dye full strength to all parts of the piece except for the drawer front, where I diluted the stain. Finally, I wiped on a coat of English brown oak stain over the piece to kill the orange hue. Before you apply a stain to a piece with an inlay, apply a 2-lb. cut of superblond shellac to the inlay using a small artist's brush to seal it, ensuring that it retains its contrast with the rest of the piece. Let everything dry.

Whether or not you stain the piece, next brush a coat of boiled linseed oil on the whole piece, then let it sit for an hour before wiping it down with a clean cloth. The oil penetrates the wood and gives maximum illumination to the fibers. Let the piece cure for five to seven days.

Apply the first coat of shellac

Lightly scuff-sand all surfaces with 320-grit self-lubricating paper to knock down any raised grain and dust nibs. Next, apply a coat of superblond shellac (2-lb. cut) to seal the dyed and oiled surface and to provide a base on which to build the finish. Be sure to use the paler superblond shellac at this stage; a deeper-colored shellac can cause color lines and a streaky effect. Use a large-capacity badger-hair mop brush to apply the shellac to every part but the top. Use a piece of folded cheesecloth to apply shellac to this area. Apply two or three coats in the direction of the grain, then leave the workpiece to dry for a couple of hours. If you live in a humid region, extend the drying times.

Brush on a pore-filler/ glaze mixture

Because a French-polished finish requires a uniformly smooth surface, the pores of open-grained woods, such as mahogany, need to be filled. Combine this step with a colored glaze that both harmonizes and ages the appearance. I mix my own glaze so that I can control both the color and the consistency. For this table, I used the following recipe: three heaped teaspoons of burnt-umber dry pigment; one heaped teaspoon of vegetable black dry pigment; four heaped teaspoons of fine-grade pumice; 1 oz. of gold size; and 4 oz. of turpentine. Turpentine extends the shelf life of the mixture, whereas mineral spirits tends to form a gel. You can adjust the pigment colors, but do not add more pumice than pigment, which can lead to specks of gray pumice showing up in the grain.

Brush the filler/glaze mixture onto a small section at a time, then wipe it off with a clean cloth. Use a circular or figure-eight motion to remove the bulk of the liquid, then wipe across the grain to deposit more into the pores. If an area dries and becomes difficult to remove, dampen the clean cloth with turpentine. As the photo of the filled top shows (bottom right, facing page), the glazed area is smoother and has the dark appearance of a mahogany antique.

Rub all surfaces with 0000 steel wool to remove any excess filler. In addition, wrap a turpentine-dampened cloth around a block and rub the surface to further remove any filler from the tabletop and deposit it in the pores.

There is one final step before the actual polishing can begin. After forming a rubber

The right rubber for the job

Every French polisher has a favorite design of rubber. If you have a preference, stick with it. For a table this size, I cut a cotton bedsheet roughly 8 in. square, removing any hems. I then cut a piece of cotton cloth approximately 6 in. square and folded it into a wad roughly 2 in. wide and 3 in. long, with a blunt point at one end.

Charge the wadding with denatured alcohol to increase its absorbency, then squirt shellac onto one surface of the wadding. Place this surface down into the center of the cloth, bring each corner of the cloth to the center, maintaining the point on one end, and twist the ends of the fabric together. Use this twist of fabric as a grip for the rubber. It is critical that the fabric be very smooth against the wadding because this is the surface that does the polishing. Smack the rubber against the palm of your hand so that the shellac penetrates the cloth, then you are ready to begin French polishing.

Start with a clean sheet. Use a white 100% cotton bedsheet as the exterior, or linen, of the polishing rubber. Cut off any hemmed edges of the sheet. The cloth encloses a wadded piece of cotton.

Charge the rubber. The shellac should be applied directly to the wadding before the rubber is used and each time it needs recharging. When not in use, store the rubber in an airtight container to prevent it from drying out.

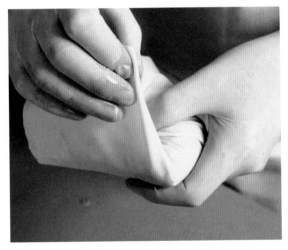

Wrap the rubber carefully. The cloth should be wrapped tightly around the wadding to form a smooth surface on the bottom that will do the polishing.

(see the sidebar on the facing page), use it to float a coat of buttonlac (2-lb. cut) across the entire workpiece. Floating refers to the process of applying shellac in straight strokes with the grain. This seals in the pore filler, while the darker buttonlac deepens and enriches the color.

Polishing starts by bodying up the finish

Let the piece dry overnight, then start building up the successive shellac coats, a process called bodying up. Still using the 2-lb. cut of buttonlac, brush a couple of coats onto every part of the table but the top. Charge the rubber with shellac, then flick a few drops of raw linseed oil onto the tabletop. The oil serves as a lubricant, allowing the rubber to float smoothly across the surface, laying down coats of shellac without abrading the previous coats. I use raw linseed oil because it has a longer cure time. If the finishing needs to stretch into several days, the oil remains workable.

Apply the shellac by moving the rubber in circles and figure-eight patterns using light to moderate pressure. Recharge the rubber, as necessary, until the finish begins to build. Brush another coat onto the rest of the table, then let the piece rest for an hour.

The last thing to do is sand the piece to remove any remaining imperfections. Flick a few drops of raw linseed oil onto some 320-grit sandpaper. The oil serves as a lubricant. Use a light touch, and avoid breaking through the finish at the edges.

Next, resume bodying up the tabletop, this time using the rubber on the legs and drawer front as well as on the tabletop. Flick the linseed oil directly onto the rubber when working on smaller areas, such as legs.

Remove the oil by spiriting off

The polishing part of a French polish is variously called spiriting off or stiffing off. This step removes the previously applied oil, which if left on would leave white traces in the cured finish. The aim is to remove the oil without displacing the coats of shellac.

First, wash out the cloth of the rubber in denatured alcohol, then wring it so that it is not dripping wet. Charge the wadding with a 1-lb. cut of buttonlac and rewrap the rubber. It is fine to go straight from bodying up to spiriting off without letting the finish rest.

Float the rubber across the surface of the table in straight strokes with slightly less pressure than when bodying up. The cloth of the rubber will start to pick up the oil in the finish. After going over the whole piece, rinse out the cloth in alcohol, but do not add shellac to the wadding. Float the rubber across the surface again and again, regularly rinsing out the cloth, which will become progressively drier. When you don't see any more oil being collected and the sheen has become an even gloss, stop and allow the piece to dry overnight.

Rub out and compound the finish

Your personal preference for final appearance decides the next step. For a high-gloss look, the finish must be rubbed out using 2,000-grit wet-or-dry sandpaper. I used the paper dry on the legs, the frame, and the drawer front of the table shown here, but on the top I used water as a lubricant. With a very light touch, sand in the direction of the grain and concentrate on not burning through the finish at the edges. Then apply a polishing compound in a circular motion using a clean cloth.

If you prefer a more satin level of gloss, rub the surface with 0000 steel wool. For

Build the finish in layers

Bodying up the finish—or applying the finish in multiple layers—
is a lengthy process, but the results will be worth the labor.

1. To apply the shellac, use a brush on all areas but the tabletop.

2. Polish the top with the rubber, using light to moderate pressure, and keep the rubber moving in circles and figure eights.

3. Add a few drops of raw linseed oil to 320-grit paper to prevent it from biting into the finish.

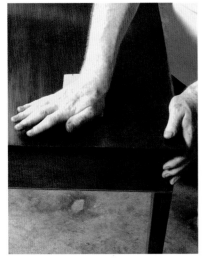

4. Rub the sandpaper across the tabletop using the heel of the hand rather than a block to lessen the chance of cutting through the finish on a high spot.

5. After sanding the piece, resume building the shellac finish. This time, use the rubber on the whole table, not just on the top, to create a smoother surface.

6. For rubbing out the finish, unroll the steel wool so that you don't cut through the finish.

the small areas of the table, I tore a strip of wool down the middle and folded it into a small pad that fit my hand. For the tabletop, I used a larger wad to distribute the pressure more evenly and to prevent the steel wool from becoming clogged. With this method, always rub the steel wool in the direction of the grain.

Last, add a coat of wax

Because I have always had a preference for an aged appearance to reproduction furniture, I like to add the step of "blacking in" to the wax polishing. I make my own blend of polish using the following recipe: one teaspoon of vegetable black pigment; 1 oz. of slow-set gold size; 4 oz. of Johnson® paste wax; and enough turpentine to dissolve the wax and make the finish easy to apply with a brush. If you prefer, you can leave out the black pigment. The gold size acts as a binder to make the pigment adhere to the finish when it dries.

Apply it to corners, crevices, feet, and any light spots. Then rub it with a clean cloth to blend it into the rest of the workpiece. To my eye, it gives character and re-creates the soft waxed luster of a piece of furniture that has been taken care of for 250 years.

A black-wax recipe. Make your own wax polish (see recipe at left) and combine it with gold size and black pigment to give the table an aged luster.

Brush on the black wax. Using an inexpensive brush, apply the wax in corners and crevices, at the bottom of the legs, and in any white pores left by the steel wool.

Instant aging. Leave the greatest concentration of the black wax in the edges of the cock beading and on the apron below the tabletop overhang. Wipe a thin layer onto the rest of the surfaces.

Padding Lacquer: An Alternative to French Polish

MARIO RODRIGUEZ

For me, French polishing is the finish of choice for the very finest furniture. When done well, a French polish has a soft but brilliant glow that brings out all the depth and color of the wood without the heavy buildup generally associated with a high-gloss finish. No other finish even comes close.

I've taught French polishing for years, and for beginners, it can be a nerve-racking juggling act. The ingredients of a French polish—shellac, oil, and pumice—must be applied at the right time and in the proper amounts. The addition of each can improve the finish dramatically—or destroy it. Padding lacquer is an amazing one-step mixture of dissolved shellac, lubricants, and nitrocellulose resins. It produces a surface virtually identical to that of a traditional French polish but without the risks. It still requires a lot of elbow grease, but because it's a premixed formula, you can concentrate on applying it and not worry about maintaining a delicate balance of ingredients. There are several brands of padding lacquers from which to choose (see "Sources" on p. 230). I haven't found significant differences among them.

In addition to being convenient and easy to apply, padding lacquer dries quickly, so you don't need a special finishing room. It can even be applied on-site, eliminating the need to bring a piece of furniture back to the shop for finish repairs. And because shellac is the primary ingredient in a padding lacquer, it can be applied over other finishes. Finally, padding lacquer has a variable sheen. The more or less sanding you do will increase or decrease its gloss.

Surface preparation

For more formal furniture pieces, which generally look best with a high-gloss finish like a French polish, scrape the wood until

Scrape the surface first. Keep scraping until it's flat and even in appearance.

Sand with the grain. Use 220- and 320-grit sandpaper to sand the surface, then wipe it down with a dry rag.

you have a fairly flat, uniform surface (see the photo above left). Then sand with 220-grit and 320-grit sandpaper (see the photo above right).

After wiping the surface with a dry rag, wash it down with denatured alcohol. This raises the grain slightly and allows you to see sanding scratches and any other flaws (see the photo at right). To fill the pores slightly for a smoother finish, wet-sand with worn 320-grit wet-or-dry sandpaper and denatured alcohol. If you want a glass-smooth, nonporous finish, use a filler (for more information, see "Pore filler gives a glass-smooth surface" on p. 112). For a moderately porous, more natural-looking finish, just dry-sand with 320- and 400-grit sandpapers once the denatured alcohol has dried.

Applying padding lacquer

When using padding lacquer, all you need is a 6-in. square of lint-free cotton. Old T-shirt scraps work great. Just make sure that there aren't any creases or seams in the center of the pad because they can mar your finish.

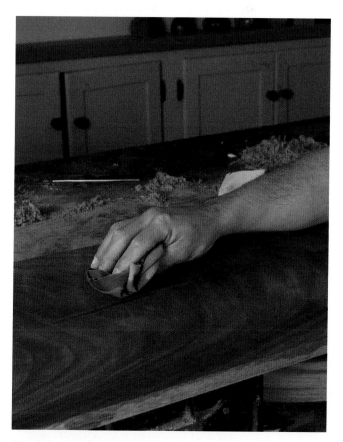

Check for sanding scratches. Flood the surface with denatured alcohol to reveal any flaws. This also raises the grain slightly, so follow up by sanding with 320- and 400-grit sandpaper.

Pore filler gives a glass-smooth surface

In traditional French polishing, pumice helps fill the pores in the surface. Padding lacquer has no pumice, so the pores don't get filled appreciably, except by the padding lacquer itself. The result, depending on how much sanding you've done, is a relatively open-pored surface.

To get a glassy-looking, nonporous surface with padding lacquer, use Behlen™'s pore-filling compound called Pore-O-Pac™ paste wood grain filler (see "Sources" on p. 230). Pore-O-Pac is available in six shades.

Applying the filler couldn't be easier. Pour some on the surface you're going to polish and wipe it all around with a rag (see the top photo at right).

Then use a scraper like a squeegee, moving the filler across the wood in all directions. This works the filler into the pores. Let the filler remain on the surface for 30 to 60 minutes before wiping it off. This filler dries rock-hard, so it's important to clean the scraper and the surface you're filling. Otherwise, it will take a belt sander to remove it. Use a clean rag and keep wiping until the rag comes off the surface without any residue.

Wait 24 hours for the surface to dry, then fine-sand with 320- and 400-grit sandpaper. After sanding, wipe down the surface with a rag soaked in denatured alcohol.

Let the surface dry and start applying the padding lacquer. A brilliant gloss will start to come up almost immediately (see the bottom photo at right).

Pour it on, and smear it around. You don't have to be fussy when applying wood filler—just fill all the pores. Move the rag around, then use a scraper.

Filled pores, satin sheen. Paste wood filler dries to a satin sheen even before padding lacquer is applied. The filler dries rock-hard, so wipe the surface clean.

Shines like a mirror. With its pores filled, this crotch mahogany panel takes on a finish that's a dead ringer for French polish—a warm but brilliant sheen.

Pour a small amount of padding lacquer into the center of the cloth, and let it soak in for a few seconds. Then with a small, circular motion, rub the polish vigorously into the surface (see the top photo on the facing page). Initially, the surface will haze and the cloth will drag a little, but with firm, steady pressure, an attractive shine will quickly start to appear. As you move from one small area to another, carefully overlap your applications for uniform coverage (see the center photo on the facing page).

A second coat can be applied almost immediately. As you build up the polish, though, you should extend the time between coats for the best results. When you get to the fourth and fifth coats, wait 12 to 24 hours.

Feathering out the finish

Even with very careful application, some areas will have more of a sheen than others, and the overall surface may look splotchy. You'll want to go over duller areas and make the surface as uniform as possible.

Then put a small amount of padding lacquer on a clean rag, and apply it over the entire surface, using a broad, circular motion. Bring the cloth just barely into contact with the work surface—almost glancing over it. This will eliminate any small streaks or blotches and leave a consistently brilliant, thin film (see the bottom photo at right).

Repairing mistakes

As easy as padding lacquer is to use, you may run into small problems from time to time. These problems usually appear as rough, craterlike patches. If they're not too severe, simply pad over them. The application of new material usually will soften the area, and vigorous rubbing will level it out. If this doesn't do the trick, let the panel dry overnight, scrape or sand the damaged area flush the next day, and then repolish. After a coat or two, blemishes will disappear completely.

Finishing on the lathe

I often use padding lacquer on lathe-turned objects, including table pedestals, spindles, cabinet knobs, and tool handles. Here, the application is even easier. Sand to 320 grit with the object spinning on the lathe. Then raise the grain with alcohol, and sand again with 320- and then 400-grit paper. You can apply the padding lacquer a little more heavily on the lathe, but don't use so much that it's spraying off the workpiece. Use gentle pressure on the rotating workpiece, and watch an incredible gloss develop.

Quick, circular motions bring up a shine. Move the pad in tight circles in a small area, applying a good deal of pressure. The surface will be hazy at first, but after just a minute or so, a shine will start to come up. Apply less pressure as the shine increases.

Overlap applications for consistency. Work just a few square inches at a time, blending adjacent areas. Apply more pressure on unfinished areas.

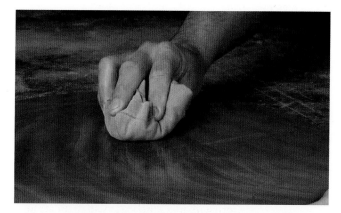

Polish the whole surface lightly. Take a clean rag, apply just a little padding lacquer, and rub lightly. The rag should just skate across the surface. Do this until the whole surface has a uniform sheen.

Wiped-On Varnish

THOMAS E. WISSHACK

The use of a bristle brush for applying varnish is so commonplace that many woodworkers don't realize there is any other way. We tend to think of varnish as a traditional finish that must be applied in fairly heavy coats, usually with a brush. This is actually a myth. Some of the oldest and most beautiful finishes relied on numerous thin coats of varnish that were rubbed onto the wood surface with a soft cloth and then polished to a delightful shine. I believe wiped-on varnish is an important addition to any wood finisher's arsenal of methods. I also think it's the most useful and versatile technique for creating a beautiful finish. The advantages of using a wiped-on finish are all related to the fact that the individual coats are extremely thin and dry quickly. Let's look at a few of these positive features:

- Dust contamination is a major drawback for people brushing varnish; it dries so slowly that foreign particles have plenty of time to land in it. But when varnish is wiped on, the individual coats of varnish dry rapidly, so dirt doesn't have much chance to adhere. This is an enormous advantage for the wood finisher because most of the time spent perfecting a varnish finish is a direct result of dust and foreign particles becoming embedded in it.

- Although varnish can be made to flow and level nicely when brushed on, it's hard to achieve a flawless surface without some sanding. If applied properly, a wiped-on varnish virtually eliminates runs, sags, and application marks. The marks that do exist are much easier to remove because the finish layer is thin.

- It's rarely necessary to build a thick layer of varnish. Aesthetically, a thinner application is more appealing. By wiping on the varnish, you have infinite control over the final thickness because you can apply as many or as few coats as you want.

Candidates for a wiped-on finish

It's difficult to build up a wiped-on varnish finish to a thickness suitable for a much-used kitchen table or bar top. I've used it on small tables, chests of drawers, frames, boxes, woodwork, and numerous other projects that don't normally receive hard use and aren't exposed to spillage or constant moisture. But I don't want to give the impression that wiped-on varnish is not durable. I've used it, with multiple coats, on dining room tabletops where an elegant finish was required. A wiped-on finish will hold up remarkably well, provided a certain amount of common sense is used in caring for it. For example, a wiped-on finish resists mild abrasion and occasional spillage, but if you plan to place a hot dish on the surface or expect it to resist deep scratches, you'd be better off with some other type of finish.

Remember that the number of coats you wipe on has a tremendous effect on the durability of the finish. One or two coats will afford only marginally more protection than several applications of a Danish-type oil finish. Six to 10 wipe-on coats begin to approach the durability of a single thickness of varnish applied with a brush. Determine whether you are willing to spend the time a wiped-on varnish finish requires.

The very nature of the process causes you to slow down and approach the finishing of your project with care.

Most varnishes can be wiped on

Virtually any kind of varnish can be applied with a cloth. It's simply a matter of learning a particular varnish's characteristics and developing a technique for applying it successfully.

Polyurethane is a good example. Strikingly beautiful finishes can be created by wiping on some polyurethanes, but polyurethane is normally thicker than standard varnish, and it takes a little more practice to master. Waterborne varnish can be built up in many layers with a cloth and rubbed to a lustrous sheen, although it tends to dry quickly when wiped on, which limits its use to relatively small projects. Certain tung oil varnishes, sold as wiping varnishes, are actually designed for cloth application and have a consistency that makes them appropriate for a good finish.

The real prerequisite for a varnish that is to be wiped on is the hardness and durability of the film it leaves on the wood's surface. Because the final layer of finish is much thinner than a brushed-on varnish finish, it only makes sense for you to work with a high-quality, brand-name product.

Certain precautions should be taken to reduce dust in your finishing area. If at all possible, do the finishing in a separate room of your shop. This is not always practical, but you can still minimize the problem by raising your work off the ground, cleaning the area, and sprinkling the surrounding floor with water. Wet a 10-ft. area around your project, as well as the path you will be using to exit the shop. For small projects, you can build a cardboard hood over the finish area, or you can place a cardboard box

The first step is the sealer. The important thing is to work the sealer—two parts thinner to one part varnish—into the wood. A natural-bristle brush works well. After the surface is completely coated, wipe off all the sealer with a rag.

For the finish coats, make a ball. Make a pillow of cotton cloth filled with cheesecloth, and hold the ball together with a rubber band. A shallow pan makes a good vessel for dipping varnish.

over a small object while it dries. Vacuum the cardboard box, and mist the inside with water before placing it over your project.

Brush on the sealer

The first step in a wiped-on finish is sealing the wood. The sealer coat makes the finish coats glide on more smoothly, and it results in a smoother, more professional-looking final product. Whatever varnish you plan to use will make a good sealer. Thin the varnish with two parts of high-quality mineral spirits or turpentine. Avoid thinning varnish with naphtha because the naphtha will cause the sealer to dry too quickly.

Apply the sealer with a natural-bristle brush to one section of your project at a time. Use the product liberally, making sure everything is covered. Work it into the pores of the wood in all directions. Let it soak in about one minute, then remove all superfluous varnish with cloths.

It's wise to let this sealer coat dry overnight—two days is even better—before attempting to apply subsequent coats of finish. This ensures that the surface you're working with is completely dry. A distinct advantage

of the sealer coat is that it stabilizes the moisture content in the wood, allowing the subsequent coats to level and dry much more reliably.

The dance of the finisher's ball

The ideal applicator for wiping on varnish is a wood finisher's ball made from a soft cotton cloth filled with cheesecloth, forming a small pillow. A rubber band holds the ball together and makes a convenient handle.

Before you use the varnish, be sure to strain it through a cone-shaped painter's strainer or a piece of lint-free cheesecloth stretched across the top of an empty can. Dilute the varnish to a 50/50 mixture with the same thinner that you used for the sealer. Then pour the mixture into a thin aluminum pan such as the type pot pies come in.

Dip your finisher's ball into the mixture, then tap the sides of the pan lightly so that nothing is actually dripping from your cloth. I always start with the smaller, more intricately detailed parts of a piece of furniture before I finish the large planes. When I applied finish to the table shown in the photos, I started with the pedestal and legs and finished the tabletop last.

Apply the finish in a circular motion, and don't worry about neatness at first. You will need to work quickly because the thinly applied coats dry rapidly. Next, use long, gliding movements, holding the wood finisher's ball in the air and landing it lightly on the wood's surface.

Work with deft strokes in the direction of the wood grain. At the far end of a flat surface, lift the ball from the surface just as you come to the edge. Repeat until you have deposited a smooth, continuous layer of varnish. Dip into the pan for fresh varnish when your cloth becomes dry or begins to drag. When you are finished with a large, flat surface, such as a tabletop, dip the ball into the varnish mixture, and gently apply a coat of varnish to the top's edges.

It's a good idea to let a coat of varnish dry overnight before applying the next coat. Here's a quick test for dryness: Lightly stroke a surface with your finest paper. If the paper produces a white powder on the surface of the wood, it's dry enough and ready for the next coat.

How many coats?

For wiped-on finish to be at all durable, four coats should be thought of as a minimum; beyond that, it depends upon the look you are trying to achieve. I sometimes apply six to 10 individual coats to a small project, such as a box made of exotic or unusual wood. I have applied as many as 20 coats to special projects. More coats give greater depth to the wood surface and are ideal when you want to show off a particularly handsome piece of wood. Keep in mind that with practically any varnish, regardless of whether it is marketed as semigloss or satin,

The second step is applying the varnish coats. Start with the intricate details, and finish the top last. For the detailed parts of furniture—pedestals, legs, carved pieces—it's not always possible to wipe on the varnish with the grain of the wood. Quick coverage and a gentle touch with the finisher's ball are what's important to avoid drips and runs.

Cover surface quickly, then go with the grain. For the finish coats of wiped-on varnish, you have to work fast before the varnish dries. After you've covered the surface with varnish, land the ball at one edge, taking a light stroke with the wood grain. Lift the ball from the surface just before you get to the far edge. It takes a little practice.

Possible pitfalls

Here are a few of the common problems that can occur when applying varnish with a cloth, along with appropriate solutions.

PROBLEM: Varnish dries before a coat can be successfully applied

You may need to practice on small boards before attempting a large piece of furniture. It takes a little time to learn to apply the finish quickly and evenly. It's also possible that your varnish is drying so quickly that you don't have enough time to apply a thin coat.

SOLUTION

Try thinning the varnish slightly, increasing the amount of solvent in small increments until it seems to be easier to work with. If a particular finish continues to give you trouble, switch to another brand.

PROBLEM: Finish appears streaky and uneven or has rough areas

Roughness usually means you have overworked the varnish and portions of it have begun to dry.

SOLUTION

Don't go back in and tamper with it. If an application is extremely rough, remove it right away with solvent rather than attempt to sand it smooth when dry.

PROBLEM: Varnish takes several days to dry or stays gummy

Chances are, the sealer coat was not given ample drying time, and trapped moisture is affecting your finish. This is common in damp weather, but it can also be caused by wood moisture.

SOLUTION

Put the object in a warm, dry place. If it does not begin to dry after 24 hours, scrub the piece with 0000 steel wool and naphtha. Wipe off all bad finish, let the piece dry overnight, and reapply the sealer. Wait several days, then apply the wiped-on coats as usual.

the gloss will increase and the grain will begin to fill when multiple coats are applied.

The final rub

Let the final coat of varnish dry about two days before attempting to do any rubbing. Less time could cause a too-soft finish to be ruined; more time could cause it to harden to the point where it's difficult to rub out. There are two important steps to the rubbing-out process: leveling and polishing.

Even a flawlessly applied wipe-on finish will need a little sandpaper leveling to remove the tiniest specks of dust that might have accumulated in the finish when it was drying. If you attempted to rub such a finish with steel wool alone, the abrasive would ride over high spots caused by debris and create a superficially smooth yet bumpy surface. Leveling cuts through these high spots and prepares the finish for the polishing of the surface.

Use new 600-grit wet-or-dry sandpaper, lubricated with a few drops of water. A soft rubber sanding block keeps fingers from digging in and aids in the leveling process. Keep in mind that a few strokes is often enough to do the job. Avoid too much pressure on the

The third step is leveling. After the last coat of varnish and before the final polishing, level the surface with 600-grit paper, a foam sanding block, and a little water. It takes a light touch. The intent is to knock off dust or debris that might have dried into the varnish despite precautionary measures.

The final step is polishing. Unfold a pad of 0000 steel wool, and dry-rub all surfaces to a dull sheen. Then mix mineral oil and powdered rottenstone into a slurry, and rub the steel wool for several minutes more. If the slurry seems dry and too abrasive, add more oil.

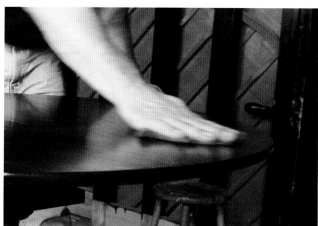

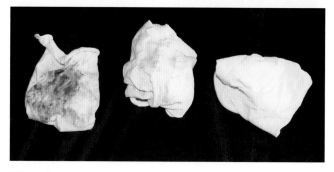

Wipe with cotton cloths to remove oil and rottenstone. Continue changing soiled cloths until the cloth stays clean when you wipe the surfaces.

ends of boards. It's fairly easy to damage a thin finish, although using the 600-grit paper makes this less likely.

Polishing is the final step in producing a superior wiped-on finish. Open a pad of 0000 steel wool to maximum size, and begin rubbing dry along the wood grain in long, even strokes. Stop before you run over the edge of the surface you are rubbing to avoid going through the finish where it is vulnerable. Rub until the surface has been uniformly dulled down, using only moderate pressure. The process will take several minutes per section. Stop frequently to examine your progress using a light held obliquely to the surface.

When the surfaces have a dull sheen, lubricate the steel wool with mineral oil and rottenstone to make a slurry, and continue rubbing in the direction of the grain for two

to three minutes. This evens out any streakiness that is a result of the dry rubbing. Also, it leaves the surface, when wiped down, with an attractive semidull sheen that will not smudge or remain oily. Special rubbing lubricants for wood finishing are made, but after trying them all, including paraffin, I find mineral oil the least greasy and easiest to remove completely.

After a few minutes of rubbing, use a clean cotton cloth to remove the rottenstone and the oil, wiping with the grain and changing cloths when they get soiled. When the cloth remains clean, picking up no more oil or rottenstone, the finish is, at last, finished. Beautiful!

Brushing on a Finish

DAVID SORG

Brushing on a finish involves considerably less expense, space, and even danger than spraying. The results can be as perfect as any sprayed finish, requiring only a little more time. I earn an added bonus when using a brush instead of a spray gun. Holding the brush, dipping it into the finish, and letting it glide onto the wood brings my project to life and provides me with a unique satisfaction. Choosing the right brush can save you hours in application speed and ease of use. Proper technique will help you avoid or minimize mistakes and brush marks.

I have two rules when it comes to buying a finishing brush. First, don't buy anything with a plastic handle. I've never seen a high-quality brush that didn't have a wooden handle. Use the plastic-handled ones for staining wood or painting your shed.

The second rule of thumb is to buy the best brush you can afford. To put things in perspective, for less than the cost of a good router you can buy a set of top-of-the-line brushes that will meet all of your finishing needs. No wonder my woodworking friends are jealous.

Brushes can be divided into four broad categories: natural bristle, synthetic bristle, artist's brushes, and nonbrushes, such as foam wedges and pads. I will guide you through each group and suggest which brushes will match your preferred type of finish and the piece you are finishing.

Brush types, sizes, and shapes

NATURAL

Natural bristles are still the standard that synthetic ones try to match. Most people associate badger hair with natural bristle, but pure badger-hair brushes are too soft for applying most finishes. The stiffest bristles are hog or Chinese bristle, which come as either white or the slightly stiffer black. Most all-purpose natural-bristle brushes are a blend of hog bristles and either badger or ox hairs. Costing $20 to $30, natural-bristle brushes are expensive. And because natural-bristle brushes absorb so much water and become limp, they are not a good choice for water-based products.

THREE SIZES TO FIT YOUR NEEDS

A 3-in. brush, a 2½-in. angled sash brush, and a 1½-in. brush with either natural or synthetic bristles cover most finishing requirements in woodworking. An angled sash brush can cover wide surfaces and get into tight spots. In general, always use the largest brush that can fit into the area to be finished. The carrying capacity of the larger brush means fewer trips to the can to reload and makes it easier to maintain a wet edge and avoid overlap streaks.

SYNTHETIC

Synthetic bristles used to be confined to water-based finishes that were unsuitable for natural bristles. They have always been less expensive and easier to maintain than their natural counterparts, and as their quality has improved, growing numbers of finishers are switching to them for all types of finishes. Names of some of the better bristles are Chinex, Tynex, and Syntox, but avoid bristles described only as nylon, polyester, or a blend of the two.

OVAL BRUSHES FOR LARGE AREAS

If you have a large surface to finish, consider purchasing a brush with an oval-shaped ferrule (the metal band between the handle and the bristles). These brushes can hold a lot of material, allowing large areas to be finished before reloading. However, it's more difficult to obtain a smooth surface using an oval brush.

ARTIST'S BRUSHES FOR SMALL AREAS

Artist's brushes can fit into tight areas. The 1½-in. wash brush with synthetic Taklon bristles will apply a final coat of thinned shellac or oil-based finish that leaves almost no brush marks.

Natural bristles are best for lacquer, shellac, and oil-based finishes

Natural-bristle brushes can hold more finish than their synthetic alternatives, an important issue for flowing shellac or lacquer. With these finishes you must maintain a wet edge, and the fewer the trips to recharge the brush, the better. Natural-bristle brushes seem to transmit a better feel for even finish distribution. I can more easily sense the degree of slickness or drag beneath the natural bristles, especially when tipping off to achieve a smooth surface. But I'd be the first to admit that it may just be the fact that I've been using natural bristles for nearly 20 years.

The disadvantages of natural bristles include a faster rate of wear and breakage of the bristles (which are a pain to pick out of your finish coat, especially if it's fast-drying lacquer or shellac), and they are harder to clean than synthetics.

Synthetic brushes are becoming more versatile

In the past, a synthetic brush was only used with a water-based finish. But synthetic brushes have come a long way since the early days of blunt-ended nylon bristles. Tynex and Chinex are among the brand names you'll see on better full-sized brushes. The latest addition from Purdy is Syntox. When applying alkyd varnish, a Syntox brush leaves as few brush marks as a natural-bristle brush does, and it works as well with water-based finishes as any other brush I've tried.

Use an artist's brush for smaller areas

Artist's brushes are made from a variety of natural and synthetic materials. For less than $10, you can get ⅛-in. and ¼-in. brushes made from synthetic Taklon that are useful for touch-ups. A 1-in. brush is handy for small

Small brushes for tight spots. Artist's brushes can reach areas that larger brushes can't.

projects, such as drawers, or thin edges. The most useful artist's brush for applying shellac or solvent varnishes is the 1½-in. or 2-in. wash brush. Offered by companies such as Winsor & Newton™, a wash brush is a soft blend of Taklon and natural bristles (or pure Taklon). It allows you to float or "wash" on thinned-down finishes (see "All about Thinning Finishes" on p. 94) with virtually no brush marks.

Use foam pads and wedges for stains and first coats

Last, and generally least, are the nonbrushes—foam wedges and pads that come on the end of a handle. These are inexpensive and useful for staining and applying first coats of most clear finishes where much of the product will be wiped or sanded off. But be cautious using them with lacquers, which may melt the foam. Also, the alcohol in shellac may dissolve the glue that attaches the foam to the handle.

Because material from these pads is squeezed out by applying more pressure, achieving an even finish is difficult. Particularly with pieces that have lots of edges, moldings, or carvings, you're more likely to get runs as you try to make the pad conform to the contours of the piece.

Don't be in a rush to brush

Much as the steering wheel of a sports car transmits the feel of the road, with experience you'll be able to sense when the brush is flowing material onto the surface at the proper rate. You'll feel the subtle differences between areas that are puddled too thickly and the extra drag from spots that have been skipped entirely.

Developing this feel takes practice. Make up a sample in the same wood and in some of the same profiles that appear in your project. Aside from helping you decide which brush feels right for the job, the sample will help you determine a finishing schedule; the correct stain color; how many coats to apply; whether thinning is necessary; when to sand and with what paper; and how the final finish will feel and look.

The easiest way to finish a project is to take it apart into its smallest components. It is also important to determine what order you will brush the various surfaces of your project. Dovetailed drawer fronts, in particular, are much easier to finish cleanly when not yet attached to their (usually) unstained and/or unfinished sides.

Remove all hardware or carefully mask any that must remain. In general, work from the top down, from the inside out, from a panel to its stiles and rails. The goal is to reduce the number of wet edges that you must try to keep so that the finish can integrate or melt into itself without leaving brush marks or ridges. Try to break down everything to a series of small panels, strips of moldings, or blocks of carvings.

Getting the brush wet

After straining the finish into another container and adjusting its viscosity if necessary (see the photos below), load the brush with the finish material. It's important to pay attention to how much finish you are placing into each brush load. Too much material, and you'll drip finish across the surface as you head for the area to be worked, or it will puddle the moment you lay the brush on the surface. If you pick up too little, it will mean more trips to the can and more

Strain the finish. After a can has been opened several times, dried finish collects around the lid and bits of skimmed-over finish may be floating inside. Remove all of this debris by passing the finish through a paint strainer.

Clearly better. Pouring some finish into an empty container allows you to thin only the finish you'll use. Select a container that the brush easily enters, and adjust the volume to reach halfway up the bristles.

Adjust the load. Push the brush gently against the side of the container to strain out the desired amount of finish. Do not scrape the brush against the rim of the container because it can cause bubbles in the liquid.

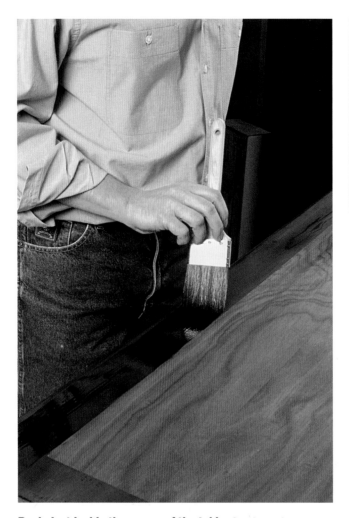

Begin just inside the corner of the table. Continue about ⅛ in. from the edge closest to you. After exhausting the finish, come back and brush off the edge where the stroke began.

Then pull off the edge. Short strokes with the tip of the brush finish the edge of the table. A curved profile is the hardest edge to finish because of the lack of a clearly defined boundary.

Continue the first strip. Start in the dry area and brush back into the feathered edge before reversing direction and carrying on to the far edge.

time for wet edges to set up before the next brush load gets there.

Adjust each brush load for its intended surface; for instance, a flat tabletop takes all you can give it, while a ¾-in.-wide by 12-in.-long drawer edge barely needs the tips of the bristles wetted.

Start each panel at the edge farthest from you. This way, if you drip onto unfinished areas, you'll be able to go right over the drips. If practical, work with the grain.

Takeoffs and landings on tabletops

On your first stroke, you have two edges— one parallel to the grain and direction of the brush stroke and one perpendicular to the grain and stroke. Land the brush just in from the perpendicular edge and move it about ⅛ in. from the parallel edge until you run out of finish (see the left photo above). Don't lean on the brush. Now return to where you started the stroke and brush off the perpendicular edge (see the top right photo above). The biggest cause of runs and drips is brushing onto an edge, which allows surplus liquid to dribble down the side of your project.

Finally, reverse the direction of the brush and lightly glide it from where the original stroke ended and go off the perpendicular edge. This process is called tipping off and should leave an even amount of finish that is as wide, or slightly wider than, the width of the brush. On a small surface, you may be able to go right off the other perpendicular edge as well. In this case, your tip-off stroke will be more like an airplane touch-and-go landing, coming in lightly an inch or so from one edge and taking off at its opposite edge.

On a larger surface, you have two choices for beginning your next stroke with a recharged brush. Some prefer to bring down the brush just inside the wet area where it began to thin out, then continue on toward the far edge. Others prefer to begin a few inches into the dry area, brushing toward the feathered edge and into it, then reversing the stroke and carrying it toward the far edge (see the bottom right photo on the facing page). Which technique you choose will depend partly on how fast you work; for

Prevent pooling. With thicker finishes, leave a gap between strokes.

Blend the lines together. The tip-off stroke fills the gap, creating a finish of uniform thickness.

Look out for puddles. Occasionally look at your work from a low angle to check that the finish is being applied evenly. Slow-drying finishes can be leveled simply by rebrushing.

Begin with the bevel. Bring down the brush away from a corner to avoid pooling the finish. Brush with the grain whenever possible. Once the stroke has been completed, use the tips of the bristles to push a small amount of finish into the corner.

Think of the panel as an aircraft carrier. Land the brush inside the near edge of the panel and continue the stroke until you "fly off" the far edge.

example, with lacquer and shellac you run a risk of pulling out the drying finish if you start inside of it.

Continue your finishing pattern until you reach the far edge—spreading out a brush full of material, then tipping off to merge the stroke with the previous one.

Begin the next stroke by laying down the edge of the brush either immediately next to the first stroke or slightly separated from it. With thin shellacs and lacquers that will melt into each other, I usually lay up the edges to the previous stroke or even overlap them slightly. With thick varnishes, I keep the strokes separated, then blend the edges by tipping off (see the top and center photos on p. 125). Water-based varnishes require this blending to be done quickly; oil varnishes give you plenty of time.

Continue until you complete the panel, checking the adjacent edges for any rollover that can be wiped off an otherwise dry surface. If the other surface is wet, it's best to let the drip dry and sand it rather than try to brush it out.

Run-free raised panels

Start with the bevel surrounding the center panel. Beginning the brush stroke right in a corner tends to cause pooling. If anything, interior corners can be starved of finish to yield a crisper look. Start the stroke ⅛ in. away and discharge the brush as you head for the opposite corner. Come back with the nearly dry brush to blend the beginning of the stroke into the first corner (see the left and center photos above).

Brush the flat section of the panel the same way you would a small tabletop: Start the stroke just inside one edge and brush off the far edge (see the right photo above). Return to brush off the first edge, and finally tip off the whole strip with a touch-and-go pattern, avoiding brushing onto either edge.

Then do the strip of molding that surrounds the panel, or the entire rail or stile if there is no decorative edge. If the rails butt into the stiles, brush the rails first, starting and stopping as close to the joint as possible (slightly over the edge onto the stile is better than coming up short of it), as shown in the top left photo on the facing page. For these strokes, you'll want a slightly less loaded

The rails need special attention. If the rails butt into the stiles, brush the rails first, starting and stopping as close to the joint as possible.

Brush the stiles as you would a tabletop. Start inside the near end, continuing to the far end, then come back to brush off the near edge.

Leave the edge until last. Apply a line of finish using the tip of the brush, then pull it off each edge.

brush because you're going to stroke to a line instead of going off an edge, and you don't want to leave a roll of material. With oil-based varnishes, you can just stroke right out onto the stile because it will stay wet long enough to be picked up when you brush the stile. Finally, finish the edges of the whole assembly.

Brushing narrow boards

Brushing a board that is wider than the width of your brush but not as wide as two brush widths is tricky. Brush a coat of finish down the middle of the board, stroke out to each of the three remaining edges, then tip off with a couple of strokes parallel to the grain.

If the board is narrower than your brush, turn the brush on an angle to make its effective width the same as the wood. This is where an angled sash brush is often convenient. When you are brushing edges of boards or doors, hold the brush perpendicular to the surface and use just the tip to lay a bead of finish down the center of the strip from one end to the other. Again, using the tip of the brush, spread the center roll of

material to each edge across the grain. Last, do a long, light tip-off stroke following the grain.

Carvings and latticework

Carvings can be finished in shellac or lacquer by using a small artist's brush. First, coat undercuts and recesses with a lightly loaded brush, then brush the tops and primary surfaces, allowing the edges of the finish to melt together. Additional coats are usually just placed on highlights that can be lightly sanded, if necessary. Surfaces that will be rubbed and polished require more finish.

When brushing oil varnish, apply it more liberally, then pick out any pools with a discharged brush. To even out the coverage in the area, use a dry brush and work in short, vertical motions (called stippling). Water-based finishes can be worked in a similar manner but in small sections to keep the working area wet.

High-Gloss Finish Made Simple

SEAN CLARKE

Nothing matches a high-gloss, rubbed-out finish for enhancing the color, depth, and figure in wood. However, you won't get this flawless and glossy look from brushing or spraying alone: It is achieved by applying certain types of film finish and then polishing them either by hand or machine.

I recommend shellac or lacquer (not water-based) for this process. While I'll demonstrate by brushing on lacquer, I'll also give recipes for spraying lacquer and for brushing or spraying shellac (see "Two alternatives to brushing lacquer" on p. 131).

Although certain styles of furniture such as Art Nouveau may have the whole surface polished (or "rubbed out"), with other styles it is quite acceptable to rub out just the most noticeable surface, such as a tabletop. Or, you can start the rubbing-out process but stop before a high gloss is reached, and instead achieve a flawless, semigloss sheen.

A perfect surface is critical for a perfect finish

For this highly reflective finish, the surface of the wood must be absolutely flat and smooth. This means that all milling marks, whether the telltale ripples of a power planer or the ridges from a handplane, must be removed. Start sanding at P150 grit and work up to P220 grit. If you are working with a harder wood such as maple, you may need to start with P120 grit. If you plan to use a water-

128

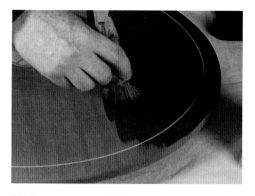

Shellac prevents stains. When using grain filler, first apply a washcoat of shellac to prevent the filler from staining the wood.

Use a stiff brush. Apply the filler using an old, paint-stiffened brush, going across the grain. Commercial fillers come in neutral, light, and dark tones, but you can tint them with dye powder to match the finished wood.

Remove the surplus. After the filler has started to dry but before it becomes hard, use a plastic spreader or an old credit card at 45° to the grain to scrape away surplus filler on the surface.

Clean the surface. Use a piece of burlap (or a white abrasive pad) to remove remaining surface filler that the scraper missed. Work at right angles to the grain so you don't pull the filler out of the pores. Let the filler cure overnight, then sand the surface lightly with P220-grit paper.

based dye, wet the surface with water to raise the grain, let the wood dry for one to two hours, and sand lightly with P320-grit paper to remove the raised grain. Apply the stain, allow it to dry for at least four hours, and lightly sand with P220-grit paper.

When applying a film finish to open-grained species such as oak, walnut, and mahogany, you must use grain filler (see the photos above). You'll need fewer coats of finish and less sanding between coats to achieve a flat surface, and you'll avoid the risk of the grain structure reappearing as the finish cures and shrinks down into the pores.

Cherry and maple are sufficiently close-grained, so they do not need filling. Before applying grain filler, apply a washcoat of dewaxed shellac to prevent staining.

You can use oil-based filler (I like Bartley; www.bartleycollection.com) or water-based (I use Behlen; www.woodcraft.com). Both come in light, dark, and neutral, but you can tweak them with water- or oil-soluble dye powders (www.woodworker.com) to customize the color. The oil-based filler gives you a longer working time, which first-time users may appreciate, but the water-based is ready sooner for topcoating.

Two sealcoats. Working with the grain (top), apply a coat of lacquer sanding sealer using either a conventional flat brush or a mop brush, which can hold more finish. Wait an hour, then apply a second coat, but this time go across the grain (above). Let the sealer dry for at least four hours.

Apply the filler with an old natural-bristle brush, working across the grain. Wait about five minutes, then use a plastic scraper or credit card to gently remove the excess from the surface. Wait about 15 minutes, then use a piece of burlap or a white abrasive pad to remove the remaining excess. The next day, lightly sand to leave the pores uniformly filled but with no filler on the surface.

Build a finish thick enough to sand flat

Whether working with lacquer or shellac, I recommend two to three fully cured coats depending on how thickly you apply it. This gives you enough material to sand flat and then polish out. After applying a sealer, don't go beyond four coats, or you risk achieving a thick, plastic look. I'll focus on brushing lacquer; see "Two alternatives to brushing lacquer" on the facing page for spraying lacquer and using shellac.

I use M. L. Campbell's MagnaSand® sealer and MagnaMax® clear gloss lacquer. Sold by the gallon, they are designed to be brushed or sprayed. Alternatively, Deft, Watco, and Behlen sell quarts of sealers and lacquers. Begin by applying two coats of

Block keeps surface even. After the sealer dries, sand it with P220-grit paper wrapped around a cork block. Sand across the grain, then with the grain.

Layer on the topcoats. Thin the lacquer, then brush on two coats across the grain. After an hour, brush on two coats with the grain. Let the finish dry for four hours.

Two alternatives to brushing lacquer

Spray lacquer and normal shellac are both easy to apply and repair. While the former has greater resistance to impact, chemicals, and heat, thick coats can look synthetic. Shellac gives rich amber tones with a deep, organic feel.

FOR A FAST BUILD, SPRAY LACQUER

Apply two coats of lacquer sanding sealer in quick succession, allowing them to dry for four hours. Sand with P220-grit paper, and spray on two coats of clear gloss lacquer reduced by 20%. Wait at least four hours and then block-sand with P320-grit paper. Wipe off the sanding residue and apply two more coats of the clear gloss lacquer, also reduced by 20%, and allow at least eight hours of drying time. Now follow the rubbing-out process described in the chapter.

SHELLAC CAN BE BRUSHED OR SPRAYED

Brush on two coats of shellac sanding sealer such as SealCoat. Allow to dry for a minimum of four hours, then block-sand with P220-grit paper. Brush or spray on two coats of a 2-lb. cut of superblond shellac, allowing 15 minutes between coats. You can use either SealCoat or dissolved flakes. After four hours, block-sand with P220-grit paper, first across the grain, then with the grain. Apply two more coats. Let dry for one or two days before starting the rubbing-out process.

lacquer sanding sealer, brushing with the grain. Wait one hour, then brush on two more coats across the grain. No sanding is necessary between coats as long as you recoat within four hours.

Reduce the lacquer by 25% to 50% with lacquer thinner until it flows out evenly on a test board, and brush on two coats across the grain. Within two hours, brush on two more coats, this time with the grain. These four coats count as one fully cured coat. Allow four hours of drying time, then sand with P220-grit paper and dust off the residue.

Repeat the four coats as described above. Depending on how thickly the lacquer was applied and how lightly you sanded, the build might be adequate at this point. To be safe, once this application has dried for four

hours, sand with P320-grit paper, brush on two more coats with the grain, and let it dry overnight.

You are now ready to begin flattening the surface with increasingly finer grits of wet-and-dry sandpaper (all wet-and-dry grits specified are CAMI grade). To lubricate the paper, add one drop of hand soap per 8 oz. of warm water, and change the water each time you move to a higher grit. Start by wrapping a piece of 600-grit paper around a solid cork block (or stick some cork flooring tile to a block of wood), splash a little water on the surface, and sand across the grain in straight strokes. Wipe off the sanding residue frequently with a cotton cloth to monitor your progress and to prevent the paper from clogging too quickly.

Start sanding across the grain. Wrap some 600-grit paper around a cork block and start sanding. Stop frequently to check your progress, and rinse the paper in warm water to resist clogging. Sand away almost all the low, shiny spots, but use caution near edges to avoid sanding through.

Uniformly dull. Work your way up through the grits until all the shiny spots are removed.

Although you aren't aiming to eliminate 100% of the shiny brushed surface, you should come very close, with only a few slight depressions unsanded. Use caution near edges so that you don't sand through the finish. Switch to 1,000-grit paper and sand with the grain, removing the 600-grit lines. Repeat with 1,500 grit across the grain, then 2,000 grit with the grain until all the sanding lines have been removed and the surface is dull but flawless. (see "Alternate directions when leveling the finish" on the facing page).

At this point, if you choose a hand-rubbed, semigloss sheen, wrap a cork block with Liberon 0000 steel wool and buff with the grain, applying firm, even pressure in long, straight strokes to dull the surface. Apply paste wax, then buff with a clean cotton cloth.

Rub the finish out to a high sheen

In the past, woodworkers used pumice and rottenstone, lubricated with oil, to rub out a finish. Today's automotive polishing compounds are much easier to use. Try 3M's Perfect-It™ Rubbing Compound from www. levineautoparts.com (or ask at your auto-parts store for an alternative).

Hand-polish small surfaces

If the surface area is small, I polish it by hand. Wrap a cork block with a clean, damp cotton cloth. Apply a small amount of compound and a few drops of water directly to the surface. Begin to polish in a circular motion, working in an area about 8-in. square. As the compound starts to dry out, add a few more drops of water and continue to polish. Apply more compound and water until a high gloss appears and all of the 2,000-grit sanding lines are gone.

Change often to a fresh section of cloth and move across the surface, adding water and compound until all areas are covered. When the whole surface has a high gloss with no lines, wrap a clean cloth around the block. Sprinkle water on the surface, add a small amount of compound to the cloth, and do a final polish with the grain. Finally, use another clean, dry cloth or paper towel to polish off any residue.

Use an electric polisher on larger areas

On a larger surface, I use a polisher with a sponge pad attachment. A right-angle grinder also can be used, if it has variable speed. If you

New material, traditional method.
Automotive polishing compound is less messy than traditional pumice and rottenstone, but you can still work small surfaces and edges by hand using a damp cloth wrapped around a cork block.

Alternate directions when leveling the finish

Your first shop teacher told you never, ever to sand across the grain, but here is an exception to this rule. Level the surface with 600-grit paper, then progressively reduce the size of the scratches until they are small enough to be rubbed out with polishing compound. It is critical to remove all the scratches, and by alternating the sanding direction, it is much easier to see any scratches that remain from the previous paper.

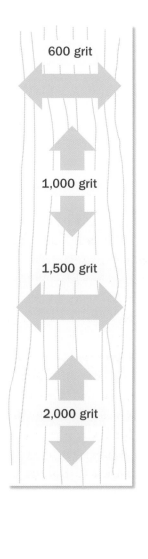

600 grit

1,000 grit

1,500 grit

2,000 grit

Labor-saving method. An electric polisher with a sponge pad brings up a high-gloss shine in a matter of minutes. Keep the machine moving to avoid overheating the finish.

don't have a polisher, you can use a variable-speed electric drill or a random-orbit sander and polishing pads. Be careful to keep water away from electrical parts.

Moisten the sponge pad to soften it, then spin the disk a few times to remove surplus water. Apply a few drops of compound directly to the surface, start at one end, and slowly move the buffing wheel back and forth across the grain, polishing out the 2,000-grit sanding lines. Use a slow speed to reduce friction that could blister the finish. Apply more compound and water as needed. Be cautious near the edges where the finish may be slightly thinner.

Once the sanding lines begin to disappear, reduce the amount of compound and increase the water to keep the surface lubricated and cool. Now work the buffer in a circular motion. The surface should take on a high gloss. Once all of the sanding lines are gone, finish polishing by hand using a dry cloth or paper towel.

Wet-look wood. Remove any remaining compound with a dry cloth or paper towel. This leaves a rubbed-out, high-gloss finish that gives the wood great clarity and depth.

All about Wax

PETER GEDRYS

There is a quality to a wax topcoat that can't be matched by more durable, modern finishes. The soft sheen and tactile quality of a waxed surface just begs to be touched. Not only does a waxed surface look good and feel good, but it also helps protect the finish underneath.

Besides being a final coat on finished wood, wax has a number of other uses. It can serve as a minimal finish to maintain a wood's natural beauty, or it can give a just-made piece an antique look. Colored waxes can create special effects. Best of all, the tools are simple and the techniques are easy. Whatever your furniture-making ability, your projects will look and feel better after a proper waxing.

Wax polish finishes a finish

The most common use for wax is to apply it as the final layer of finish. It can go on top of any type of finish, from an in-the-wood couple of coats of oil to high-gloss, rubbed-out shellac. The wax helps to even out the sheen and adds a measure of protection that can be renewed easily. However, don't be in a rush to apply it: Almost all waxes contain solvents, which can damage a film finish that isn't fully cured. For most finishes, this means waiting a week, but wait at least a month before applying a paste wax to solvent-based lacquer.

Meet the waxes

Wax can be used to perfect a finish or create special effects. The first step in working with wax is to understand it.

CLEAR WAX

Although brands of wax vary greatly in price, they all draw from the same limited number of raw waxes and solvents.

The best-known wax is beeswax. After the honeycomb has been melted and refined, it can be left dark or placed in the sun and bleached. Medium-soft, beeswax produces a medium-gloss finish.

The cheapest component is paraffin wax, derived from refining crude oil. Relatively soft and colorless, it serves as the base for many wax blends. Also obtained from petroleum is microcrystalline wax, a highly refined and expensive wax that has

Raw waxes. Shown from left are beeswax, paraffin, and carnauba flakes.

excellent resistance to water. It is favored by museums because of its neutral pH.

To offset paraffin wax's softness, manufacturers add harder waxes. Carnauba, obtained from scraping the leaves of a Brazilian palm tree, produces a high shine but is also hard to buff out when used alone. Candelilla, obtained from the leaves of a Mexican plant, is much like carnauba but somewhat softer.

The speed at which a solvent evaporates will determine how long you have to wait before you can buff the wax. Traditionally, turpentine was used to dissolve beeswax, but its relative expense means this medium-paced solvent is rarely used in commercial waxes.

Mineral spirits is the most common solvent and can be formulated for slow- or medium-paced evaporation. Faster-evaporating solvents include naphtha and toluene. I avoid toluene waxes such as Briwax® (top photo on the facing page) for a number of reasons. First, I dislike their strong odor; second, toluene is most likely to damage a finish that is not fully cured; and third, I find they harden very fast, making them somewhat difficult to work with.

COLORED WAX

As this piece of walnut (at right) shows, a clear wax on a dark, open-pored wood can leave white residue in the pores. Even if the pores are filled, the clear wax can leave a slight haze on a dark surface. Conversely, wax the same color or darker than the wood can enhance the appearance. See pp. 140–141 for more detail and to learn how dark wax can be used to give an aged look.

You can buy wax in a range of wood tones, or you can take clear paste wax and color it yourself. You must first melt the wax, but because wax is flammable, never heat it over an open flame. Instead, place it in a container over heated water, a device known as a double boiler. Add artist's oils or universal colorants, and mix them in thoroughly. Let the wax solidify before use.

Clear wax

Dark wax

Buy the right color. If you find a dark wax that matches the wood, it won't show in pores and recesses.

Color your own wax. If you need only a small amount of colored wax or you want an unusual color, melt some clear paste wax in a container over hot water, then mix in artist's oil colors.

Choose a wax made for furniture. In general, if the first use mentioned on a can of wax is polishing wood floors, don't use it on furniture. It is likely to contain a high percentage of carnauba wax and is designed to be buffed with a mechanical floor buffer. You'll have a hard time buffing it by hand. Butcher's® Bowling Alley Wax and Minwax finishing wax fall into this category. However, these hard paste waxes can be used as a clear base for custom coloring. In general, waxes designed for furniture are easier to use. They usually are softer in consistency due to their higher percentage of solvent, which makes them easier to apply. You'll get good results with Antiquax; Fiddes dries fast and has a low odor; Liberon's Black Bison goes on smoothly but has a strong odor; and Goddard's™ has a pleasant lemon verbena scent.

For best results, use an applicator

Using widely available but hard paste waxes, beginners tend to put on too much and then wonder why the surface smears when they try to buff it. The answer is to make a wax applicator.

Take some good, dense cheesecloth and fold it over. Place a small amount of wax on the middle of this pad. Gather up the edges and twist them to form a small knob that encloses the wax. As soon as you rub the surface, the wax will start coming through the cloth evenly and thinly. Although you can use softer semipaste wax this way, you gain the most benefit when using harder paste waxes. For closed-pore, light-colored woods such as maple, I use a clear wax, but for open-pore woods such as oak or mahogany and darker closed-pore woods like cherry, I use a colored wax.

Create a wax applicator. Place some wax in the center of a double thickness of cheesecloth, gather the edges of the cloth together, and twist them closed.

When you rub the surface, you will apply a very thin film of wax. The applicator prevents you from applying too much. I begin by applying the wax in circles, forcing it into any open pores, then I give it a once-over with the grain to straighten everything out. If you run out of wax, don't apply more to the outside of the applicator; just unwrap it and replenish the inside. When finished, you can store the applicator inside the can of wax.

To get the best results, you must wait for the solvent to evaporate before you remove the excess wax and buff the surface. If you do this too soon, you'll either remove the wax or

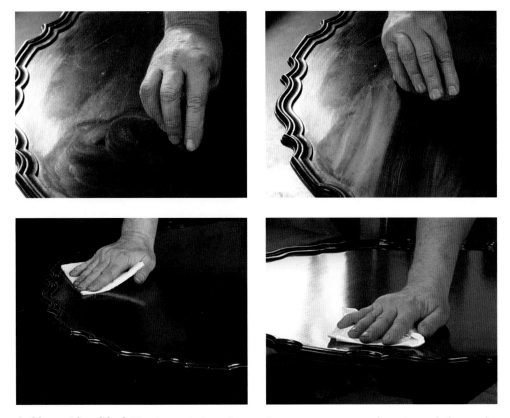

A thin coat is critical. The cheesecloth applicator allows an even amount of wax to reach the wood. Apply the wax in a circular motion (top left). Follow up by giving some light strokes with the grain (top right). Before buffing, wipe the surface with a white nonabrasive pad; the open weave picks up any residue (bottom left). Don't use a colored pad; many contain abrasives. To raise the shine (bottom right), you can do the final buffing with a cotton cloth or a paper towel. Turn it frequently to keep removing surplus wax.

just move it around. If you wait too long, it becomes progressively harder to remove the surplus. Although the wax won't get hazy like car polish, it will change from glossy to dull. The time this takes varies by brand and atmospheric conditions, but 20 minutes is average.

Although using the applicator should prevent excess wax, I still rub the dried wax with a white nylon nonabrasive pad (www. woodworker.com). The open weave picks up any thicker patches or small lumps of wax. The final step is to buff the surface with a soft cloth like terry cloth, an old T-shirt, or even a paper towel. Rub the surface vigorously and turn the cloth frequently so that you burnish the wax rather than just redistribute it.

At this stage, if you find you simply can't get the surface to shine, you probably put on too much wax or let it harden for too long. Rub the surface with a cloth dampened with mineral spirits to remove most of the wax. Wait an hour for the solvent to evaporate, then reapply the wax more carefully.

Rub out the surface with wax

If you prefer a medium luster, an option when waxing a cured finish such as shellac, varnish, or lacquer is to apply the wax with 0000 steel wool or a gray abrasive pad. This will reduce the sheen and soften the look. To better lubricate the steel wool, use a softer semipaste wax. To avoid cross-grain scratches, apply the wax with the grain only. It is easy to apply too much wax with this method, so you'll probably need to go over the wax once it has dried with clean steel wool or a white abrasive pad. When the wax has cured, buff the surface in the same way as previously described.

Waxing intricate shapes and carvings

By highlighting areas that are proud and leaving recesses dull, wax can give carvings and moldings a more three-dimensional appearance. The softer the wax, the easier it is to work into the corners using either a cloth or a small, stiff brush. When dry, a vigorous buffing with a dry and moderately stiff-bristle brush will yield good results.

Renewing a waxed surface

When a waxed surface begins to look dull, try buffing to renew the sheen. If this doesn't do the trick, simply apply and buff another layer of wax in the same way as described earlier. When done correctly, the layers of wax are so thin you need have no concern about wax buildup.

If the surface becomes worn or dirty, wax can be removed with mineral spirits or one of the proprietary wax washes. If it is very grimy, use either 0000 steel wool or a gray abrasive pad with solvent to loosen the wax. Wipe well with paper towels, then rewax the surface.

Wax bare wood for a natural look

Wax also can be used on its own as a finish. It has the advantage of barely changing the natural color of the wood, just giving

Steel wool and wax. You can combine rubbing out the finish and waxing it by using steel wool to apply the wax. Liberon's 0000 steel wool gives the most even scratch pattern (above). To avoid cross-grain scratches, rub the steel wool with the wax in the direction of the grain only (right).

Not just for shoes. You can buff wax with a brush. This works well in carved areas and produces a slightly lower shine than a cloth.

Simple steps. For objects rarely touched and that don't need a protective finish, wipe on a single coat of shellac, sand when dry, then wax and buff.

the surface a slightly higher sheen. The downside is that it gives minimal protection, but this is not a problem for objects such as picture frames that are subject to infrequent handling. As with waxing a finish, you need to match the wax color to the wood.

A variation on this is one of my favorite finishes. I seal the bare wood with a coat or two of a 1- to 2-lb. cut of shellac, lightly sand it when dry, and then apply the wax. I've used it with great success on lightly used furniture and on architectural components such as paneling. The thin barrier of shellac barely changes the wood's appearance yet makes it smoother and less porous, allowing a more even luster. It also allows me to easily remove the wax at a later date, if required.

Colored wax gives a range of looks

Wax comes in a range of colors, from wood tones to specialty colors such as black and white. These colored waxes can be used either for decorative finishing or for replicating antiques.

A limed finish on white oak is the most famous decorative wax finish. First, open up the pores with a brass brush or a slightly stiffer bronze brush, then vacuum and blow

Prepare the wood. Open the pores by brushing the wood with a bronze or brass brush. After removing the dust with a vacuum or compressed air, apply a single coat of shellac.

A limed finish. Fill the pores with white liming wax, then remove the surplus. Later add a coat of clear wax, or for a higher gloss, a coat of shellac.

Color wax with powders. You can color clear wax by adding dry pigments or mica powders. Afterward, topcoat with either clear wax or shellac.

Dirt in the crevices. Apply softened paste wax into the nooks and crannies of carvings. Then tap in some rottenstone using a stiff-bristled brush (above). When the wax has dried, rub the area with crumpled newspaper to remove the bulk of the rottenstone, then burnish the high points with a cloth (right). This leaves a line of gray similar to that found on antiques.

Simulate wax buildup. To replicate the dark recesses found on antiques, use dark wax in these areas (above), or apply dry pigments to freshly applied clear wax (left). When the wax is dry, burnish the high points with a cloth or a brush (below).

out the pores thoroughly. Seal the surface with a thin coat of shellac, then rub white wax well into the pores. Wipe off the excess and apply either a couple of coats of paste wax or, for a higher sheen, a coat of shellac. Other applications include adding colored pigments or mica powders to clear wax to color the pores.

If your taste runs more toward period than contemporary, wax can give furniture an aged appearance. Using wax a shade or two darker than the wood will add accent lines around moldings and carvings. There are brown and black waxes sold as patinating waxes, but you can make your own or use dry pigment powders on top of a clear wax.

Don't use shoe polish. Many include silicone, which will play havoc with any film finish that you apply afterward.

Spray-Finishing Basics

JEFF JEWITT

It's a pity that so few woodworkers have taken the plunge and begun spray finishing. Lack of information is the main reason, and manufacturers bear much of the blame. Makers of professional spray systems assume you're already familiar with spraying, while the manuals for entry-level equipment give only basic details, and instructions on cans of finish tell you to consult your spray-gun manual.

To remedy this dearth of useful information, I'll describe the main types of spray guns and show you how to match the gun to the finish. By spraying various pieces of furniture, I can demonstrate the different spray strokes that will work best on each kind of surface. This information will allow you to begin finishing the way the pros do.

Set up to spray

Few woodworkers can afford a purpose-built spray booth, especially one that meets health and safety codes for spraying solvent finishes. At the other extreme, waiting for a fine day and spraying outside also is fraught with problems: The wind blows the spray back in your face, and every bug in the neighborhood dive-bombs the wet finish.

The spray booth and accessories shown here are inexpensive and will allow you to spray indoors in a controlled environment. The booth is designed just for water-based finishes. I advise you not to spray flammable materials indoors unless you have a dedicated

Choosing a gun

Newcomers to spraying should use a high-volume, low-pressure (HVLP) spray system for the efficient way it converts liquid to droplets (atomization) and transfers those droplets to the object being sprayed.

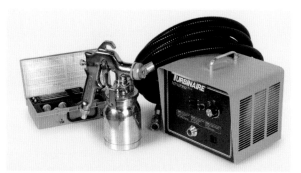

TURBINE-DRIVEN HVLP

The first HVLP guns were powered by converted vacuum-cleaner motors, which evolved into two-, three-, and four-stage fans known as turbines. These HVLP systems offer a number of advantages to novice sprayers: They're normally sold as a packaged set, including the turbine, an air hose, a gun, and multiple needle/nozzle sizes for different finish viscosities, and generally come with good directions.

COMPRESSOR-DRIVEN HVLP

If you already have an air compressor, you may want to consider buying a gun that will use the air from this source (see below). Known as conversion guns, they convert the high-pressure air from the compressor to a high volume of low-pressure air at the spray tip.

Suction feed

Air expelled through the front of the gun creates a venturi effect, pulling the finish into the gun. Although it's fine for medium- and low-viscosity finishes, this conversion spray gun can't pull up thick finish with enough speed to spray efficiently.

Gravity feed

With the finish container mounted above the gun, this system lets gravity push the material down into the gun. Not only can you spray thicker materials more efficiently, but the gun also is easy and quick to clean. However, it is harder to get the gun into tight spaces.

Pressure feed

You can pressurize either a cup attached to the gun or a remote pot that delivers the finish to the gun through a hose. The latter system makes the gun smaller and more maneuverable, but there are more parts to buy and clean.

Anatomy of a spray gun

The components of most spray guns are the same as this typical HVLP conversion gun.

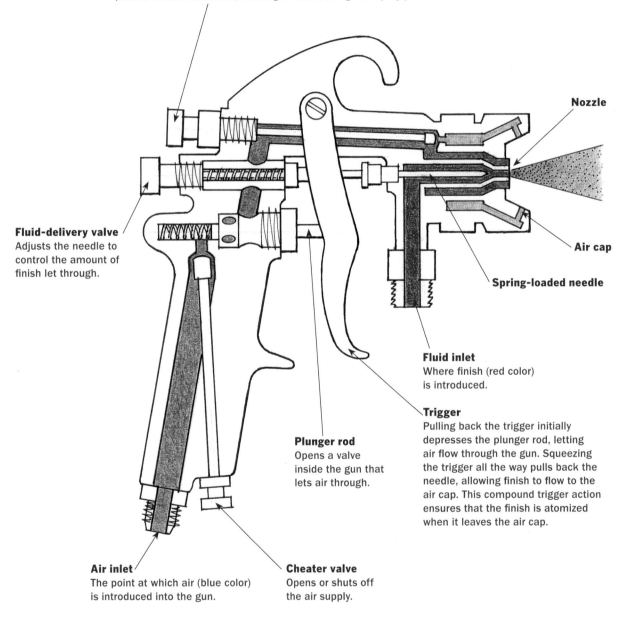

Fan-width control valve
When the valve is closed, air is directed through the center and small annular holes of the air cap, resulting in a small, round spray pattern. Opening the valve lets air (blue color) into the outer horns of the air cap, which pushes the round pattern in from the sides, creating a flatter, elongated spray pattern.

Nozzle

Fluid-delivery valve
Adjusts the needle to control the amount of finish let through.

Air cap

Spring-loaded needle

Fluid inlet
Where finish (red color) is introduced.

Trigger
Pulling back the trigger initially depresses the plunger rod, letting air flow through the gun. Squeezing the trigger all the way pulls back the needle, allowing finish to flow to the air cap. This compound trigger action ensures that the finish is atomized when it leaves the air cap.

Plunger rod
Opens a valve inside the gun that lets air through.

Air inlet
The point at which air (blue color) is introduced into the gun.

Cheater valve
Opens or shuts off the air supply.

room outfitted with an explosion-proof fan and explosion-proof lighting fixtures.

Booth controls overspray

When spraying indoors, it's important to evacuate the overspray produced by the gun, not only for health reasons but also to prevent the atomized overspray from settling on your furniture and creating a rough surface. A simple approach is to construct a booth using three panels of foil-faced rigid-foam insulation joined with duct tape. Furring strips glued to a fourth panel form the top, which keeps the booth stable.

Cut a hole in the center panel about 30 in. off the floor. Slide a furnace filter in front of the hole, and rest a box fan on sawhorses on the outside. Use a cheap, open-weave filter; the more expensive kinds designed to trap minute particles will get clogged with finish too quickly. The 4-ft. by 8-ft. foam panels can be cut easily to fit any location, and when folded for storage, the booth is less than 2 ft. deep and light enough to be carried by one person.

Spraying accessories

Unless you don't care about spray getting on the floor, lay down a cotton drop cloth. Don't use plastic sheeting because it becomes slippery when wet.

Save large sheets of cardboard packaging to use for test spraying when setting up the gun or altering the fan pattern.

Drive multiple nails or drywall screws through a piece of inexpensive plywood (see "Spray-finishing accessories" on p. 146). This nail board supports the work during and after spraying. Finish the nonshow side of the piece first; place that side on the points while you finish the show side. Because the workpiece needs to remain on the board while drying, you will need a separate board for each part you spray during each session.

A finishing turntable allows you to turn the workpiece instead of walking around it, and remain spraying toward the fan. A simple finishing turntable can be made by placing a 12-in.-dia. lazy-Susan swivel plate on a plywood base and then resting a nail board on top of the plate.

Place the finishing turntable on a pair of sawhorses to bring the workpiece up to a comfortable height and even with the fan for better fume extraction. For larger pieces, place the finishing turntable on the floor or rest the work on a dolly.

Spray-gun holders provide a resting place for the gun. Most cup and pressure-feed guns have a built-in hook and can be hung from plastic-coated hooks. Gravity-style guns require a gravity-gun filling station, which doubles as a convenient strainer support. Attach a piece of ¾-in.-thick plywood to the foam spray booth with construction adhesive, then screw on the gun holder.

To remove impurities from the finish, always strain it through a cone filter into the gun. A medium-mesh filter works best for most water-based clear finishes.

To prevent contamination from the compressor reaching the gun, invest in some inline air filters, which are available from auto-supply stores.

You will require bright lighting in the booth to differentiate between wet and dry areas when spraying. I like to use halogen work lights on a tripod.

Match the finish to the gun

A spray gun mixes pressurized air and liquid finish in a process known as atomization. For proper atomization, it is critical to adjust the gun to the thickness, or viscosity, of the finish you want to spray.

Spray-finishing accessories

CONE FINISH FILTER
All finishes should be poured into the gun through a filter to remove impurities that might plug the gun.

GUN HOLDER
Gravity-feed guns need a special holder. This one includes a filter holder for straining the finish.

AIR REGULATOR
This miniregulator is installed to set the air pressure coming into the gun.

INLINE AIR FILTER
Disposable filters trap water, oil, and other impurities coming from the compressor that would interfere with the finish.

LAZY-SUSAN TURNTABLE
A turntable allows you to spin the workpiece to finish all sides instead of walking around it.

WORKPIECE SUPPORT
Nail boards can be made with nails or screws driven through a piece of plywood. Spray one side of a panel, then rest the wet surface on the nail board while the top surface is sprayed.

Measure the viscosity. Submerge the viscosity cup in the finish, and time how long it takes for the stream of finish to break.

Measure the viscosity of the finish

A viscosity measuring cup is small with a precisely machined hole in the bottom. Most turbine-driven spray guns come with this type of cup, but owners of conversion guns can purchase one. I use a Ford no. 4 cup, which is standard. If your cup is different, a viscosity conversion chart is available at www.finewoodworking.com.

Viscosity is affected by temperature, so before you try to measure it, make sure the finish is at 70°F. Begin by submerging the cup in the finish, then take it out. Start timing when the top rim of the cup breaks the surface of the finish. Raise the cup 6 in. over the can, and when the first break appears in the fluid stream, stop the clock. The number of seconds passed is the measure of the finish's viscosity (see the chart on the facing page).

Viscosity Chart

GENERIC FINISH VISCOSITY	VISCOSITY TIME[a]	APPROPRIATE NEEDLE/NOZZLE SIZE[c]		
		GRAVITY FEED	SUCTION FEED	PRESSURE FEED
Thin	10–15 sec.[b]	1.1 mm	1.3–1.4 mm	0.7 mm
	15–23 sec.	1.2–1.3 mm	1.5 mm	0.8–1.0 mm
	23–35 sec.	1.5 mm	1.7 mm	1.1 mm
Medium	35–40 sec.	1.5–1.7 mm	1.9 mm	1.1–1.2 mm
	40–45 sec.	1.7 mm	—	1.2–1.3 mm
	45–55 sec.	1.9 mm	2.2 mm	1.3–1.5 mm
Thick	55+ sec.	2.2 mm	Not rated	1.5–1.7 mm

[a] Measured in a Ford no. 4 viscosity cup with finish at 70°F.
[b] Water = 10 seconds.
[c] To convert millimeters to inches, multiply the millimeter figure by 0.03937.

Select the appropriate needle/nozzle

Once you know the viscosity of the finish, the next step is to choose the matching-size needle/nozzle and sometimes air cap. Keep in mind that the different styles of gun (gravity, suction, or pressure feed) use different-size needle/nozzles for the same finish. Always use the smallest needle/nozzle that you can, as the smaller-diameter ones generally atomize finishes best. Try thinning the product before you select a larger needle/nozzle.

Some cheaper guns may come with only one size needle/nozzle, and in extreme cases the manual may not even specify what size needle/nozzle that is. In this case, you'll have to thin the finish until you achieve good atomization. Manufacturers of water-based finishes typically recommend thinning with no more than 5% to 10% of distilled water. Beyond that, you will have to use a viscosity reducer dedicated to that finish. Add the water or reducer in increments of 1 oz. per quart of finish until it sprays properly.

For the best finish "off-the-gun," it is a good idea to strain all finishes as you pour them into the gun. A fine- or medium-mesh

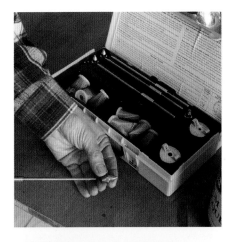

Choose the right-size needle/ nozzle. The higher the viscosity of the finish, the larger the needle/nozzle is needed to achieve good atomization.

Filter the finish. Strain the finish through a cone filter to catch impurities that could clog the spray gun.

Hose-Pressure Drop

INSIDE DIAMETER OF HOSE	PRESSURE AT COMPRESSOR	PRESSURE DROP		
		15-FT. HOSE	25-FT. HOSE	50-FT. HOSE
5/16 in.	40 psi 60 psi	1.5 psi 3 psi	2.5 psi 4 psi	4 psi 6 psi
3/8 in.	40 psi 60 psi	1 psi 2 psi	2 psi 3 psi	3.5 psi 5 psi

Pressure drop is the amount of air loss from the compressor regulator to the gun's air inlet. For pressures less than 40 psi, the pressure drops in the hose are negligible.

Set the air pressure. With the gun's trigger depressed to allow only air to pass, set the outlet air pressure at the compressor, taking into account the hose-pressure drop (see the chart at right).

cone filter works well to strain impurities from water-based clear finishes; a medium-mesh filter works for paint.

Create a good spray pattern

Once you've matched the finish to the gun, make final adjustments at the gun. Also, select a respirator with cartridges suitable for the type of finish you will be spraying.

Setting up a conversion gun

HVLP spray guns have a maximum inlet pressure of 20 to 50 pounds per square inch (psi); the exact figure is either stamped on the gun's body or given in the instructions. Conversion, or compressor-driven, HVLP spray guns are designed to reduce this inlet pressure to 10 psi at the nozzle, enough to atomize most finishes. With the trigger of the gun slightly depressed to release air but not finish, set the compressor's regulator to slightly above this maximum inlet pressure. This allows for the hose-pressure drop (see the chart above), which is caused by friction as the air passes through the hose. To avoid

this calculation, install a miniregulator (see "Spray-finishing accessories" on p. 146) at the gun to set the pressure.

Turn the fan-width and fluid-delivery valves clockwise so that they're closed. If your gun has a cheater valve (a built-in air regulator), make sure it's open. While the trigger is fully depressed, open the fluid-delivery valve a few turns, which regulates the amount of fluid going through the nozzle. Set it low for delicate spraying of edges and small areas, or open it up for spraying large surfaces. Spray a piece of scrapwood or some corrugated cardboard. Ideally, you want a fine and uniform pattern of droplets across the width of the spray. If you have coarse, large droplets, either the finish is too thin or the needle/nozzle is too large. The reverse is true if the gun sputters or spits. If the finish looks good, keep turning down the air pressure in 5-psi increments until you start to see the finish form a dimpled surface resembling an orange peel. Then raise the air back up 5 psi. Note this as the proper air pressure for the finish you're using. Operating the gun at the lowest pressure possible saves material by reducing bounce-back and overspray.

The fan-width control valve on the gun regulates the spray pattern. As you open the valve, the spray pattern becomes elongated (for more on spray patterns, see "Dial in the spray pattern" at right). When you open the valve, you also may have to turn up the air pressure going into the gun, so it's a good idea to keep an eye on your regulator.

Setting up a turbine-driven gun

Fully open the cheater valve on the gun. The correct air/liquid balance is established the same way as on a conversion gun. However, on most turbine guns, the position of the air cap determines the shape and orientation of the spray pattern (see the bottom photo at right). When the air cap's horns are in the horizontal position, the spray pattern is wide and oriented vertically. When you rotate the air cap 90°, the spray pattern is horizontal. The intermediate position makes the spray pattern tight and round.

Mastering the art of spraying

Before spraying any piece of furniture, dismantle large items as much as you can. Remove backs from carcase pieces and remove drawer bottoms, if possible. If you have a complicated project that includes a lot of slats, consider finishing them before final assembly.

How much finish to apply

Novice sprayers often get carried away with the ease of laying down a finish, and so they apply too much at once.

You should aim for each coat to be about two thousandths of an inch thick, or in spraying terms, two mils. A mil gauge is a piece of metal with teeth in mil increments. To use the gauge, spray some finish onto an impermeable surface such as laminate or glass. Drag the gauge through the wet

Dial in the spray pattern

The type of gun will determine the method of adjustment for the shape and orientation of the spray pattern.

Rather than alter the way you hold the gun, adjust the spray pattern to suit the object being sprayed. For vertical surfaces, a horizontal pattern gives optimum coverage; when spraying flat panels in the crosshatch pattern, adjust the gun to get a vertical pattern. A tight circular pattern reduces overspray when finishing narrow parts, such as slats and legs.

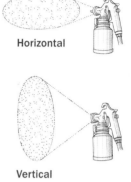

Horizontal

Vertical

Circular

Conversion guns require two adjustments. A valve at the back changes the pattern from circular to elongated. Twisting the air cap changes the orientation of the spray pattern.

Turbine guns are adjusted at the front. To adjust the pattern from circular to horizontal to vertical, just turn the air cap.

The basic spray stroke

Hold the spray gun at the same distance from the workpiece for the entire pass over the surface. Start spraying off the edge of the workpiece and proceed over the surface. Stop spraying off the other edge.

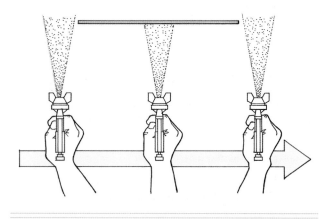

finish, keeping it 90° to the surface and pressed down. Withdraw the gauge and note the first tooth that isn't coated with finish, as well as the one next to it that is coated. Your depth of finish will be an intermediate thickness between these marks. If you have trouble seeing clear finishes on the gauge, sprinkle talc on the wet teeth and blow it off. The talc will stick to the wet teeth.

The fundamental spray technique

Lay a flat board or a piece of cardboard on a pair of sawhorses to practice on. Hold the gun perpendicular to the surface, about 6 in. to 8 in. away and about 3 in. off the bottom left-hand corner. Depress the trigger until finish comes out, and move the gun across

Spray-finish a flat panel in four steps

To achieve a good finish on a flat panel, you need even coverage on all surfaces. The use of a nail board and turntable (see "Spray-finishing accessories" on p. 146) allows you to finish the top surface while the bottom is still wet and to direct the spray (and the overspray) toward an extractor fan.

1. Spray the edges. With the gun parallel to the panel's surface, make one pass on all four edges.

2. Recoat the edges. With the gun now at a 45° angle to the panel, give the edges a second coat of finish.

the board until you get 2 in. to 3 in. past the far edge. Do not arc your pass; rather, lock your forearm so that the gun moves across the board at a constant height and in a straight line. As you make another pass, overlap the first by 50% to 75%. Move the gun fast enough to avoid puddles of finish but not so fast that the surface feels rough when it has dried.

I start with the surface closest to me and work toward the exhaust fan in my spray booth to reduce overspray landing on the wet finish and leaving it rough. Practice this basic stroke until it becomes second nature because it is fundamental to all spraying.

Flat surfaces

The basic spray technique for flat surfaces is called a crosshatch. Begin with the underside of the piece: At a 90° angle to the grain, start your first pass at the edge closest to you and spray a series of overlapping strokes. Then rotate the top 90° (it helps to have it on a turntable) and spray with the grain.

Holding the still-dry edges, turn over the panel and place it back on the nail board. Spray the edges with the gun parallel to the surface, then bring the gun up to 45° to the top and spray the edges again to get extra finish on them. Finally, repeat the cross-hatching on the top side.

If you get a drip, and you won't be damaging a delicate toner or glaze underneath, wipe

3. Spray across the grain. Maintaining the gun at an even height over the surface, spray overlapping strokes across the grain.

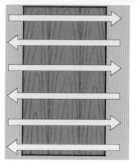

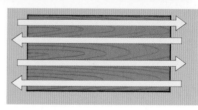

4. Then spray with the grain. Turn the workpiece 90°, and spray with the grain in the second half of a crosshatch pattern.

TIP If you spot an area with too much finish, quickly wipe away the surplus and apply another light coat.

the drip immediately with your finger and lightly respray the area.

Inside cabinets

Spraying inside a cabinet is a lot easier if you remove the back. If you cannot remove the back, you'll get a face full of overspray unless you turn the air pressure way down, which may result in a poorly atomized finish. Start on the underside of the top and then the two sides, leaving the bottom last so that overspray doesn't settle there and create a rough finish. For each panel, spray all four edges first before doing the center. Rotate the piece so that you always spray toward the back of the booth; this way, the fan will draw the overspray away from the piece. Blow away the cloud of finish left inside by depressing the trigger of the gun slightly so that air but no finish comes through.

Get down, and get under your cabinet. Spray the underside of the shelves first (above). Then complete the inside of a cabinet by spraying the sides (right) followed by the tops of the shelves. In this way, the most noticeable surface is sprayed last and won't be affected by overspray.

Avoid runs on vertical surfaces. Apply overlapping strokes from bottom to top, but do not apply a crosshatch spray across the grain, as too much finish likely will sag or run on a vertical surface.

Verticals

Start at the bottom and lay down a continuous layer of finish until you reach the top. Overlap each pass 50%—as though you were spraying a flat surface—but don't crosshatch because the extra finish will cause runs. For face frames, adjust the fan width to match the width of the frame members, if possible.

Complicated pieces

To spray a stool or a chair, work from the less-visible parts to the most visible. With the piece upside down, spray the underside and inside areas. Although less visible, they still have to be finished. Turn over the stool and rest it on four screws driven into the feet (see the photos at right) to prevent the finish from pooling around the bottom of the legs.

Now spray the sides of the legs and the slats, working quickly to apply light coats. Finally, finish the outside surfaces that are most visible. As with vertical surfaces, the trick is to keep the coats of finish thin and to avoid sags and runs.

Slats and spindles. With the stool upside down (top), spray the underside of the rails and the inside surfaces that are least visible. Flip the stool (above), and spray the visible areas, keeping the spray gun the same distance from the workpiece.

Spraying other complex pieces. For raised panels (above), the procedure is identical to that of a tabletop, with the addition of a first pass with the gun angled around the inside edge of the frame. Treat grids and frames for glass-panel doors (right) as a flat, continuous surface, and apply a crosshatch spray pattern.

Troubleshooting Spray-Finishing Problems

JEFF JEWITT

As the technical troubleshooter for my business, I've been asked to solve just about every spray-gun problem imaginable, from a new gun that just hisses air to an old gun that used to spray perfectly and now leaves a horrible finish. The good news is that in most cases, you can diagnose the cause of the problem by analyzing the spray pattern. In a few other situations, a slight change in your spraying technique can help. Even if you're just considering taking the leap into spray finishing, knowing how to achieve and maintain a good spray pattern will give you the confidence you need.

Because all spray guns operate on the same basic principle, it doesn't matter whether you have a high-volume, low-pressure (HVLP) gun or a non-HVLP gun, a turbine-driven system or a compressor-driven system. When differences exist, I'll call them out.

Most of the time, some finish comes out of the gun, just not in a manner to give that thin, even coating that makes spraying so worthwhile. One of the most common problems is uneven coverage, which leaves a repeating light/dark effect when the finish dries. You can study the spray pattern with a light shining through it. If you find this difficult, spray some dark finish or stain onto cardboard. If you substitute a dark finish for a clear one just to test the pattern, be sure that it has a comparable viscosity.

Pattern is heavy on one side

The typical culprit for this is a plugged or partially clogged air-cap port. It's easy to diagnose: Just rotate the air cap 180° and if the problem side reverses, then it's the air cap. Remove the air cap and soak it in lacquer thinner. Use micro-brushes to clean the air-cap ports as best you can. The ports meet inside the air cap at a 90° angle, so come in from both sides. A blow gun that has a protective rubber tip can be used to blow out the ports, but wear eye protection in case some thinner splashes out (I speak from painful experience).

Test your gun. You want the gun to spray an elliptical pattern consisting of fine, even-sized droplets like the far-right pattern. Most of the time, spraying clear finish onto cardboard will give you a legible spray pattern while the finish is wet. For an even clearer pattern, spray black stain or paint onto the cardboard as shown in this chapter's test panels.

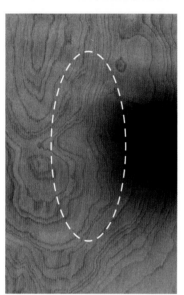

One side clogged. To find out if a clogged port on one side of an air cap is causing the spray pattern to be heavy on one side (photo at left), rotate the air cap 180° and see if the heavy pattern also changes.

Blow out the problem. Air ports have a 90° turn in the air cap, so the easiest way to clean them is to blow out any obstruction with compressed air.

Which type of spray gun do you have?

Spray guns come in two basic designs. Siphon cups (also called suction cups) have the storage cup under the spray gun, while gravity guns have it on top. To troubleshoot correctly, you need to know which type you have.

SIPHON CUPS

In a standard siphon cup, air exiting the front of the gun creates suction, pulling the finish up into the gun through a metal tube. With a pressurized siphon cup (usually called a pressure cup), the cup is pressurized by an external or internal tube that diverts a small amount of air from the gun. This pushes the finish up into the gun. All turbine systems use pressurized siphon cups.

GRAVITY CUPS

With the cup on top, gravity alone pushes the finish down into the gun. Gravity guns range from full-size cups (20 oz. to 25 oz.) to detail guns (4 oz. to 5 oz.) used for touch-up and small projects. These small gravity guns don't use much air (4 cubic feet per minute) and typically can be run using a small portable compressor.

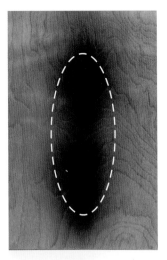

Less pressure. If there is no finish in the center of the spray pattern, try turning down the air pressure on the compressor or turbine.

Adjust the nozzle. If adjusting the air pressure doesn't solve the problem, switching to a smaller fluid nozzle may help.

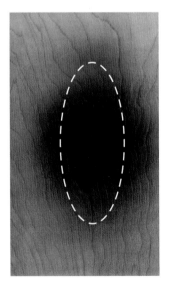

More pressure. If most of the finish is in the center of the spray pattern, turn up the air pressure.

If the pattern does not reverse when you rotate the air cap, then it is the fluid nozzle that is clogged, causing the spray to veer to one side as it exits the gun. If you have a gravity gun, you can easily diagnose a partially obstructed nozzle by unhooking the air line and pulling the trigger completely back with solvent or finish in the gun. The liquid should come out in a steady stream if the nozzle is clear. If you have a compressor-driven pressure cup and the gun has a cheater valve (an internal air shutoff), simply close the cheater valve and pull the trigger. Again, the finish/solvent should come straight out the front. On suction and turbine-driven pressure cups, you can't do this, so you'll just have to see if cleaning the nozzle helps.

Pattern is split or heavy in the center

If there is no finish in the center of the spray pattern (top left photo), more than likely the air pressure is too high. Lower it and see if the problem gets better. On the few turbine models that lack air regulation, switch to a smaller fluid nozzle.

If most of the finish is in the center (bottom left photo), the air pressure is too low. If you can adjust the pressure, turn it up. On a compressor-driven system, turn down the atomizing air using either the compressor output regulator or a secondary supply regulator. This regulator can be wall-mounted if you have a metal air pipe, or a miniregulator attached to the base of the gun. With turbines, all you can do is to turn down the atomizing air with an air-control valve mounted on or near the base of the gun. If your turbine has a speed control, you can adjust it for a slower speed, which reduces the air. If you can't adjust the pressure, try thinning the product or switching to a larger fluid nozzle.

You can't get a wide fan pattern

On a suction-feed gun, try thinning the finish or even just spraying some solvent to see if you can get a wide pattern. If that doesn't help, try increasing the atomizing pressure. If both these steps fail, then install a larger nozzle.

Though unlikely, both air ports on the air cap may be clogged, so remove and clean them as explained earlier. As a final cause, the fan-width adjustment valve assembly may be damaged or faulty, in which case you should return the gun if it is under warranty or seek out a repair shop. On gravity and pressure-cup guns, follow the same sequence of steps, but don't increase the atomizing pressure.

Coarse spray pattern

If your dried finish has little dimples all over it resembling the skin of an orange, you have "orange peel." Poor atomization (large droplets) is the main culprit, and this is often easiest to see if the spray pattern is backlit.

On all compressor-driven guns, try increasing the air pressure and see if the coarse pattern improves. If it doesn't, you can try thinning the product in 10% increments until it improves. If neither works, try a smaller nozzle.

With a turbine gun, make sure the air control (if you have one) or the speed control for the turbine is opened all the way. If this doesn't work, try thinning the material and then switching to a smaller nozzle.

Too much overspray, dry or rough spray, or no spray at all

HVLP systems should limit overspray to 20% to 30% of the finish. If you think you're getting more, you can reduce it by turning down the air pressure. Just keep in mind that when you do this, the finish quality will

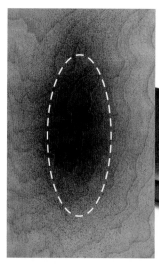

Orange peel. Poor atomization is the cause of this coarse spray pattern.

Bounce-back. Old-fashioned spray guns created large amounts of overspray. Modern HVLP guns are designed to avoid this.

Throttle back the air. To reduce overspray, simply reduce the air pressure. If you build a dedicated spray booth, consider installing a combination regulator and air cleaner attached to the wall. The cleaner ensures that no contaminants reach the finish.

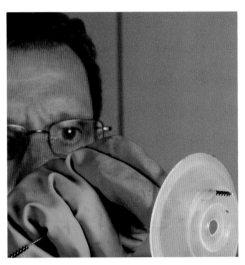

Clean the splash guard. The small pressure vent can get plugged with dried finish, interrupting the flow. Use micro-brushes in a spray-gun cleaning kit to clean the hole.

Get closer. If you use an HVLP gun more than about 6 in. from the surface, you run the risk of creating a rough surface.

Slow things down. A finish that dries before it can flow out will leave a rough surface. Adding a suitable retarder slows the evaporation and lets the finish dry smooth.

Remove dried-on finish. Soaking gun parts in lacquer thinner is the best way to remove hardened finish, but first remove nonmetal parts.

start to suffer, at some point resulting in the orange-peel effect described on p. 157.

If the finish feels rough when it dries, there are some possible causes common to all guns. You may not be depositing enough finish: Try slowing down your motion as you spray to leave more finish on the surface. Likewise, the gun may be too far from the surface. The correct distance is 4 in. to 6 in. for HVLP and 6 in. to 8 in. for non-HVLP.

It could be that the overspray is landing on your work after you spray. Use a fan to remove the overspray. Last, the finish may be drying too fast because it's hot and dry. Use a retarder specified by the manufacturer to give the finish a longer time to flow out into a smooth film.

In extreme circumstances, you may get no finish coming out of the gun. You pull the trigger and hear air coming through the front but no finish comes out, or it sprays a little and then stops. All standard siphon and gravity cups have a small vent hole that allows air to enter the cup to displace the finish volume as it's pulled out through the fluid nozzle. Use a toothpick or micro-brush (see "Regular cleaning prevents most problems" on p. 160) to clear the vent hole. If there's a fair amount of hardened finish in the hole, soak the top in lacquer thinner, but be sure to remove any gaskets first.

If that doesn't work, remove the fluid nozzle and see if it's clogged. Soak it in lacquer thinner to soften any dried finish, and ream it clean with a micro-brush. Finally check the fluid pickup tube and see if it is clogged.

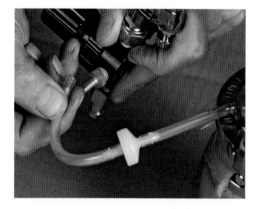

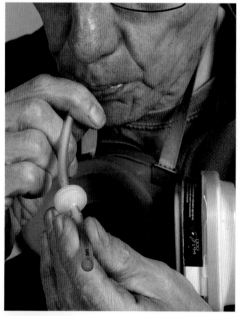

Trouble in the tube. If the tube that pressurizes a pot is clogged, finish will not fully flow to the gun. Remove the tube from the base of the gun and the top of the pot (above), then blow through the tube to see if the check valve or tube is blocked (right).

A thorough going-over. After spraying waterborne or oil-based finishes, guns need to be stripped down and thoroughly cleaned right after use.

Regular cleaning prevents most problems

If you are spraying a fast-drying finish such as shellac, solvent-based lacquer, or a water-based finish, each coat is likely to be one to two hours apart, so leaving finish in the gun between coats doesn't cause problems. However, if the finish needs to dry overnight, or if you change to a different finish, you should clean the gun.

Buy a full cleaning kit. To keep spray guns working properly, a cleaning kit should contain special brushes and needles to access the different parts of the gun.

When you use solvent-based lacquer and shellac, any new finish in the gun will re-melt any dried finish, so you typically don't have to clean the gun thoroughly. Just run some lacquer thinner or denatured alcohol through it, depending on the finish.

Finishes that require more diligence in cleaning are water-based and oil-based products (including latex and oil paint) because the cleanup solvent won't remove the dried finish. Therefore, you should clean the gun soon after use. When cleaning guns that sprayed paints, remove the air cap, fluid nozzle, and needle so you can clean more thoroughly. The chart below tells you which solvent works best to clean the different finish types, or you can check the finish container for the proper solvent. Note that some products require a different cleaner once they have dried.

For Cleanup, Match Solvent to Finish

FINISH	TO RINSE/CLEAN	TO REMOVE DRIED FINISH
Shellac	Denatured alcohol	Denatured alcohol
Solvent lacquer	Lacquer thinner	Lacquer thinner
Waterborne finishes and latex paint	Water followed by denatured alcohol	Acetone/lacquer thinner
Oil-based finishes and oil paint	Mineral spirits/paint thinner/naphtha	Lacquer thinner

Let fluid flow. Use a large brush to clean the main nozzle in the center of the air cap where finish exits the gun.

Air supply. The small holes on either side of the fluid nozzle supply air that atomizes the finish. Clean them using thin needles.

Don't forget the needle and nozzle. After removing the air cap, unscrew the nozzle (left), and use a micro-brush to clean inside it (right).

The 10 Best Fixes for Finishing Mistakes

TERI MASASCHI

Hobbyists and professionals alike make mistakes in the shop. When you're building a piece, fixing an error is fairly straightforward: Back up and start again by milling a new piece, recutting a joint, or fitting in a patch. But finishing mistakes can be harder to overcome—hence the dread many woodworkers feel.

Problems can pop up at any one of three points in the finishing process—surface preparation (and assembly), staining and coloring, and applying the topcoat. I'll show you some of the methods I use as a professional to back out of a mistake and to try to keep it from happening in the first place.

The best way to avoid mistakes altogether is to practice on a sample board. Testing the colors and materials you want to use will alert you to problems before you risk ruining an expensive project. Also, resist the urge to rush through the finishing process. You can nearly always tell when someone has taken a shortcut.

And finally, even if you make mistakes you can't fix, after suffering through them you probably won't repeat the same ones again.

Surface flaws

The most common surface flaws are sanding swirls and tearout, glue squeeze-out, and sanding through the veneer of hardwood plywood. Many of these maladies can occur even if you're trying to be meticulous. And you might not see the problem until it glares at you through a freshly applied coat of oil or stain.

1. Scratches and tearout

Problem: A random-orbit sander left its signature pigtail marks, or you didn't use the right paper to eliminate scratches left by coarser grits. Or, cutting or planing tore out some wood fibers, leaving a divot in the surface. If the first swipe of stain shows vivid swirls or scratches all over the work, stop.

Solution: Sand the piece again, this time changing paper frequently and working your way systematically through the grits. If you've oiled or stained the piece and find that swirls show up in only one or two spots, sand those areas by hand with P220-grit wet-or-dry paper, wetting it with some of the same finish you used. This method works well with most oil finishes or oil-based pigment stains. If you used stain, reapply it carefully to match the surrounding stained areas.

If you used a dye, resand a stand-alone area, such as an entire stile. If it is a large surface, sand the damaged area, feathering the edge between sanded and unsanded parts. Then apply more dye.

To eliminate tearout, sand, plane, or scrape the surface. Wipe the surface with mineral spirits to check the smoothness. If the imperfections are small enough (generally no larger than a pinhead), you can fill them after you've stained and sealed the piece, using fill sticks, the wax crayons sold for touching up scratches.

If you aren't coloring the wood, small amounts of tearout can be OK in some places (legs, frames, etc.). But stain makes them pop.

Not smooth enough. Swirl marks tell you that you haven't done enough sanding to eliminate scratches.

Smoothing slurry. Wet-sanding with the oil or stain you used helps eliminate swirls more rapidly without ruining the color.

2. Glue residue

Problem: You used too much glue, leaving squeeze-out around the joint. Or you got sloppy and left a gluey fingerprint on the workpiece. Oil or stain won't penetrate the glue residue, leaving an unsightly light spot.

Solution: You can get rid of some fingerprints by wet-sanding with the stain you used, or by lightly sanding and reapplying the stain.

Use a sharp chisel to eliminate dried glue from around a joint. Use sandpaper to clear up areas where you didn't completely wipe away squeeze-out. Wrap P220-grit paper around a hard block, and sand with the grain, using firm pressure. To avoid scratching adjacent surfaces, use a 6-in. flexible drywall knife as a shield.

3. Sand-through

Problem: You sanded away some face veneer on a large, expensive piece of plywood after you had glued up everything.

Solution: Use a scrap of the same plywood to duplicate the mistake and serve as a sample board for the remedy. Apply the same finish you plan to use on the piece, then sand through a portion of the face veneer to give yourself a place to experiment with a repair.

Uneven oiling. Glue residue on this mortise-and-tenon joint prevents the wood from absorbing oil evenly.

Touch-up. When removing glue squeeze-out, sand with the grain using P220-grit sandpaper. Keep the block flat against the work to avoid rounding over an edge. Shield adjacent surfaces with a wide drywall knife.

Mix thin shellac with a touch-up powder such as Behlen Master Furniture Powder (www.woodworker.com) or Mohawk Blendal® Powder Stain (www.mohawk-finishing.com). Put a piece of glass next to the sand-through on the practice board and begin developing your color (see the center photo below). Quickly dip the brush into the shellac, then into one of the touch-up powders. Swirl the brush around on the glass to incorporate the powder and shellac. Dab on more shellac and a different powder to blend the color you need. Work in thin layers, sneaking up on the color rather than painting it in. If you aren't happy with the results, wipe away the color and start over.

When you've done a reasonable job of covering the sand-through on the scrap, take a deep breath and do the same thing on the real project. A glaze—a type of stain used on a semisealed surface—brushed on and then lightly wiped off will help blend in the patch.

Overdone. It doesn't take much to sand through the face veneer on hardwood plywood.

Practice patch. Make a similar burn-through on a scrap of the same plywood. Mix touch-up powders with thinned shellac to match the color of the face veneer and hide the sanded-through spot.

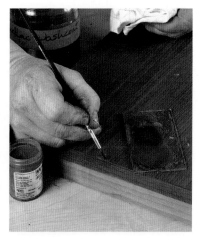

Faux finish. Carefully paint the tinted shellac over the sand-through. Apply a glaze to help blend the patch into the surrounding wood.

How to prevent surface flaws

Sand with progressively finer grits, ending with P220. Finish by hand-sanding with the grain with P180- or P220-grit paper. Vacuum or blow off the dust. Wet the surface with mineral spirits or shine a bright light across it to reveal flaws. If you're working with hardwood-veneer plywood, sand with a very light touch and check your progress often. Use glue sparingly and remove squeeze-out carefully.

Sand by hand. To eliminate cross-grain scratches, finish sanding by hand, always moving with the grain.

Check your work. Wipe on mineral spirits before applying the finish. This will reveal any lingering scratches or patches of tearout.

Easy fix. This maple door didn't take dye well, leaving lap marks on the frame. A wet rag rubbed over the dye will even out the color, minimizing blotchiness.

Color mistakes

By far the biggest finishing problems can occur when you apply dye or stain. A color you thought would look great comes up garish. Or the first coat of color takes unevenly, leaving blotches or streaks. Here's how to get around drawbacks like these.

4. Uneven dye stain

Problem: A dye-based stain looks stronger or more intense in some areas than in others. Consequently, you have an unevenly colored surface or lap marks where you wanted uniformity.

Solution: Pull a damp rag over the surface. That will lift the dye so you can "move" or remove it to make the color even. Work the rag around to blend the color evenly. Then apply a washcoat of shellac and the stain you want to use.

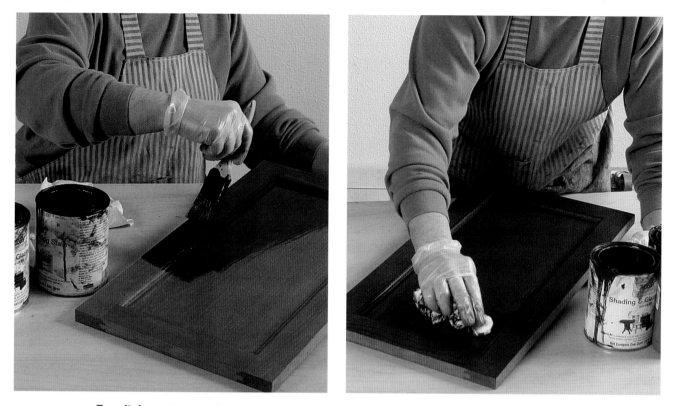

Tone it down. A contrasting glaze usually will correct a color that's wrong. Here, black glaze will tame a too-red stain on this oak door (left). Wipe off the excess glaze almost immediately, revealing a better color (right).

5. Wrong stain color

Problem: The stain you applied threw the wood color way off. Generally, a stain will appear either too red or not red enough. Either way, it spoils the appearance of the piece.

Solution: Correct the color with a glaze. I've had good results with Behlen or Mohawk glazing stains. Apply a washcoat of shellac over the stain, then gently scuff-sand with P320-grit paper when it's dry. Use a glaze that contrasts with the stain to bring the color back into line.

For example, if the stain looks too red, tone it down with a raw umber glaze, which is greenish in tone. Alternatively, you can use a black glaze to change the color's tone.

If the stain doesn't have enough red, warm up the color with burnt umber or burnt sienna, which is predominantly reddish.

Brush on the glaze liberally, let it sit for a minute or so, then lightly remove most of it with a clean rag, leaving a thin film of color. Once you've corrected the color to your liking, protect the glaze with another washcoat of shellac before you apply the topcoat.

6. Blotchy stain

Problem: You chose a pigmented stain that didn't take evenly on the wood. Pine, cherry, maple, birch, and alder are the most likely to blotch.

Solution: If the surface is very blotchy, you'll have to remove the stain by stripping, sanding, or both, and start over. This time, apply a washcoat of shellac and then the stain.

If the blotching isn't too severe, try using a glaze to soften the contrast between the deeply colored and lighter areas. Once the initial stain is dry, apply a washcoat of

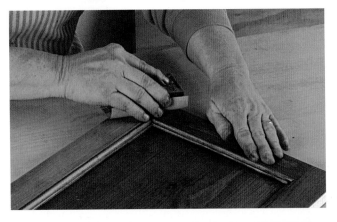

Sand lightly. Pine is one of several woods that blotch easily. To even things out, begin by scuff-sanding.

Apply a glaze and wipe it off. Brush on a glaze to help cover up the blotches. Wipe away the excess glaze to reveal a much more uniform color.

shellac. Let it dry, then gently scuff with P320-grit paper. Brush on a burnt umber or other brownish glaze; wipe gently to remove most of the excess.

Topcoat trouble

Problems can occur in laying down the final coats, whether you brush, wipe, or spray. Apply multiple light layers of the topcoat rather than one or two thick ones. Sand carefully, wiping away the sanding dust to check surfaces frequently. Rubbing out, the last step, is incredibly important because it "finishes" the finish. However, the idea of abrading a carefully applied topcoat scares many people, and rightly so. You don't want to have problems so close to the finale. Use a light touch.

7. Drips and sags

Problem: You used too heavy a hand in applying the topcoat, so the coating drools down the side of your beautiful project.

Solution: Wait until the sag is totally dried. It should feel hard, not resilient, when you push on it. Wrap a cork or hardwood sanding block with P320-grit paper and lightly sand to level the mess. If you start sanding while the sag is still gummy, you'll just make the mess worse. Check your work frequently and change the paper often. You want to flatten the lumps without going through the stain color or down to the bare wood.

Or, if you only have one or two drips, you can use a fresh single-edge razor blade to scrape them off. Be sure to scrape carefully to avoid cutting through the finish.

8. Contaminated finish

Problem: Flat surfaces are pockmarked with small craters. Often from the first brushful, the coating literally "crawls" into an odd formation that resembles a crater or fisheye. You can't do anything ahead of time

How to prevent color mistakes

To avoid problems with stain or water-based dye in the first place, use a sample board to test the finish you want to use. You'll greatly increase the odds of having the color go on evenly if you apply a washcoat of thinned shellac beforehand. That will help ensure that subsequent coats of color take uniformly. A good washcoat is a 1-lb. cut: Combine premixed shellac (which is a 3-lb. cut) and denatured alcohol in a 3:2 ratio.

Control penetration. A light coat of shellac thinned to a 1-lb. cut creates a good foundation before coloring the wood.

No blotching. Stain over a shellac washcoat has much less tendency to blotch.

Sample board. Test the finish you want to use on a scrap of the same wood used in the workpiece.

Scrape or sand. Once a drip has dried completely, scrape it off with a razor blade (left) or sand it flush (above).

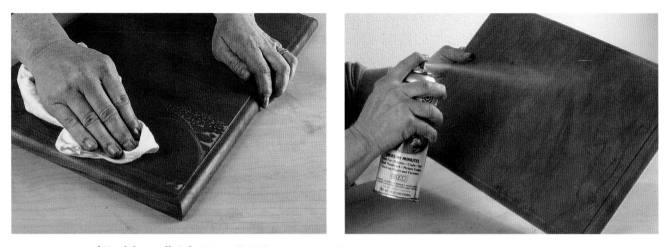

Attack immediately. Wipe off all the contaminated topcoat as soon as you see it crawl (left). A light spray of shellac (right) will isolate the contamination, so you can reapply the topcoat.

to prevent this contamination. It may come from lubricants used on a tablesaw or jointer bed. It can also occur if you put a water-based finish over an oil-based stain.

Solution: Stop. Don't even begin to think you can keep brushing to eliminate the problem. Wipe off all the coating, then brush or spray on a light coat of shellac. If spraying, use a very fine, almost dry spray. The shellac forms a barrier to keep the contaminant from coming up through subsequent layers of finish. When the shellac dries, continue applying the topcoat you want.

9. Burn-through

Problem: You have either sanded through the finish (a frequent occurrence on edges, moldings, and carvings) or burned through the color (removing both the topcoats and the stain).

Solution: If you've burned through the color, carefully apply more stain, protect it with a light coat of shellac, and then replace the topcoats. If you've only burned through the finish, delicately reapply it. When the repairs are thoroughly dry, rub out those areas to blend them in with the rest of the surface.

10. Witness lines

Problem: When rubbing out a film finish like varnish, you cut through the layers of finish. Witness lines are shadowy craters of this cut-through. Witness lines seldom occur with shellac or lacquer because new coats of those finishes dissolve into the old ones.

Solution: Keep leveling the finish, then apply at least two more fresh coats of finish (see bottom photos on facing page).

Witnesses. Sanding too much can produce witness lines, whitish areas exposing earlier coats of finish.

Burned up. If you sand the topcoat too aggressively or don't keep the sanding block level, you risk removing some of the finish.

Restore the color. Use a small artist's brush to reapply stain to the sanded-through area.

Seal the color. Brush a light coat of shellac over the stain touch-up.

Keep sanding to remove witness lines. Using fine sandpaper and a light touch, sand the surface to level it as much as possible before applying more topcoat.

Add another topcoat. Apply more of the topcoat to the entire surface, not just where the witness lines had been.

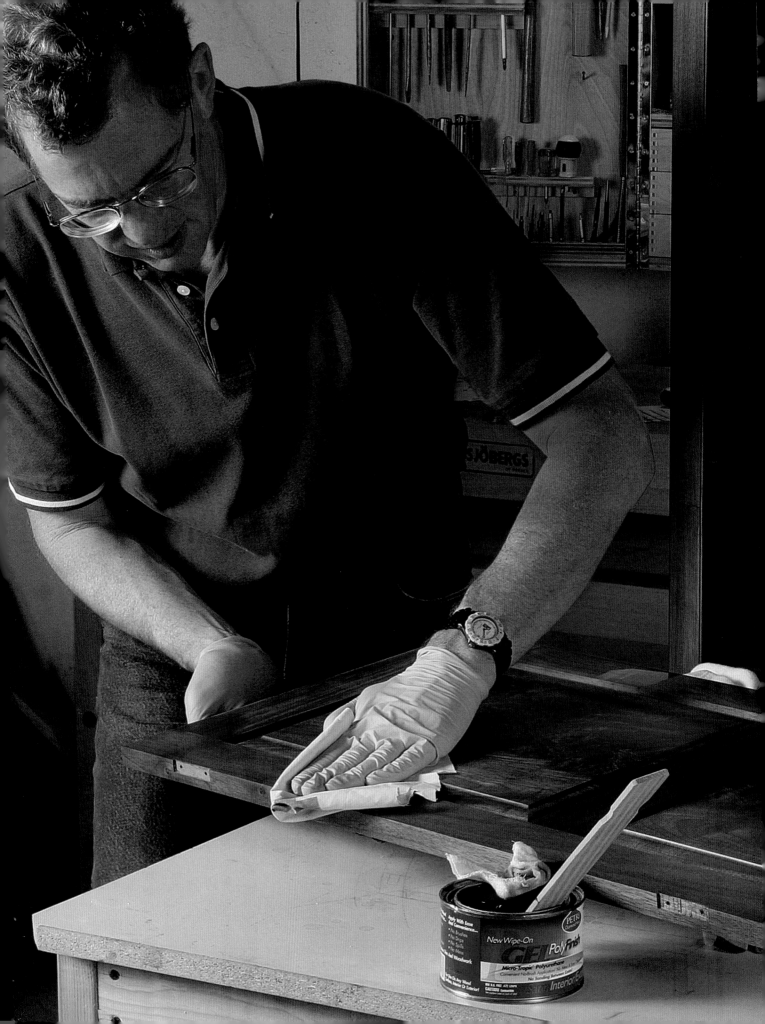

A Foolproof Finish

BY MARK SCHOFIELD

When I joined *Fine Woodworking* in the summer of 2000, I was made responsible for the finishing articles. The editor made it seem like an honor, but in truth I don't think any of my colleagues wanted the job. Like most woodworkers, they'd rather cut wood than finish it. But today, after hundreds of hours watching finishing experts such as Peter Gedrys, Jeff Jewitt, Teri Masaschi, and Chris Minick work their magic, I have a confession to make. I like finishing.

I haven't completely bought in, however. While I'll attempt a perfect French polish, I can still relate to my fellow woodworkers who above all want a finish they can't mess up.

To meet this need, I have developed what I call the "*Fine Woodworking* foolproof finish." You first seal the wood with shellac, then apply three or more coats of gel varnish, and complete the finish with a coat of paste wax. You get a medium-luster, in-the-wood finish that can be built up to give varying degrees of protection. All three steps are applied by hand, and the only "tools" are pieces of cloth. I promise you'll be proud of the results.

It all begins with careful preparation

I've lost track of how many projects I've seen (including one or two of my own early efforts) that prominently display the telltale tracks of jointer or planer knives. Like most finishes, this one doesn't hide poor preparation; it magnifies it. So the first task is to prep the wood's surface.

If you have mastered the bench plane and/or the scraper, you can remove machine marks fairly quickly. Then use a random-orbit sander with P180-grit sandpaper followed by P220-grit paper, and finally hand-sand with the grain using P220-grit paper wrapped around a sanding block. Remove the dust with a vacuum or compressed air. If you don't handplane, start power-sanding with P100 grit, move to P150 grit, and then follow the steps above.

The second step is to create a sample board on scraps from the project. After making the cabinet shown here, I could tell after wiping the bare wood with denatured alcohol that the walnut crotch used for the panels would appear darker under a finish than the walnut used for the rest of the project. I did the full finishing sequence on samples of both woods and found that a dark wax would bring the plain walnut close enough in color to the crotchwood (which gets clear wax).

Seal with shellac, then apply gel varnish

If your project includes a floating panel, it is always a good idea to finish it before inserting it into the frame. In this way you won't see a strip of unfinished wood when seasonal changes cause the panel to shrink. I also finish the inside edges of the frame components with shellac and gel varnish

Dip and squeeze. Fold up a small piece of clean cotton cloth, and dip it into a can of dewaxed shellac. Squeeze out the surplus so that it doesn't drip.

Seal the surface. Wipe the cloth over the surface no more than a couple of times to leave a thin film of shellac on the wood (left). Use P320-grit sandpaper wrapped around a sanding block to smooth the surface (above). Remove the dust with a vacuum or compressed air.

before assembling them. This is much easier than trying to finish the narrow strip of frame and not get finish on the panel.

I've found that giving bare wood a single coat of dewaxed shellac has a number of benefits. On blotch-prone woods like cherry or pine, shellac helps prevent the uneven shading you can get from applying gel varnish to bare wood. On dyed wood, the shellac prevents pulling away some color when you rub on the gel varnish. And finally, sealing the wood with shellac and then sanding it gives a smoother base than bare wood for the gel varnish. Use a dewaxed shellac, like Zinsser's SealCoat. It comes as a 2-lb. cut, and I apply it as is, by dipping a small piece of cloth in the can, gently squeezing out the surplus, and then wiping the wood with the cloth. A couple of strokes over each area is usually sufficient. Let the shellac dry for

about 30 minutes, then lightly hand-sand the surface with the grain using P320-grit sandpaper. Vacuum or blow the dust out of the pores.

A gel varnish (also known as gel polyurethane or gel topcoat) has much the same resin, oil, and mineral spirits as a liquid clear finish, plus a thickening agent. This makes it much easier and less messy to wipe on. And because the product is designed to be wiped, it needs no thinning. Best of all, each layer dries too quickly to attract dust, so there is no need to sand between coats.

To apply, you simply dip a cloth into the gel, work it into the wood, and remove the surplus with a clean cloth. There are a few tricks to getting the best results. First, don't apply too much gel or work on too large an area at once. The varnish gets tacky in minutes and becomes progressively harder to remove. If you find yourself trying to wipe away gel the consistency of lard, simply dampen a cloth with mineral spirits, wipe away the gel, let the surface dry, and then apply the finish again.

Start with an area of about 2 sq. ft. You can increase the area if you find you are having no trouble removing the surplus. I rub the gel well into the wood. After you first wipe off the surplus, small wood pores appear filled; however, as the gel cures, it sinks down to line the inside of the pores, leaving an open-grained look.

When removing the surplus gel, keep refolding the cloth so that you don't smear the finish. The final rubdown should be with the grain. You can let the finish cure overnight, but in reasonably warm and dry

TIP Because gel varnish is thick and quick-setting, applying too much of it to your cloth can make it difficult to wipe away the surplus before it tacks. The easiest way to control how much gel varnish goes onto the cloth is to place it on using a stirring stick.

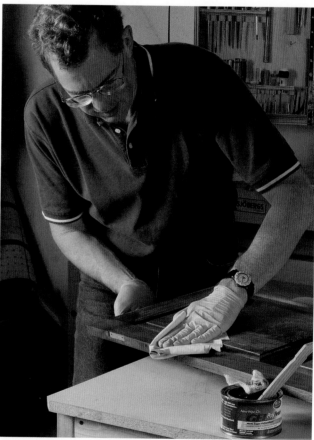

Rub on the gel varnish, then wipe off the surplus. Work the finish into the wood using small, circular movements, then wipe with the grain to remove any thicker deposits (top). Don't try to cover too large an area or the finish will become tacky before you can buff it. Use a clean cotton cloth to wipe away the surplus gel varnish (bottom), turning the cloth frequently to keep exposing a clean surface.

Apply dark wax directly.
If you want dark wax to enter the pores to change the tone of a piece, wipe the cloth into the wax (left). Work it into the wood, then wipe with the grain to remove the surplus (below). Buff the wax, clear or dark, until the surface is silky to the touch (right).

conditions you can apply two coats in a day. To avoid spontaneous combustion, always spread used finishing cloths outside to dry before throwing them away.

You should apply at least three coats to build an even luster. On a piece like a side table, where the top will get slightly heavier use, you can apply four or five coats. But don't try to build up a plastic-looking finish. In theory, you could wipe on enough coats to protect a kitchen tabletop, but liquid polyurethane would be quicker. By the way, all gel varnishes leave a satin finish.

Top it off with wax

After the last coat of gel has cured for at least three days, I give the workpiece a coat of paste wax. (Peter Gedrys describes the numerous benefits of wax in "All about Wax" on pp. 135–141.) Although gel varnish, applied and wiped off correctly, leaves a very smooth surface, it still has a slight grab to it when you touch it. Nothing beats the silky feel of a surface that has been waxed and buffed. Wax also gives some scratch protection, since objects are more likely to slide across the surface than to dig in and

Apply clear wax thinly. Fold over a piece of cheesecloth a couple of times, then place a lump of paste wax in the center (right). Gather the corners of the applicator, and press down until the wax begins to ease out through the rounded face of the applicator (below). To avoid having light wax show up in the pores of dark wood, use light pressure on the applicator.

TIP Colored wax can be used to subtly change the tone of a whole piece or to harmonize sections. I used a really dark brown wax on most of the walnut but a clear wax on the panels. Allow wax to dry for 20 or 30 minutes and then buff the surface with a clean cloth.

scratch it. And wax conceals any differences in sheen, though these should be minimal if you removed all the surplus gel.

Finally, dark wax left in corners and crevices emphasizes the three-dimensional aspects of the piece, and it can cover up minor blemishes in craftsmanship. You may never build the perfect piece, but at least it'll have a perfect finish.

An Oil-and-Wax Finish

CHARLES SHACKLETON

I strongly believe that a finish should not come between the end user and a piece of furniture. Hence, I stay away from plastic-type finishes, such as polyurethanes and lacquers or varnishes. These finishes tend to sit on top of the wood rather than soak into it, obliterating the subtle textures left by handplanes. One of the most frequent comments from visitors to my showroom is, "We saw the furniture and came in to feel it." I use an oil-and-wax finish instead.

All finishes have their drawbacks; this one lacks durability and high-gloss sheen. However, I am prepared to forego the durability because I get repairability (without having

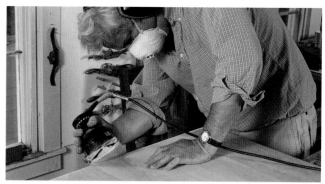

Sand only where needed. Use a palm sander with 220-grit paper to break sharp edges and smooth the end grain. Don't stray onto areas already planed smooth.

Smooth all surfaces. Begin by handplaning the surfaces to level and smooth them (above). Clean up any torn grain with a card scraper (right).

to refinish the whole piece) and better aging. My furniture is meant to be functional as well as beautiful: Even if it gets dinged and scratched, an occasional rewaxing and reoiling allows these defects to become part of the piece, making it feel like an antique that has weathered the storms of time. With a high-gloss finish, the repair of scratches and dings can become a horror story.

Equally important, this finish is low tech. It requires no special tools or a spray booth. In my shop, I don't employ a dedicated finisher. Each craftsperson builds his piece from rough lumber to buffing the wax finish, a method most readers should relate to.

Surface preparation is the key to this finish

After the wood has been through a thickness planer, handplane all surfaces. On areas

in which the grain has torn out, use a card scraper. The aim is for the surface to have that smooth and fresh, straight-from-the-blade look.

Selectively sand with 220-grit paper

There's still quite a bit of sanding involved, mostly in areas that won't cut clean, such as difficult grain patterns, end grain, and edges. Sand large areas with 220-grit paper on a palm sander, but be careful not to stray into cleanly planed areas.

When working on confined areas, it's better to fold the sheet of sandpaper into quarters and sand by hand, working with the grain or close to it. Sandpaper is powerful stuff, and things can happen faster than you imagine, so be careful not to create hollow areas in the surface.

Raise the grain. Dampen the wood (left) and let it dry. Then sand with 400-grit paper, and rub the surface with either a gray abrasive pad or 0000 steel wool. Burnishing the surface this way (below) lessens the chances of unequal oil penetration and blotching.

Raise the grain and resand the surface

Wipe down the whole piece with a damp cloth, being careful only to dampen the surface, not wet it. Use distilled water, which doesn't contain minerals that can react with tannin in the wood and cause stains. The moisture causes grain that has been crushed by the planing to rise. After about half an hour, the surface will be dry and noticeably rougher.

Lightly hand-sand every surface with 400-grit paper in the direction of the grain. Working by hand gives you a better feel for what's going on. Don't underestimate the cutting power of even 400-grit paper—you'll be amazed how quickly you can remove the crisp texture of a handplaned surface. A bright light held at a low angle is a great help, but monitor your progress by checking the texture of the surface with your hands.

The final step before applying the oil is to rub down the whole surface with Liberon 0000 steel wool or a gray abrasive pad. This further smooths and slightly burnishes the surface, which will allow the oil to penetrate the wood more evenly, reducing the chances of blotching.

Be generous with the oil

On most woods, I use boiled linseed oil because it gives a dark, aged appearance to the furniture. The exceptions are maple and ash, on which I use pure tung oil to keep the wood's appearance as light as possible. In either case, pour the oil from the can into a container 6 in. dia. by 6 in. deep. Put on a pair of disposable gloves, immerse an 8-in. by 8-in. bit of toweling in the container, and use it to apply the oil. Slosh the oil over the surface liberally, but make sure you do end grain early on, or you may wind up with drip marks there. As with all finishes, be

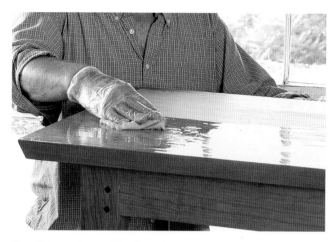

Flood the surface with oil. Soak a small piece of toweling in a bowl of boiled linseed oil and wipe the oil generously onto the wood.

Don't forget the end grain. If you leave the end grain until last, it may be hard to blend in darker drip marks.

Wipe off the surplus oil. After an hour, use a series of clean, dry cloths to remove any oil that remains on the surface. Wipe the wood thoroughly to avoid a sticky residue.

sure to coat both sides of all surfaces. Let the oil soak in for about an hour, then wipe off all of the excess, using pieces of clean cloth.

Let me repeat the warning I give all of my employees about disposing of oily rags in a safe manner: When wadded up, the rags are highly combustible, so hang them outside to dry or immerse them in water before disposing of them.

After wiping off the excess, let the workpiece dry for two days. Then apply a second coat of oil in the same manner as the first coat. This time there should be no areas where the oil soaks in completely, as the first coat should have formed a barrier. If there are areas where the oil does soak in, particularly on surfaces that will be subject to wear, you will need to repeat the oiling process a third time after the second coat has dried for two days.

You may find the dried oiled surface slightly rough, so before going onto the final step of waxing, burnish the surface using a very fine white abrasive pad.

Apply the wax sparingly

The purpose of applying wax is not to feed the wood, as commercials are fond of implying, but rather to give the surface a soft luster and a silky-smooth feel. You also can alter the wood's tone subtly by using colored wax. Apply thin coats of the wax in a circular motion using a 6-in.-square piece of toweling furled into a ball. This circular motion ensures that the wax gets worked into all of the pores and acts as filler.

On surfaces where there are multiple boards glued together, work across the surface board by board. Every 20 seconds or so, go back over the last section, wiping it with the grain. This avoids any swirl marks in the dried wax. Check that the wax is being applied evenly and smoothly; little lumps of

wax cause big problems later as they smear around when you are trying to buff a shine.

Leave the wax to dry for at least half an hour, then buff it using another piece of toweling and plenty of elbow grease. Your piece should now have a lovely shine.

Any wax finish will lose its gleam over time, particularly if it's a dining table that gets wiped down with a damp cloth after meals. But it is a simple task to apply and buff up another coat of wax. If moisture from a cold glass of water leaves a white ring, you can fix the problem by rubbing the area with 0000 steel wool or a gray abrasive pad.

As I said, I have used this finish for nearly 18 years and have had few complaints. For some odd reason, the most common complaint (about three times) has been from people who had left a pumpkin to rot on their table. This required us to replane the surface, but I'm sure *Fine Woodworking* readers take better care of their furniture.

Burnish and wax. After the last coat of oil has dried for two days, burnish the surface with a white abrasive pad (top) to smooth the surface prior to waxing. Finally, sparingly apply paste wax (left), rubbing first in a circular motion to fill any pores, then with the grain. A colored wax can be used to darken the appearance of a piece.

Hot-Rod Your Varnish

ROLAND JOHNSON

We'd all like a finish that can be applied easily by hand, stands up to the rigors of everyday use, and is easy to repair or renew. Several years ago, in my search for this Holy Grail finish, I started sampling varnishes. I rejected polyurethane because it's hard to repair and worse to remove if a piece needs a total refinish. I narrowed my search to alkyd-based varnishes, eventually choosing Pratt & Lambert®'s No. 38 clear. However, I wanted it to have more water resistance and to dry faster, and I wanted to wipe it on.

So I started tweaking the stock No. 38 and, through trial and error, came up with a brew that fulfilled my needs. I mixed equal parts of No. 38 and pure tung oil, added some pure spirits of gum turpentine, and zapped the mix with a dose of Japan drier.

This custom oil-varnish mixture has a number of advantages. It is easily wiped on and off with a paper towel. It can be wet-sanded into the grain to act as a pore filler. The thin coats dry quickly, reducing the opportunity for dust to get trapped in the wet finish. Often I apply finish in an area that is less than white-room clean, so eliminating the worry about dust is a real bonus. This finish is water-resistant and tough enough to hold up to everyday use, it's easy to repair or replace, it resists yellowing, and it dries hard enough to be rubbed out to a high-gloss sheen if desired.

There are a couple of drawbacks, though. It has a short shelf life (a few weeks before it

starts to solidify), so mix only the amount you'll need for the project. More than with other oil-based finishes, cloths used with this mixture must be laid out to dry because the fast catalytic reaction caused by the Japan driers may create enough heat to spontaneously combust if they are left wadded up.

Flood on the first coat

A clear finish looks only as good as the wood beneath it, so good surface preparation is important. I typically sand to P240 grit, then use compressed air or a shop vacuum to clean

Mix what you need. Because this finish goes hard in the container after a few weeks, mix only what you'll need for each project.

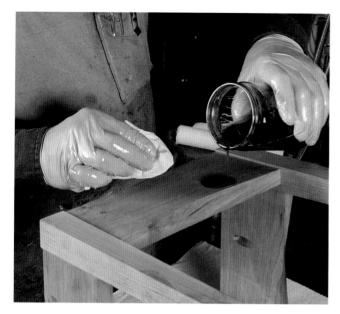

Pour it on. Flood the surface with the first coat of finish, moving it around with a disposable brush or a paper towel.

Look for an even sheen. It is important to apply an even coat. Check your progress using a low-angle raking light.

off the dust, and wipe the surface with a tack rag before applying the first coat.

On horizontal surfaces, pour some finish onto the wood and use a disposable foam or bristle brush or a good-quality paper towel (Bounty® works well) to cover the surface with varnish. On vertical areas, apply the finish with the brush. The key to success is an even coating. Keep applying finish until it is no longer absorbed quickly. Areas that absorb the finish will have a dull appearance. A raking light across the surface will help you see the dull spots.

You've applied an even film when the sheen across the entire piece is reasonably consistent. At that point, wipe off the excess with a dry paper towel or a lint-free cotton cloth, then allow the finish to dry thoroughly. If the temperature is at least 65°F, 24 hours should be enough time for this first coat.

First coat can also fill the pores in open-grained wood

If you want a glossy film finish on open-pored wood, you will need to fill the pores.

Spread on the finish. Liberally cover the surface with the oil/varnish mix. Using P400-grit paper, sand the surface with the grain to create a slurry that fills the pores.

Remove the surplus. Wipe the surface with a paper towel across the grain. The aim is to remove surplus slurry from the surface without pulling it out of the pores.

Spread on the first coat as shown in the center photo on p. 183, then sand the surface with P400-grit paper. The resulting slurry will form a paste that fills the pores. Lightly wipe the excess finish off the surface, going across the grain, and allow the finish to dry for 24 hours. To avoid pulling the filler out of the pores, don't sand the next one or two wiped-on coats (see the bottom right photo on p. 183).

Sand between coats and build the film

I sand between each coat of finish with P400-grit paper. The real importance of sanding between coats is to even the surface tension of the next coat of finish. If the surface is left shiny, or with an inconsistent gloss, the wet finish will not flow out evenly.

The varnish is dry enough to sand when the sanding dust is white and doesn't gum up

Dry enough to sand. If the sandpaper produces a white powder (top), the finish is ready to sand between coats. If the sanding residue is brown and sticks to the paper (above), let the finish dry longer.

Picking your paper. Hand-sand between coats using a ¼ sheet of P400-grit paper, folded once.

Build the finish. After sanding the first coat, vacuum the dust and wipe on the next coat. Three or four coats are enough for most surfaces, but tabletops need at least six for sufficient protection.

the paper: "When the swarf is white, the drying is right." If the dust is brown and forms tiny clumps on the paper, the finish isn't ready for sanding. Vacuum the dust.

After the first coat, where the wood absorbs a lot of finish and needs longer to dry, successive coats may be applied as quickly as every three or four hours, depending on the temperature and humidity. However, I wouldn't apply more than three coats in one day as you might trap solvent under the topcoat, resulting in a prolonged curing time. For most surfaces, three or four coats give a nice, even build. For tabletops or other surfaces likely to receive occasional liquid spills, I would apply a minimum of six coats.

Rub out and wax the surface

I prefer medium-luster finishes, and to get there I use steel wool and wax. Unfold a pad of 0000 steel wool and lightly rub the surface. Keep checking the surface under a raking light until it shows an even dullness. At that point, vacuum away the steel-wool dust and rub on a thin coat of clear paste wax. Let this dry for 30 minutes, then buff the surface with a clean cotton cloth.

If you prefer a higher gloss, wait several weeks for the varnish to harden, then sand the surface with 600-grit (CAMI) paper, rub it with car polish, and finish with a coat of paste wax. Your piece will now have a finish worthy of your craftsmanship.

Rub out and wax. Steel wool and wax quickly produce a medium-luster look.

Rub out with 0000 steel wool. Rub the surface with the grain until you achieve a uniformly dull sheen.

Bring up the shine. Wipe on a coat of paste wax, wait 30 minutes, and buff the surface with a cotton cloth to leave a silky surface with a medium luster.

One Fast Finish

JEFF JEWITT

I've had to learn to do quick finishing jobs and make fast fixes in my refinishing business. This method is both fast and attractive, whether you're working on a holiday gift on Christmas Eve or you just prefer no-fuss finishes. I came up with the technique based on necessity, but I'm sure it will save you when time is tight.

This finish is ideal for a low-build, "in-the-wood" type of look, where durability is not the key factor. However, you can build the shellac to increase the level of protection. The ingredients—boiled linseed oil, denatured alcohol, a can of amber shellac, and a few rags—can be found in most woodshops or at the nearest hardware store. The wipe-on technique avoids the hassle of most oil finishes, which can take days to complete. In fact, it works so well that it might become your favorite finish.

Begin with a light coat of linseed oil

For surface preparation, scrape, plane, or sand the wood with the grain to P220 grit. Wipe with naphtha or denatured alcohol to remove dust, dirt, and sanding debris. The solvent will highlight potential problems like glue spots and scratches.

Applying boiled linseed oil is the first step in French polishing, a more tedious and time-consuming technique from which this finish is derived. In fact, you could call this a "down and dirty" French polish.

I'm a big fan of boiled linseed oil for this step because it contains driers that cause it to cure faster than tung oil. Pour a small amount onto a small cotton cloth. Apply just enough oil to make the wood appear "wetted," which is about a teaspoon per square foot depending on wood species. Don't use the "flood on, let sit, then wipe" method. If you do, the oil will seep from figured areas through the thin shellac that is applied in the next step.

Remove excess oil with a clean rag, then lightly buff the surface with a gray synthetic abrasive pad such as 3M Scotch-Brite™ or Mirka Mirlon. The pad will pick up residual oil and will smooth the wood surface further.

A thin coat of oil lays the foundation. Because this finish does not provide time for the oil to dry, compensate by using a whisper-thin coat (above). Use just enough to bring out the beauty of the wood. Immediately remove any residual oil with a clean, lint-free cloth (left). A good rubdown with a synthetic pad (below) will smooth the surface and add a nice sheen.

Pad on shellac right away

Normally, you would let the oil cure for 24 to 48 hours. You can wait, but if you go directly to the shellac application, it will speed things up and the oil will provide a bit of lubrication for the shellac. The thin coat of oil cures fine below the shellac.

Plain, orange, waxy shellac (sold in a can as amber shellac) works well and is easy to find. The brand I use comes in a 3-lb. cut that I dilute by mixing two parts denatured alcohol with five parts shellac. Put the mixture in a squeeze bottle with a dispensing spout.

I use a padding cloth to wipe on the shellac. It should be as absorbent, clean, and lint-free as possible. Old, clean T-shirts work fine. Cotton is preferred because polyester does not hold or absorb liquids as well. Wad up the cloth so that the bottom part is as smooth and free of wrinkles as possible. Make the pad a manageable size. Large pads are great for big, flat surfaces but don't work for smaller and more intricate projects.

Dispense about 2 oz. of denatured alcohol into the pad, and compress the pad with your hand several times to work the solvent through it. Then squeeze the pad to remove excess solvent. Pour about 1 oz. of shellac solution onto the pad bottom.

Wipe on shellac. Thin the shellac you'll use by mixing 5 parts shellac with 2 parts denatured alcohol. This thinner shellac is easier to apply, especially on small or intricate surfaces. Wipe it on thinly with a cloth pad, starting with flat surfaces (top) and then working the sides and edges (middle). Use 600-grit sandpaper to smooth out application marks or remove debris (bottom).

2 parts alcohol

5 parts shellac

Padding shellac simply means wiping it on thinly with this cloth pad. It is best to practice on a flat surface to get a feel for applying it smoothly and evenly.

Finishing different surfaces requires a variety of techniques

For flat surfaces, bring the pad down lightly near one edge and drag it across the top and off the opposite edge, like an airplane landing and then taking off again. Come in from the other side and repeat the stroke. Continue down the board in alternating stripes, with the grain. When you've reached the bottom, start again at the top. One of the great benefits of shellac is that it dries quickly enough for you to repeat the sequence rapidly. Work the sides and edges in a similar fashion. As the pad starts to dry out, reload it with shellac.

For complex surfaces such as furniture interiors, tight corners, or other challenging areas, you'll need to modify things a bit. Start with the pad anywhere that's convenient and move it toward corners, right angles, and such. Always keep the pad moving. When you recharge, make sure you don't put too much shellac in the pad or you'll pool it. Bring the pad down on the surface and immediately begin to move it using just the pressure of your fingers or the weight of your arm.

To finish routed or other three-dimensional surfaces, wad up the cloth and compress it into the profile of the edge. Use a small, well-wetted portion of the pad to get the shellac into small or tight areas. But again, don't get the pad too wet or you'll create problems.

It probably took you longer to read about the shellac application than it will to actually do it. For a medium-size project like a small cabinet or table, I spend only about 30 minutes with the shellac. Smaller projects are a little harder because you risk returning to an area before it dries and dragging the gummy shellac. Move the pad more slowly, or try using a smaller pad.

You may encounter streaks or fibers in the sticky shellac. Any application marks or debris can be rubbed out with some 600-grit (CAMI grade) sandpaper followed by 0000 steel wool after the shellac has cured for about eight hours. Because there are no "coats" of finish in the conventional sense, just keep applying the finish to achieve the look you want.

Applying the final touch

Near the end of the process, if you use all the shellac in the pad and keep rubbing with the dry pad, it will burnish the surface and give it a nice, soft glow. For a lower luster and extra protection, wait a day and then apply some paste wax with 0000 steel wool. Buff the wax with a soft cloth.

Finish with steel wool and wax. Paste wax adds a more even sheen and a nice feel to your project. Apply it with 0000 steel wool. When the wax appears hazy, buff it with a soft, clean cloth.

An Easy, Durable Finish

LON SCHLEINING

I wasn't asking for much: I wanted a finish with a rich, hand-rubbed luster, neither too glossy nor too dull, that illuminates rather than hides the grain—one that would offer real protection from moisture and sunlight and yet still feel like wood, not plastic. I also wanted a finish I could apply quickly and easily, and something I could use right out of the can. And it would be awfully nice if it smelled good. That isn't too much to ask of a finish, is it?

The answer turned out to be rather simple: high-gloss spar varnish, turpentine, wet-or-dry sandpaper in various grits, a few rags, and a bit of elbow grease. Simply rubbing plain gloss varnish into the raw wood provided the protection, sheen, feel, and ease of application I was looking for.

Start with a well-prepared surface

The key is to scrape, plane, or sand each of the pieces of your project before you assemble it. Even if you have to touch up the sanding after final assembly, this step will save lots of time.

During the building process, I sand by machine (belt sander, 120-grit sandpaper), then sand by hand with a wood sanding block padded with felt. The sanding sequence will depend on the type of wood. On hard maple, use 100 grit, then 120, 150, and finally 220 grit. With mahogany and its much more open grain, stop dry-sanding at 150 grit. Be sure to change sandpaper frequently.

Make sure the surface is clean by using a vacuum to pull out the sanding grit from the pores of the wood. Don't worry if the surface is less smooth than what you normally shoot for. The sanding doesn't stop when the finishing begins. I wet-sand with finer and finer grits during the application of the finish itself.

Preparing to finish

The heart of my finish is a high-gloss spar varnish, which has several advantages: Unlike plain oils, it hardens overnight; it's readily available; and it has much greater clarity than semigloss or satin finishes, whose additives not only dull the finish but also cloud the grain. Spar varnish also contains ultraviolet protection that will help keep the wood from fading or yellowing. I've used this varnish for years on boats, protecting the wood from salt water and abuse, so I know it provides the tough tabletop film I'm looking for. As an added bonus, this finish is quite easy to renew by scuff-sanding with 220-grit paper and simply wiping on an additional coat of varnish if the surface ever needs it. In addition, this finishing method will also work with other types of varnish, urethanes, and even some finishing oils.

Though it's counterintuitive, gloss varnish does not produce a glossy surface when it's rubbed on. Because you're wiping off any excess varnish, not letting it stand on the surface, it doesn't get a chance to build up to its normal gloss.

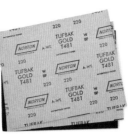

Three parts varnish + **One part thinner** + **220-grit wet-or-dry sandpaper**

Apply the finish liberally. It is important to coat the whole surface as quickly as possible to avoid creating lines where the finish overlaps. Use gloved hands to spread the thinned varnish over the surface before sanding it in with 220-grit wet-or-dry paper.

Grain filler with a perfect color match. Sanding the varnish with the grain creates a slurry that fills the pores of open-grained wood.

To thin the varnish for the initial coat, I like to use natural turpentine instead of paint thinner, simply because it smells good. As a general rule, thin a finish with whatever the label suggests for cleanup.

You will need a few sheets of 220-, 320-, 400-, and 600-grit wet-or-dry sandpaper for sanding in the varnish. For dry-sanding between coats, use open-coat, self-lubricating, 320-grit paper. A box of soft cotton rags from a paint store ensures that you won't run out of clean rags just when you need one. Lastly, disposable gloves are essential. Not only will they protect your skin from solvents, but they also make the job a lot less messy.

Before starting, spread out a plastic sheet to contain drips and spills. This is also a good time to change into an old shirt and pants. (I might even follow my own advice about this one of these days.)

First coat: thinned varnish

Pour a small amount of varnish into a container using a piece of nylon panty hose as a strainer. Thin with one part turpentine to about three parts varnish. The first coat saturates the wood more effectively if it is thinned down a bit.

Wearing gloves, quickly flood the entire surface on all sides until it's coated, adding more varnish as needed. It's important to cover the piece completely, not in sections. Working on a small area at a time may leave a line where different areas of finish overlap.

Sand the wet varnish into the wood using 220-grit wet-or-dry paper. Sand with the grain until you produce a slurry. This helps fill the pores of open-grained woods, such as mahogany or oak, and the color match is perfect. While the varnish is still wet, wipe with a soft cotton rag to remove any varnish that has not soaked into the wood. When removing the excess varnish, there's a point at which the varnish gets quite sticky and

Sand on and wipe off. Before the varnish becomes tacky, wipe off the surplus using clean cotton rags. Keep changing the rags until no more finish can be removed and the surface can be buffed smooth.

No place for surplus varnish to hide. No matter how much you wipe, varnish has a habit of oozing out of joints after you have done your final buffing, creating sticky and glossy areas. Remove surplus varnish using compressed air, and wipe the area clean.

difficult to wipe. Working on something like a large tabletop might require a helper. Rub across the grain to avoid pulling the slurry out of the wood pores. Be sure to spread out the oil-soaked rags to dry before disposing of them, to avoid the danger of the rags spontaneously igniting.

Buff with a fresh cloth until the surface is slick and smooth. Polish the piece every half hour or so to make sure no wet spots emerge on the surface. Joints, such as on the breadboard ends of a tabletop, will absorb excess varnish, which will gradually seep out after the rest of the surface has dried. To avoid this, blast the joint with compressed air, forcing the surplus varnish out of the gap.

Let the piece sit at room temperature overnight. You can carry on working in the shop because it doesn't matter if dust lands on the piece, but it is a good idea to ensure adequate ventilation to avoid a concentration of fumes.

Additional coats: unthinned varnish

The next morning the surface should feel smooth and dry. Lightly dry-sand it with 320-grit nonloading, or stearated, paper. Use a felt-padded block, and sand with the grain. Clean the surface with a vacuum or compressed air. Apply a flood coat of unthinned varnish, and use 320-grit wet-

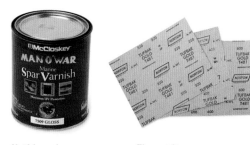

Unthinned   +   Finer-grit paper
varnish

Scuff-sand the surface the following day. Between coats, lightly sand the surface using 320-grit nonloading, or stearated, paper under a padded block. Always sand with the grain.

Build the finish. Apply subsequent coats the same way as the first coat. Rub in each coat with a higher grit of wet-or-dry paper. Rub the last coat in with 600-grit paper to create a very smooth surface.

A final buffing. After the final coat has dried, the surface will be silky smooth with the pores filled. Rub the surface briskly with a clean cotton rag.

or-dry paper to sand the varnish into the surface. Wipe and buff the excess varnish as before.

Repeat this process each day, wet-sanding with finer and finer grits until you have at least three coats. Additional coats will produce slightly more luster. Some folks like to wax the surface when it's dry, but I prefer to leave it unwaxed because it's easier to recoat should the surface become damaged over time.

I haven't yet been tempted to throw away either my spray guns or my badger-hair brushes, but after using this finishing process on several projects, I can't remember the last time I used those tools. This simple technique meets all of my criteria for an ideal finish and produces consistent results, all without a large investment in equipment.

Finishing Mahogany

JEFF JEWITT

When the cabinetmakers in England and America who built early 18th-century furniture fell in love with mahogany, most of the wood was of a color and quality that few woodworkers will have the chance to work with ever again. Those old-growth trees of Cuban and Santo Domingan mahogany (*Swietenia mahagoni*) yielded lumber with a much darker color and a finer texture than what's commonly available now. I first saw that wood up close many years ago, when I toured the collection of American furniture at a museum in Williamsburg, Virginia. The first thing that struck me was the color of those pieces: It wasn't just the patina—it was simply awe-inspiring wood. So when I recently had the chance to put a finish on a piecrust table made with a single-plank top, I knew I had to come up with a way to coax that rich, dark finish from the lighter color of the Central and South American (also called Honduras) mahogany (*S. macrophylla*) available today.

Lay on the first layer of color

It is not uncommon to find wormholes in otherwise perfectly sound mahogany lumber. To avoid wasting a lot of wood, you can fill and color them easily (see "Filling the inevitable wormholes" on p. 196). After that, you can lay on the first level of color. I use an amber-colored water-soluble dye as a base coat to mimic an old finish. The amber

Filling the inevitable wormholes

In most extrawide mahogany boards, you'll often find large wormholes near the edges. You can cut them out, but then you risk losing your chance to make a one-piece top, and you waste a lot of lumber. I've used all sorts of putties and fillers, and I've come to the conclusion that the best solution is to use a nonshrinking auto-body filler, such as Bondo® brand. I have used Bondo for 20 years in repair work, and while I suspect that some purists may despise it, the product has several things going for it.

First, it's absolutely nonshrinking, so after two or three years, you won't notice any depression where the hole was. Second, the color of the mixed putty is a pinkish red that matches the natural color of the mahogany, and it's easy to tweak to get the final color of the finish. When you apply Bondo to an open-grained wood such as mahogany, it's important to apply masking tape around the hole so that you don't get any Bondo in the grain, which will show up later in the finishing process. Let the Bondo dry several hours, then remove the tape and sand the surface level. After the subsequent staining and first coat of shellac finish, you can further refine the putty with some dry pigment colors mixed with shellac, if necessary.

1. Mix dry pigments into a little shellac. After doing this a few times, you really can develop an artist's eye for color.

2. To cover the distinct black line left around the rim of the hole, paint over it with a nearly opaque coating of color.

3. Add some faux grain. Small, darker-tinted lines will look like grain texture after a finish goes on over the repair.

4. After the sealer coat of oil goes on but before the topcoat, tweak the final color of the repaired area.

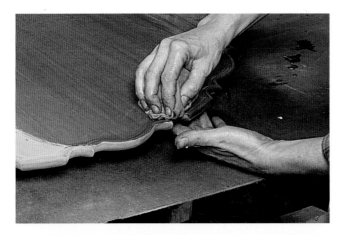

Raise the grain before the first coat. Before applying a water-based dye stain, wet the surface thoroughly to raise the grain, then let it dry. Sand down the raised fibers before applying the dye stain. The result is a smoother finish than you'd get without taking this preliminary step.

Start with a water-based dye stain. Using an amber-colored stain as the first coat of color does two things: It gives the lumber an aged look, and it evens out different shades inherent in the wood.

Spray it on for even coverage. An inexpensive plastic spray bottle is a great tool for applying water-based dye stain quickly and evenly.

Abrasive pads conform to tight spaces. To smooth out intricate shapes after staining, abrasive pads work better than sandpaper, and they last longer.

undertone evens out color variations in the wood and adds depth to the final finish. I prefer water-soluble dyes because they're easier to control. Also, they tend to absorb more evenly into the wood than alcohol-based dye stains, which dry faster and leave behind unsightly lap marks.

Before applying the stain, sand the piece with 220-grit paper, then raise the grain by wiping the surface with distilled water to minimize any further grain-raising. (Tap water can contain mineral impurities that may discolor the wood.) Wait several hours for the water to dry, then resand with the 220-grit paper.

Use a plant mister to spray on the amber dye, saturating the surface quickly and thoroughly. Water-based dyes are forgiving compared with alcohol-based dyes, but make

sure you soak up any excess with clean rags. After the amber dye has dried, scuff the dry surface using a gray synthetic abrasive pad such as Scotch-Brite brand; go lightly so that you don't cut through the dye.

Mix the second color into an oil-sealer coat

Now it's time to add the second, primary overtone of color. With this table, I used a technique that I first heard about from Rob Millard, who builds reproductions of 18th-century furniture. To get an aged effect and a rich color, use boiled linseed oil colored with dye. You can use an oil-soluble dry powder or a liquid concentrate like I used on this table (see "Sources" on p. 230). Practice on some scraps first to get the effect you want. To enrich the yellow undertone of the first color, I used equal amounts of TransTint brown mahogany and reddish-brown liquid dyes, mixing 5 ml of each into 100 ml of boiled linseed oil.

Mix the color into the oil in precise amounts, and keep a record so that you can duplicate the mixture if you run out. Apply the oil by vigorously wiping it on with a rag in a circular motion; you can use a small brush for intricate shapes. Don't add thinners to the oil because it causes dark circles to form around the pores where the color becomes too concentrated. If the piece becomes too dark, just wipe the colored oil with a new coat of clear oil or a rag dampened with alcohol to remove some of the color.

Fill the grain with a rottenstone slurry

As an option, you can fill the grain in the tabletop at this stage, rather than waiting for the oil to dry and using a paste wood filler. Filled grain results in a smoother surface after the topcoats have been applied. Or you can leave it unfilled. My preference for tabletops is for a filled surface, so I added some more clear oil, sprinkled some rottenstone on the surface, and padded the slurry mixture into the grain of the wood with a circular motion. The rottenstone isn't as abrasive as pumice, which might cut through the dye and the undertone color. Also, the gray rottenstone adds a bit of darker

Seal the wood with a coat of tinted oil. Powdered or liquid dyes mixed with oil, in this case boiled linseed oil, will stain and seal the wood in one step. Be precise and keep track of the amounts that you mix so that you can duplicate the same concentration if you run out.

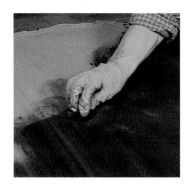

Elbow grease is appreciated here. Saturate a wiping rag with the dyed-oil mixture and apply it quickly and efficiently, wiping in a circular motion.

Use a brush to do what the rag couldn't. The dampened rag may not effectively stain detailed areas, such as the carved edge of this table.

Even out the color. After applying the first coat of tinted oil, a rag dampened with alcohol or a new coat of clear oil will help even out the color. The alcohol will dilute the dye without affecting the oil sealer.

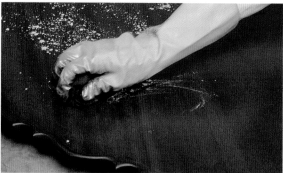

Fill the grain for a smooth top. Fill only the top surface of the tabletop. Apply a second, fresh coat of oil, and sprinkle some rottenstone over the surface (left). Rub it in using a circular motion to form a gray slurry that fills the open grain, leaving a smoother finish after topcoats are applied over it (below). This step is not recommended for intricately carved details, like those on the table legs of this project.

color when it's mixed with the oil. After the rottenstone filler has set up for several hours, use a wadded clean cloth to wipe off any excess slurry remaining on the surface. Let that last coat of oil dry for at least three days. If it's cool (65°F or lower) and damp in your shop, let the coat dry for a week.

Build up the topcoats in thin layers

You can choose from a wide range of topcoats—a solvent-based wiping varnish, spray lacquer, or even water-based finishes if you apply dewaxed shellac first—as a barrier coat over the oil. For this job, I opted for the classic and traditional shellac finish. For brushing shellac, I prefer a 1½-lb. cut. Because a gallon of shellac was much more than I needed, I just factored the ratio down to 3 oz. of shellac flakes mixed into a pint of alcohol.

I really like the subtleties of texture you get with a brushed-on shellac finish. I use a technique I learned from Don Williams at the Smithsonian Institution many years ago. The trick is to apply the fast-drying shellac in whisper-thin strokes with a finely bristled

synthetic brush, such as the Taklon brushes sold in specialty catalogs and art-supply stores. For this table, I used two widths—a 2-in. brush for the flat top and a 1-in. brush for the intricately carved base. A single 1½-in. brush would suffice if you don't want to buy both sizes (these brushes are rather pricey).

To apply, dip the brush about halfway into the shellac solution. With shellac, bubbles aren't a problem as they are with brushing varnish, so you can scrape off the excess shellac by dragging the bristles across the lip of the jar. The raised, molded edge of this table can be a challenge for laying on a finish, but this brush excels at the task. Because it doesn't hold a great deal of finish (as a larger brush with an internal reservoir would), this small brush doesn't deposit a pool of shellac when it first touches the surface. And because it has a finely chiseled edge, you can place the brush down lightly right where the edge of the raised molding meets the flat surface of the tabletop and drag it gently toward the center.

Use minimal pressure and leave just a whisper-thin film of shellac. When you start to run out, dunk the brush into the shellac

Build up the finish with thin coats. Seedlac shellac adds more color to the surface and dries quickly, so three thin coats can be applied in one day. Shellac also bonds well to a surface that was sealed with linseed oil.

Dewax your own shellac. Mix shellac several days ahead of time to allow impurities to settle out of the mixture. Skim the clear shellac off the top with a syringe.

Small brushes are better for tight spaces. Slap on several thin coats with a small brush to avoid muddling up carving details.

again and feather each new stroke into where you left off with the last one. Brushing shellac this way takes a bit of practice, so start on the undersides of a project to get the feel for it. For the intricately carved parts, I use a slapping or flicking motion to apply the shellac. The fast-drying nature of shellac keeps dust pimples from forming in the finish, and you can keep building up new coats quickly.

I usually build up at least three coats in a day, let it dry overnight, and then lightly sand the surface with 600-grit wet-or-dry sandpaper for the flat areas and gray synthetic pads for the complex shapes. Once the shellac has dried for at least three days, you can dull the surface with 0000 steel wool if you want more of a matte sheen. Because all of the layers of shellac melt into one another as the last one dries, there's little danger of rubbing through the finish. If you have to remove some brush marks, use 600-grit sandpaper first, then follow with the 0000 steel wool. A light coat of paste wax will bring up a dull surface to a satiny sheen.

Work toward the center. Lay down each brush stroke of thin shellac quickly. Brush from the outside edge toward the center of the table to keep the finish from pooling at the shaped edge.

The Best Finish for Pine

TOM WISSHACK

Ihave never understood why so many woodworkers consider pine an inferior wood. I think it's one of the most beautiful woods available, and it only gets better with time, taking on a marvelous color and patina. But poor staining and finishing techniques have given pine a bad rap.

Pine does present unique challenges. You want the wood to look as if it has aged naturally to its present color. You'll never achieve that look if you apply stain directly to pine because the color penetrates deeply and unevenly. Softer portions of the wood become very dark, while the harder and more resinous areas resist the stain. Worse, this blotchiness is irreversible. That is, the drastic measures you'd have to take to correct the blotchiness could ruin the piece.

Fortunately, you can achieve superior results if you apply thin layers of shellac and stain with patience and a delicate touch. When you wipe away the excess stain, some will remain in the crevices of moldings and joints, giving the subtle feeling of age that I prefer on pine.

Let the pine age naturally

I smooth my pieces with a handplane and polish them by hand with P600-grit wet-or-dry paper. If you use sandpaper alone, begin with P120- or P180-grit, then work up to P320 or P400 grit.

Whenever I build a piece from pine, I sand it and then allow it to stand in the shop for at

First, do nothing.
Unfinished pine will take on a golden color naturally after a few weeks' exposure to the air, as the top half of the sample board shows. This patina will enhance any color you apply.

least a month before finishing. Pine will take on a natural patina, which I call shop aging. When I apply the finish, the resulting color is always deeper and richer than it would be if I finished the piece right away, so a very light stain normally is adequate. Waiting for the wood color to change is a luxury, but the results are worth it. Applying a finish too soon after constructing a piece of furniture is, in my opinion, a mistake.

Seal the grain

A washcoat of shellac comes first. This serves as a sealer; it's essential to close the pores of the pine and provide a foundation for the stain. Shellac dries quickly and gives the wood absolute clarity. You can stain over it and—what's critical—remove most or all of the stain if you make a mistake or don't like the look.

I have had good luck with Zinsser shellac, which is widely available. I usually mix the clear and amber varieties, which gives the wood a warm, antique hue. Fill a quart glass jar about one-fourth full of clear shellac. Add small amounts of amber shellac until the mixture is about the color of honey. Note how much shellac you have, then add about half that amount of denatured alcohol. The result is close to a 2-lb. cut, but exact proportions aren't critical.

Brush the shellac onto one horizontal surface at a time, using long, even strokes. Rotate the piece as needed to coat all the surfaces with this thin washcoat. When covering a wide surface, work quickly, overlapping

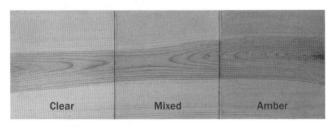

Clear   Mixed   Amber

Shellac prevents blotching and adds subtle warmth. A washcoat of thinned shellac partially seals the wood pores, ensuring that subsequent coats of stain will be absorbed evenly. The washcoat also can add a hint of color, as shown in the panel above. Mixing clear shellac (left panel) and amber (right) produces a nice intermediate shade (center).

strokes only slightly. Seal a piece of scrap, too, so you can dial in the stain color before tackling the workpiece.

For best results, apply two washcoats. Wait about an hour between coats and two hours after the second coat. Then scuff-sand with worn P600-grit wet-or-dry paper.

Mix and apply the stain

Oil-based stain is the best type for pine. It can be brushed or wiped on, and it dries relatively slowly. Regardless of the brand, thin it with mineral spirits. That not only gives you more working time but also keeps the addition of color subtle. A small amount of boiled linseed oil makes the stain more translucent.

Off-the-shelf stains vary considerably in the amount of pigment they contain. The Olympic® stains I usually use are heavy-bodied and require considerable thinning. Stain/sealer products that contain some tung-oil varnish are watery and weaker.

Don't be afraid to experiment with color, intermixing stains and trying different dilutions to get just the shade you want. See "Stain recipe for pine" on p. 204 for a good basic stain recipe to use as a starting point. The amount of thinner required depends on the opacity and thickness of the stain you choose. Start with a mixture that's roughly 30% mineral spirits to 70% stain. If that's too intense or opaque, add more spirits. Very often, I end up with 60% thinner to 40% stain.

When the color is right, brush a liberal amount of stain onto the wood, let it stand about five minutes, then remove the excess very lightly. A soft cotton cloth works well; quilted bathroom tissue is even better.

The stain mixture normally will stay workable for 15 to 20 minutes. If it begins to set up, lay down another coat of stain before continuing to wipe. A single coat of stain

Two washcoats, light sanding. Brush on the shellac with long, single strokes (top). Two coats are best. (For this project, the door was left attached, an unorthodox technique, to ensure that the stain was applied uniformly and to allow the finish to build up on the brass, giving it a patina similar to the wood.) Lightly scuff-sand the dry shellac with P600-grit paper (above).

Stain recipe for pine

This recipe makes about 1 qt. of stain. It uses three Olympic oil stains, which I've found to be very heavily pigmented. If you use another brand, it may not contain as much pigment, so you may have to adjust the amounts.

- 1 pt. mineral spirits
- ⅓ cup boiled linseed oil
- ⅔ cup Olympic Dark Walnut oil stain
- ⅔ cup Olympic Colonial Maple oil stain
- ⅔ cup Olympic American Cherry oil stain

Mix the ingredients and stir well.

The resulting mixture should have a medium golden-brown look and the consistency of 2% milk. Test the stain on a sample board. If the stain looks too dark, add more Colonial Maple; too light, more Dark Walnut; too brownish, more American Cherry.

Apply stain generously. Brush on a thick coat of stain, working in a defined area such as this door panel. Use the brush to work the stain into corners and the recesses of moldings.

Mix well. Fill a jar with the mineral spirits and linseed oil, then add the stains. You don't have to measure precisely. Let the color of the mixture tell you when you have the right amounts. Err on the side of making the stain too thin.

Test the stain. Test the color on a sample board that's been given a washcoat of shellac. This lets you tweak the proportions of the stain recipe before finishing the real piece.

Wait, then wipe lightly. Let the stain dry for 15 to 20 minutes (temperature and humidity will affect drying times). Then wipe away the excess. Work in a circular motion at first, then with straight strokes. Use a very light touch—no pressure on the wood at all.

may have a minimal effect on the wood's color. But if you layer three or more coats of stain, you will steadily achieve a rich and increasingly aged look. Let the individual coats of stain dry for at least a week.

Add another coat of shellac, then the topcoats

Once you are happy with the color of your pine, protect the stain with another coat of shellac. If you don't, the stain may dissolve when you apply a topcoat. Use a somewhat thicker mixture this time, say 70% shellac to 30% denatured alcohol.

Don't overbrush or overwork the barrier coat because the alcohol can dissolve the stain beneath. Allow the barrier coat to dry several hours or overnight.

I've found that varnish makes the best topcoat because it adheres well to shellac and gives the wood an additional amber tint. Avoid polyurethane varnish, though; it won't adhere well to the waxy shellac.

Lightly scuff-sand the piece with P400- or P600-grit paper, dilute the varnish by 30% to 40% with mineral spirits, and brush on three thin coats. Smooth the final coat with P600-grit wet-or-dry paper, and rub the surface with 0000 steel wool and mineral oil for a satin sheen.

More stain if needed. Brush on a second coat of stain (left), then wipe carefully (right) to avoid hitting an area you've already wiped. If you slip, dab on more stain, then wipe again.

Brush on more shellac. Let the initial coats of stain dry thoroughly, which can take as long as a week. Then brush on another washcoat of shellac. Rotate the piece as needed so you're always working on a horizontal surface.

Add protection with a topcoat. Use a mixture of varnish and mineral spirits, brushing it on with long, smooth strokes.

Blotch-Free Cherry

MARK SCHOFIELD

Cherry's popularity for fine furniture is no surprise: It is hard but not heavy; it cuts easily with power tools or by hand; the grain is restrained but interesting; and over time it takes on a beautiful deep, red-brown color.

However, like a scorpion, there is a sting in the tail for the unwary. Many woodworkers apply an oil-based clear finish only to see the wood break out in random, dark, ugly blotches. Those who stain the wood, intending to instantly turn pallid, freshly cut cherry into the rich look of a 200-year-old antique, can see even worse results.

Not all cherry behaves like this. I'll show you how to spot the problem areas in advance. I'll also give you tips on how to pretreat your project before you apply a stain or a clear coat. When you start with a wood as nice as cherry, it's worth learning how to finish it.

Everyone agrees blotching is caused by uneven absorption of a liquid, whether it is a dye or a clear finish. There is less agreement on the causes. Some say it is resin

deposits from kiln drying, while others point to alternating grain, similar to that found in curly wood.

No matter the cause, to locate these blotch-prone areas and to anticipate the degree of blotching, wipe all of the wood with a cloth soaked in denatured alcohol. Most of the wood should stay a uniform shade, but certain parts may soak up the alcohol, turning the wood much darker. These areas, which also will take longer to dry, are the ones that will blotch when a dye or oil-based finish is applied.

Now that you know trouble lies ahead, forewarned is forearmed. You can use a variety of different products and techniques, depending on the severity of the blotching, to pretreat the wood before applying a dye, stain, or clear finish. However, even if there are only one or two problem areas, the whole workpiece will need to be treated to achieve an even appearance when finished.

A blotch-control test

The objective of all blotch prevention is to even out the absorption capacity of the wood, and there are at least a dozen products and techniques that claim to achieve this. The majority aim to restrict the wood's ability to absorb a dye or clear finish by burnishing or semisealing the surface. The second method is to saturate the wood with another liquid prior to applying the finish.

To discover which methods worked best and how much time and effort they took, I initially made three sample boards of blotchy cherry. I sanded half of each board to P150 grit, while the other half was treated with six methods of blotch control. One board was finished with Danish oil, another wiped with a water-based dye, and the last was wiped with an oil-based pigment stain. After discussing the results with the other editors at *Fine Woodworking*, I did further

Figure is one cause of blotching

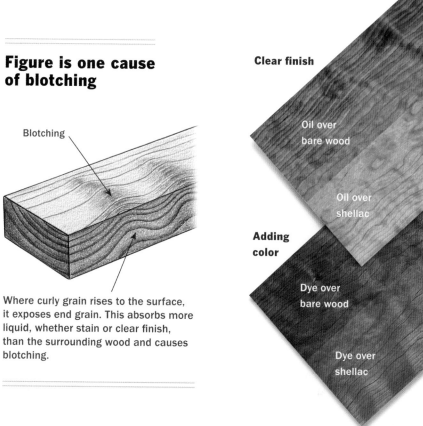

Blotching

Where curly grain rises to the surface, it exposes end grain. This absorbs more liquid, whether stain or clear finish, than the surrounding wood and causes blotching.

Clear finish
Oil over bare wood
Oil over shellac

Adding color
Dye over bare wood
Dye over shellac

Alcohol reveals trouble spots. It is difficult to spot blotch-prone areas on bare boards, especially after sanding. The best way to find them is to wipe the wood with denatured alcohol. This will leave blotch-prone areas that are darker than their surroundings and take longer to dry.

How blotch prevention works. The near side of the board was washcoated with shellac, while the far side was left bare. Then the surface was flooded with Danish oil. After 30 minutes, the bare wood had absorbed almost all the finish, while the washcoated side had absorbed far less.

testing using larger areas, to explore various grain situations and types of stains.

Some clear finishes cause blotching

We've all sighed with content as that first coat of Danish oil reveals the true color and shimmering depth of cherry. This is what woodworking's all about, we think, and happily press on. The next morning is when the shock hits: What is that dark area on that drawer front? Why doesn't it disappear when you look at it from a different angle? It's not poor sanding because the surface feels uniformly smooth. Welcome to the world of blotchy cherry.

It's not just oil/varnish blends like Danish oil that cause blotching but also wiping varnishes such as Waterlox Original and oil-based alkyd varnishes or polyurethanes. Any blotching will be less noticeable than when dyeing or staining, but the darker patches still will be blemishes. The three most effective ways to control blotching are described on the facing page, while two techniques to avoid are on p. 210.

Add color to cherry but not bare wood

While many woodworkers recoil from the concept of coloring wood, with cherry in particular it's tempting to fast-forward the aging process and achieve an antique look in hours. Alternatively, you may be trying to blend cherry boards with different tones or to match an existing piece of furniture.

As well as the sample boards tested with water-based dye and oil-based pigment stain,

Three ways to reduce blotching from clear finishes

Oil-based finishes are the most likely of the clear finishes to cause blotching on cherry. These include wiping varnish, oil/varnish mixes, Danish oil, and polyurethane, and the blotching can occur whether the finish is wiped, brushed, or sprayed on. The sample board shows how Watco Danish oil is affected by various treatments.

The entire board was coated with Danish oil.

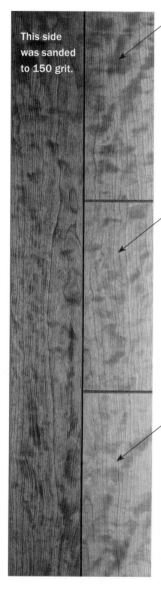

This side was sanded to 150 grit.

FOR MINIMAL BLOTCHING, KEEP ON SANDING

If the alcohol test reveals that only minimal blotching is likely, the simplest method of blotch control is to sand to a higher final grit. Instead of stopping at P150- or P180-grit sandpaper, carry on through the grades until you reach P400 grit. This smooths and burnishes the wood, making it less able to absorb a liquid. It will still allow the deep, lustrous look associated with oil-based finishes, but it does involve more time sanding—a task that few of us find appealing.

A WATER-BASED CONDITIONER SEALS IN MODERATE BLOTCHING

Minwax's Water-Based Pre-Stain wood conditioner feels and looks like a greatly thinned water-based clear finish and dries to a thin film on the surface. Brush on a single coat, let it dry thoroughly, and sand it with P320-grit paper. Remove the dust and apply the oil-based clear coat of your choice. This method works well on wood with moderate blotching, yet the results still resemble a penetrating finish. Don't be tempted to thin a water-based finish by 50% and use that as a blotch controller; it won't work.

NOTHING BEATS SHELLAC ON SEVERELY BLOTCHY WOOD

If the alcohol test reveals severe blotching is likely, stop sanding at P180 grit and apply a single coat of a film finish that has been heavily thinned. Known as a washcoat, the most common choice is a 1-lb. cut of dewaxed shellac. The blotch-prone areas will soak up the washcoat more than the rest of the wood. After the washcoat dries, sand it lightly with P320-grit sandpaper. You'll remove much of the sealer but leave the blotch-prone areas lined with it, allowing the surface to absorb clear finish more evenly. This will almost eliminate blotching, but the reduced oil penetration will also leave more of a film-finish look.

Two blotch-control methods to avoid

GLUE SIZE: EFFECTIVE BUT TIME-CONSUMING

You've probably noticed how remnants of glue squeeze-out leave annoying pale areas after you've applied a dye or an oil-based clear finish. You can exploit this by diluting some yellow glue with about eight parts of water to create a glue size. Brush on a single coat, let it dry, then sand the surface with P320-grit paper. Like a washcoat of shellac, this seals the blotch-prone areas so they will end up the same color as the rest of the board. However, the water-based glue size raises the grain more than shellac, takes longer to sand smooth, and can't be used under a water-based dye or water-based clear coat. So stick with shellac.

SOLVENT-BASED CONDITIONER LEFT SPLOTCHES

Just as an inoculation gives your body a small amount of the disease, in theory you can treat blotching by first applying a much-diluted coat of a penetrating finish. The directions call for flooding the surface and wiping off the surplus. Then you apply the dye or clear coat. I found presaturation less effective than sealing the wood, especially on heavily blotchy cherry. I applied a coat of Minwax's Pre-Stain wood conditioner (not to be confused with the water-based product of the same name, which actually seals the surface), but it left orange splotches on the wood that showed through the clear finish.

I also tried a gel stain and colored Danish oil. Without exception, all of the coloring methods looked better when applied to cherry that had been pretreated with a washcoat of shellac. On bare wood, all of the dyes and pigment stains caused blotching to a greater or lesser extent.

On the facing page, there are three ways to color cherry based on the amount of color you want to add, the ease of application, and the number of colors available. On p. 212, you'll find a couple of coloring options to avoid.

The bottom line? Never apply any pigment stain or dye to blotch-prone cherry that has not been treated with a washcoat. Whatever dye or clear finish you use, try it on a sample board from scraps of wood left over from your project. Discover the hidden surprises there and not on your cherry workpiece.

This side has color over bare wood.

This side has color over shellac.

Three ways to add color to cherry without blotching

To narrow down the options, a number of dyes and stains were tested on separate sample boards, each treated with various stain controllers. Then the board at left was made to illustrate how the best stain controller—a washcoat of shellac—can help with three good methods of coloring cherry.

TINTED OIL ADDS MINIMAL COLOR WITHOUT FUSS

Watco's cherry Danish oil is a pigmented stain, and as expected it caused severe blotching on bare cherry. However, on blotch-prone cherry washcoated with shellac, the result was a light but even application of color. If you want only a slight change in your cherry's

Penetrating pigment. Tinted oil was liberally applied (left) and then wiped off (right). The washcoated side didn't blotch; the bare-wood side did.

tone (remember, cherry will darken as it ages, even under a dye) and prefer the look of a penetrating finish, this is the way to go.

GEL STAINS ADD EXTRA COLOR WITH EACH COAT

While Bartley's Pennsylvania cherry left bare wood blotchy, it left wood washcoated with shellac evenly colored and blotch-free but with the grain slightly highlighted. Each coat of gel stain adds incremental color with minimal fuss, so if you are looking for an easy way to harmonize different-colored boards, try a gel stain. However, because gel stains are mostly pigment-based, each extra coat after the second or third will gradually make the finish more opaque, hiding the wood's figure.

WATER-BASED DYES OFFER CLARITY AND COLOR CHOICE

With dyes, the particles of color are far smaller than in pigment stains, so they remain suspended in the liquid (there's no need to stir the container) and they don't collect in the wood pores, highlighting them. However, they will still create darker areas on blotch-prone wood, so pretreating is advisable. A washcoat of shellac will reduce the overall impact of the dye when compared with bare wood, but you can get around this by mixing a more concentrated batch.

Shellac prevents blotching. A thin coat of shellac, known as a washcoat, is the most effective form of blotch control. However, it is important that you use dewaxed shellac, as waxy shellac can prevent some topcoats from adhering. Among the brands made by Zinsser, make sure you choose SealCoat, which is dewaxed, and dilute it 50% with denatured alcohol.

Avoid oil-based pigment stains for cherry

Walk into any hardware store or home center and the first choice for coloring wood will be rows of wood stains. The choice of colors is extensive, and the application method (apply, leave on for five minutes, and then wipe off with a clean cloth) seems simplicity itself. Just say no. On this sample board, I applied a single coat of Minwax Wood Finish, an oil-based pigment stain. On the right-hand side of the board that was sanded to P150 grit, it brought out the worst in this blotchy cherry. Various methods of blotch control on the left-hand side had mixed results. From top to bottom: An oil-based conditioner and a water-based one reduce but don't eliminate blotching; a coat of glue size or a washcoat of shellac eliminates blotching and most of the color but still leaves pigment in the grain; and sanding to P400 grit and P220 grit makes little difference.

An Antique Finish for Tiger Maple

LONNIE BIRD

I've always admired the distinctive stripes, three-dimensional depth, and rich amber color of antiques made from tiger maple. The challenge is to replicate this century-old appearance on creamy white, fresh-cut maple. The steps I take to transform tiger maple aren't difficult and can be done by hand, but the process will stretch over days as you wait for each step to dry. Of course, that's a lot quicker than waiting for the piece to become an antique.

The finish rewards good surface preparation

It's important to remove all marks left by saws, planers, and jointers because this finish will display them prominently. A bench plane is the fastest way to get rid of these marks and beats the tedium, dust, and noise of machine sanding. However, because cautious when handplaning tiger maple because the dramatically figured grain tears out easily. I avoid this problem by using a razor-sharp plane equipped with a high-angle frog to give a cutting angle of 50°, sometimes referred to as a York pitch. You can achieve the same angle by grinding a 38° edge on a bevel-up low-angle plane.

Sometimes, despite your best efforts, you still will get minor tearout. I use a sharp card scraper to smooth it away and blend the area with the surrounding surface. Of course, some surfaces, such as curved legs and moldings, can't be planed. I scrape these areas

and then lightly hand-sand with P220-grit sandpaper to smooth the surface further and remove any facets left by the scraper. I use the same paper to lightly sand the flat areas that were planed; otherwise, they'll accept the dye differently than the sanded areas.

Develop the figure with dye

The widest selection of dye colors comes in powder form in formulas that can be mixed with water, alcohol, or oil. I use water-based dyes because they make it easier to control lap marks and streaking than faster-drying, alcohol-based dyes, and they are reportedly more lightfast than oil-based dyes. The disadvantage is that the water in the dye raises the grain, so I preraise the grain by wiping the wood with a damp cloth. Once

TIP To keep the end grain from absorbing too much dye and becoming too dark, wet it first with water and immediately apply the dye. This will dilute the color.

Raise the grain. To prevent a water-based dye from raising the grain, preraise it by wiping the wood with a damp cloth (top). After the wood is dry, lightly sand the surface (above).

the surface is dry, I lightly sand the wood with worn P220-grit or P320-grit sandpaper to smooth the fuzzy grain before applying the dye.

Another advantage of powdered dyes is that you can control the intensity of the color. The manufacturer recommends 1 oz. per quart of warm water, but I start with half that strength. Experiment on scrap tiger maple until you find a color you like. Two of my favorites from the J. E. Moser brand (www.woodworker. com) are russet amber maple and honey amber maple. Both yield the golden color of old maple furniture. For this project, I prefer the redder tones of the russet dye.

I dye the edges of floating panels before inserting them into their frames. This way, if seasonal movement causes a panel to shrink, I'm spared the embarrassment of undyed edges appearing. To reduce the chance that drips or runs will go unnoticed, I dye small areas one at a time and wipe spills immediately. If you do have faint drip or lap marks, go over the entire piece with a damp cloth when you've finished dyeing it. Don't get the wood dripping wet, as too much water can cause surfaces to warp and panels to swell. When satisfied, let everything dry overnight.

Add luster with oil

One reason oil finishes are so popular is that they enhance wood's natural appearance. They have the same effect on dyed wood. I flood the surface with an oil-based wiping varnish such as Waterlox or Formby®'s tung oil, making sure to cover all the crevices and details (if you prefer, you can use a pure oil finish such as boiled linseed oil instead). After a few minutes, wipe away the excess. Let the finish cure overnight, and dispose of the soiled rags in a safe manner.

Apply the dye. A quick way to test how the dye will look is to use a stirring stick made from the same wood as the workpiece (left). Then brush on the dye (right), and wipe with a clean cloth while still wet.

Enhance wood's appearance with oil. Apply a generous amount of oil to the wood, let it soak in for a few minutes, then wipe off the surplus. This gives greater depth to the appearance of the wood.

Add more color with an amber shellac topcoat

The amber shellac I use is made by Zinsser and comes as a 3-lb. cut. I reduce it to a 1-lb. cut by combining one part shellac with two parts denatured alcohol. Adding more alcohol will allow the finish to flow out better before setting up. It also lets the shellac flow into the grain, giving more of an in-the-wood finish, which I prefer over a film finish.

After each coat of shellac has dried, I rub the finish with 0000 steel wool, being careful not to rub through the finish. I then vacuum the surface thoroughly. Two or three coats of shellac are usually enough. Any more and the finish may begin to look thick, especially in crevices and details.

Glaze, shellac, and wax complete the finish

It's the details that often make a piece of handcrafted furniture successful. Moldings, corners, and even simple carvings catch light and create interesting shadow lines for a visual treat. Glazing can accentuate

Seal with shellac. Use several coats of thin shellac to give the wood a thinner, more natural topcoat (left). After the shellac has dried, smooth the surface with 0000 steel wool (above).

these details even when the lighting doesn't cooperate. Although you can mail-order ready-made glaze, an easier source is an oil-based stain from a local paint or hardware store.

It's important to choose a stain that is darker than the dye yet complements its color. For my maple finishes, I use Moorish Teak stain from Zar. With the contents unstirred, pour off the excess oil, leaving an oil and pigment mixture with the consistency of mud at the bottom of the can.

Apply the glaze to the moldings, carvings, and other details with a small artist's paintbrush. Long before the glazing dries, wipe away the excess. A cloth moistened with mineral spirits or turpentine speeds the process or enables you to wipe away all traces of the glaze should you change your mind. Because the shellac is dissolved with alcohol, the mineral spirits will have no effect on it.

After the glaze has cured overnight, I apply another coat of shellac for a protective seal. Finally, I rub out that coat using 0000 steel wool and complete the finish with a coat of paste wax.

Bring out the details with glaze. Use the pigment from oil-based stain as a glaze (top left). Push the glaze into all the corners and crevices of the workpiece using an artist's brush (top right). Wipe away the surplus before it dries (bottom). If the glaze becomes too tacky, dampen the cloth with mineral spirits or turpentine.

A final coat of shellac. After the glaze has cured overnight, seal it with a final coat of thin shellac. Finish with a coat of wax.

Finishing Walnut

JEFF JEWITT

It's no mystery why so many antiques are made of domestic black walnut: It cuts and sands well, accepts stains without blotching, and can have attractive figure. However, there are two reasons why today's woodworkers sometimes are frustrated with walnut's appearance. Harvesting of smaller trees means that a greater number of boards incorporate sapwood, whose creamy color contrasts with the dark heartwood. Most commercial walnut is steamed and then kiln-dried, which darkens the sapwood but robs walnut of the richer colors seen in air-dried lumber.

To eliminate these problems, I apply dye to blend the sapwood into the heartwood and to give the whole piece a warm tone. The first dye is sealed, then a second coat of dye provides a rich, deep color. The piece can be finished with a clear topcoat.

Conceal the sapwood

If your piece contains sapwood, the first finishing step is to blend it in with the heartwood. Because the color of heartwood doesn't change drastically over time, you can blend in the sapwood by staining it. Wipe the wood with a damp rag to preview the finished color of the walnut. Blend and dilute one or more water-based dyes, and dip in strips of white paper to judge the tone and intensity of the color. Lightly wipe the dye on the sapwood with a cotton rag; for molded edges or other hard-to-reach areas, use an artist's brush. When you've coated all of the sapwood, wipe the entire surface lightly with a water-dampened rag to blend the dyed area into the heartwood.

Reveal the contrast. To see how much the undyed sapwood and heartwood will contrast under a clear finish, wet the wood with a damp cloth.

Apply the dye with care. Stain the sapwood with a small piece of cloth to ensure that you don't color the adjoining heartwood.

How to reach small areas. Use an artist's brush with either a pointed or a chiseled tip.

Warmer, more uniform color

If you wipe bare walnut with mineral spirits or alcohol, you can see what it will look like with a clear finish. Kiln-dried walnut, either solid or veneer, likely has a grayish color. You also may notice that different boards have contrasting color tones. Linseed oil, varnish, and shellac, because of their natural amber color, mitigate the first problem, but a better way to achieve tonal uniformity is to stain the entire piece.

Apply the base stain

The best way to start making different boards (or a combination of solid lumber and veneer) look more uniform is to apply a base stain to the piece. You can spray a non-grain-raising (NGR) or alcohol-based stain and save application and drying time. A water-based dye applied by hand dries more slowly, but it reduces the chance of streaking.

Apply the base stain. If you apply the stain by hand, use water-based stains because their long drying time reduces the chance of streaks and uneven color.

If you had to blend in the sapwood (see "Conceal the sapwood" on p. 219), wait until that dye has dried and then apply a base stain of golden brown to the entire piece. Dilute the dye to the desired strength. In this case, I used ½ oz. dye to 1 qt. water. As when applying dye to the sapwood, use a small piece of cloth to color the large areas and an artist's brush for crevices and corners. To force the dye onto the parts of raised panels within the frame, use compressed air. Using this method will prevent a strip of pale wood from appearing when the panel shrinks seasonally.

Seal the dye with shellac. After the dye has dried, brush on a thin coat of dewaxed shellac such as Zinsser's SealCoat.

Seal in the dye with shellac

After the piece has dried completely, apply a thin coat (1-lb. to 2-lb. cut) of dewaxed shellac. You may want to apply a second coat to end grain to prevent these areas from absorbing the oil-based glaze and becoming too dark. When the shellac has dried, lightly sand the surface with P600-grit (FEPA grade) no-load sandpaper (400- or 320-grit CAMI grade). For moldings, use a gray fine-abrasive pad.

Add age and depth with an oil-based glaze

The process of applying stain over sealed wood is called glazing. If you don't like the effect on the color from this step, you can remove almost all of it using mineral spirits without damaging the base stain. (Obviously, it's best to work out your coloring options on scrap first.)

Making oil-based glazes the easy way

Ready-made colored glazes are sold in stores, but I like to make my own because I have more control of the color and there is less waste. You'll need boiled linseed oil, an oil-based varnish, and artist's oil colors. Vandyke brown and burnt umber are good colors to start with, and you can use lamp black and red for fine-tuning. Japan colors work almost as well as artist's oils but are a bit weaker in tinting strength.

Mix one part boiled linseed oil and one part varnish. I use gel varnish because it makes the glaze thicker and less likely to run. It also hangs better in nooks and crannies. The glaze for this cabinet was made with ¼ cup (1 oz.) boiled linseed oil, ¼ cup Bartley gel varnish, ½ teaspoon Vandyke brown, ½ teaspoon burnt umber, and ¼ teaspoon deep azo red. But feel free to experiment. To test the color and translucency of the glaze, simply smear it on a piece of white paper. Keep adding artist's oils until you are pleased with the color.

A shopmade glaze. You can make oil-based glaze using boiled linseed oil, gel varnish, and artist's oil colors (left). To check the color and translucency of the glaze as you add artist's oil colors, smear samples onto white paper (above).

Apply, then remove the glaze

With an inexpensive natural-bristle brush, generously cover the entire surface with glaze. On relatively small areas like this cabinet, you can glaze the whole door before starting the removal process. Larger surfaces have to be done in sections to prevent the glaze from setting up.

Wipe off most of the glaze with a cloth, leaving a thin film of color on the surface of the shellac. The effect of these two colors, the base stain and the glaze, is to create the illusion of depth. The glaze also darkens the pores, emphasizing the grain pattern. You can leave excess glaze in corners and crevices to simulate age.

If certain parts end up noticeably lighter in appearance, let the first coat of glaze dry overnight, then apply a second coat to the lighter areas.

Brush on and wipe off. Don't worry about applying the glaze evenly (top). It is more important to cover the whole surface and to work fast so that the glaze can be wiped off before it becomes tacky (bottom). Leaving extra glaze in the recesses replicates the dirt often found on antiques.

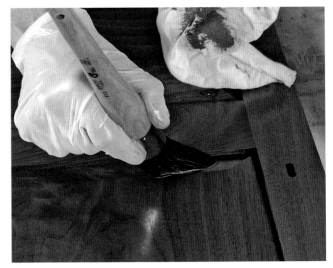

Dry brushing. To remove surplus glaze from confined areas, use a dry brush and wipe it frequently on a clean cloth.

Seal in the color with a topcoat

Any solvent-based clear topcoat can be applied after the glaze has fully cured in 12 to 24 hours. In keeping with the country-style appearance of this piece, I wanted an open-grained appearance and a satin luster. I chose to wipe on a single coat of Waterlox satin finish, an oil-based varnish. If you wish to use a water-based finish, I recommend first applying a thin-cut coat of shellac to seal the oil-based glaze.

Add a clear topcoat of your choice. A wipe-on coat of satin finish gives this piece a low-luster, country look.

Finishes for Foodware

MIKE MAHONEY

At college, my industrial arts professor cautioned me many times about the harmful finishes I was using for my wooden bowls. Specifically, he stressed that oil finishes with metallic driers were dangerous for food contact. Now that lead has been banned as a drier, studies have shown that almost all finishes are benign to humans: Ingesting fully cured finish is similar to eating a piece of plastic—the body won't digest it.

If safety is no longer an issue, how do you decide which finish to use? From the many finishes available, you should base your choices on durability, ease of application and repair, and the intended use of the piece.

Penetrating oils are most ideal for heavy-use items

For wooden items that will get constant wear and tear in the kitchen (for example, salad bowls, plates, spatulas, and butcher blocks), penetrating oils are the preferred finish. They are the easiest to apply, and the ability to reapply them easily will keep your work looking great year after year.

With penetrating finishes in particular, you need to carefully sand away any tool marks. For a turned piece, sand it on the lathe, sanding in both directions if the lathe has a reversing switch. It also helps if you raise the grain with water and let the piece dry before giving it a final sanding.

The two most popular oils are boiled linseed oil and tung oil. They are both curing oils and will slowly harden in the wood, reducing the need for reapplications. Boiled linseed oil is cheaper and more widely available, but it has a tendency to yellow the wood more than other oils. Pure tung oil gives a little more water protection but is harder to rub to an even sheen.

Oil/varnish blends such as Danish oil, if heavily diluted and thinly applied, are easy to apply and repair. Just don't apply so many coats that you start to build a film, as this will break down and be hard to repair.

Nut oils, such as walnut, macadamia, and almond, are more expensive and will cure more slowly and only partially. Mineral oil is widely available in drugstores and forms no film or sheen no matter how many coats are applied, but it also requires more frequent renewal.

I don't recommend using olive or vegetable oils for finishing. These oils will not cure at all; they can go rancid under the wrong conditions; and if kept in a closed, oxygen-deprived area, or if too much finish is applied, the piece can become sticky.

Regarding the objection that oil finishes don't offer any resistance to abrasion, my contention is that if you're using a wooden item to serve food and are worried about staining or scratching the wood's surface, you may be better off using ceramic, plastic, or glass. The lack of a moisture barrier is not important for foodware, as wood naturally absorbs and evaporates moisture. I have been using wooden butcher blocks, bowls, and dinner plates in my house for nearly 20 years and they look better than the day they were made—stains, cut marks, scratches, and all.

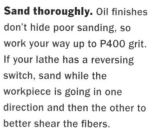

Sand thoroughly. Oil finishes don't hide poor sanding, so work your way up to P400 grit. If your lathe has a reversing switch, sand while the workpiece is going in one direction and then the other to better shear the fibers.

Raise the grain. You'll get a smoother surface if you raise the grain with water, let it dry, and then sand the wood again.

Final sanding. Give the workpiece a final sanding by hand using P400-grit sandpaper.

Pour on the oil. Boiled linseed oil is a good penetrating oil. Flood the surface, and use a disposable brush to ensure uniform coverage.

Sand in the oil. Another way to apply oil is to place a few drops on a foam-backed sanding pad chucked into an electric drill (left), and then sand it into the wood with the workpiece slowly turning (right). This deepens the penetration and brings out any curl.

Use oil/varnish mixes sparingly. You can use oil/varnish mixes and wiping varnishes as penetrating-oil finishes, but don't apply too many coats or you'll build up a film, which is hard to repair.

Renewable mineral oil. Because it never forms a film, no matter how many coats you apply, mineral oil is easy to use. But it has to be renewed frequently.

Film finishes: instant appeal but problems down the road

There is no denying the eye-catching shine that a film finish can give to a piece. However, some topcoats, such as lacquer, shellac, and waxes, while easy to apply, aren't durable enough for items that get regular use and need to be cleaned occasionally. These finishes may be relatively easy to repair if damaged, but eventually you'll get tired of doing so.

The case for or against using varnishes is more complicated. Many wooden foodware items such as spoons, rolling pins, butcher blocks, and mortars and pestles are rubbed, washed, knocked, cut on, and pounded in everyday use. A tough surface film would seem ideal to stand the rigors of time. But when a varnish or polyurethane breaks down and especially if water penetrates it, it is much harder to repair.

However, these tough film finishes may be quite appropriate for objects that contain dry goods, such as sugar bowls or lidded boxes for cookies. These items rarely receive any abrasion and usually need dusting only. Therefore, the membrane will take many years of wear.

Because oil/varnish finishes are very slow to dry, their odor can linger, sometimes for months. This is especially true on lidded containers. I would not let food be in contact with this finish until the odor has completely dissipated. Instead of waiting, you can either leave the inside unfinished or finish it with quick-curing shellac.

Natural, unfinished woodenware

A third choice is the finish left by sandpaper —in other words, no finish at all. The wooden plates I use in my kitchen have never had a finish. They are 12 years old and are barely broken in yet. A closed-pored wood such as maple, cherry, or birch is best.

However, there are some secrets to letting woodenware age gracefully. When washing these items, do not leave them in standing water; use mild dish soap, scrub gently, and rinse. Then either dry the piece with a towel or let it air-dry.

Never put wooden items in the dishwasher or the microwave. Some timbers, especially fruitwoods, are also sensitive to cold and may crack if refrigerated.

Warning: tough to repair. Film finishes eventually will break down. Once water gets under them, they are almost impossible to repair.

Natural wood. The author has a collection of unfinished foodware that still looks great after more than a decade of use.

Film finish is for show. On pieces not exposed to water or tough use, a film finish such as varnish or polyurethane can give many years of service.

Dull the shine. If you don't want the plastic look of a gloss film finish, rub out the final coat with 0000 steel wool.

The best woods for foodware

The best woods for the kitchen and dining room are what I call the soft hardwoods. These include maples, cherry, walnut, ash, birch, poplar, and sycamore. These timbers are flexible and shock resistant. In contrast, the hard hardwoods such as locust, rosewoods, hickory, and Osage orange will shatter if dropped or knocked and won't last very long in the kitchen. White oak is the exception: Tough yet flexible, it makes excellent foodware. Red oak, on the other hand, is too porous.

Metric Equivalents

INCHES	CENTIMETERS	MILLIMETERS	INCHES	CENTIMETERS	MILLIMETERS
⅛	0.3	3	13	33.0	330
¼	0.6	6	14	35.6	356
⅜	1.0	10	15	38.1	381
½	1.3	13	16	40.6	406
⅝	1.6	16	17	43.2	432
¾	1.9	19	18	45.7	457
⅞	2.2	22	19	48.3	483
1	2.5	25	20	50.8	508
1¼	3.2	32	21	53.3	533
1½	3.8	38	22	55.9	559
1¾	4.4	44	23	58.4	584
2	5.1	51	24	61.0	610
2½	6.4	64	25	63.5	635
3	7.6	76	26	66.0	660
3½	8.9	89	27	68.6	686
4	10.2	102	28	71.7	717
4½	11.4	114	29	73.7	737
5	12.7	127	30	76.2	762
6	15.2	152	31	78.7	787
7	17.8	178	32	81.3	813
8	20.3	203	33	83.8	838
9	22.9	229	34	86.4	864
10	25.4	254	35	88.9	889
11	27.9	279	36	91.4	914
12	30.5	305			

Contributors

Lonnie Bird is a woodworker, tool consultant, and author. He teaches woodworking at his shop in Dandridge, Tennessee. For information on classes, visit him on the Web at www.lonniebird.com.

Brian Boggs is a longtime contributor to *Fine Woodworking* who designs and builds Appalachian-style chairs and contemporary furniture. He is based in Asheville, North Carolina, but you may visit him online at www.boggscollective.com.

Sean Clarke is the owner of Clarke Co., www.clarkecompany.com, a furniture repair, restoration, and refinishing company in Columbus, Ohio.

Peter Gedrys is a professional finisher and the owner of Architectural Finishes, LLC, specializing in high-end restoration work. Gedrys also teaches classes in a variety of finishing disciplines in and around Connecticut.

Scott Gibson has spent many years writing and editing magazine articles about furniture making and home building. A former editor at *Fine Homebuilding*, *Fine Woodworking*, and *Home Furniture* magazines, Scott now works as a freelance writer, editor, and photographer from his home in southern Maine.

Jeff Jewitt is a frequent contributor of finishing articles for *Fine Woodworking*. He is the author of *Spray Finishing Made Simple* (2010), *Taunton's Complete Illustrated Guide to Finishing* (2005), *Hand-Applied Finishes* (1997), and *Great Wood Finishes* (1999).

Roland Johnson is the founder and president of the Central Minnesota Woodworkers Association. He divides his time between writing and building furniture for himself and his clients from his home in Sauk Rapids, Minnesota.

Mitchell Kohanek is a teacher in the Wood Finishing Technology Program at Dakota County Technical College in Rosemount, Minnesota.

Mike Mahoney is a professional woodturner, specializing in bowlmaking, from Orem, Utah.

Teri Masaschi is a professional wood finisher and writer. She is best known for teaching both simple and advanced techniques for finishing new furniture as well as ways to maintain and restore antiques. Teri lives in Tijeras, New Mexico.

Charles Neil crafts furniture for clients nationwide and teaches woodworking. Visit him on the Web at www.charlesneilwoodworking.com.

Mario Rodriguez spent most of his career teaching woodworking in the Restoration Department of the Fashion Institute of Technology in New York City. He also has taught workshops at The Center for Furniture Craftsmanship, Marc Adams School of Woodworking, Kelly Mehler's School of Woodworking, and the Connecticut Valley School of Woodworking. Currently, he builds commissions and teaches classes at The Philadelphia Furniture Workshop.

Lon Schleining is the author of *Wood Bending Made Simple* (2010) and *The Workbench* (2004). He lives in Capistrano Beach, California.

Mark Schofield is managing editor at *Fine Woodworking*.

Charles Shackleton was named Woodworker of the Year for 2006 by the Vermont Wood Manufacturer's Association, and is the president of Charles Shackleton & Miranda Thomas Ltd. in Bridgewater, Vermont.

Paul Snyder is a professional finisher near Fredericksburg, Virginia. He manages a finishing and restoration website, www.refinishwizard.com.

David Sorg is a finisher and artist who lives in Denver, Colorado.

Ari Tuckman is a woodworker in West Chester, Pennsylvania.

Tom Wisshack makes and restores fine furniture in Galesburg, Illinois.

Sources

From "Dyes Can Do It All," pp. 68–75
Dye powders, Solar-Lux, Wizard Tints:
Woodworker's Supply
800-645-9292
www.woodworker.com

TransTint, dye powders:
Homestead Finishing Products
216-631-5309
www.homesteadfinishingproducts.com

Mohawk stains:
Wood Finisher's Source
888-822-0974
www.woodfinisherssource.com

**From "Foolproof Dye and Gel-Stain Recipes,"
pp. 81–86**
Lockwood powdered dyes:
W. D. Lockwood & Co., Inc.
866-293-8913
www.wdlockwood.com

General Finishes gel stain:
General Finishes
800-783-6050
www.generalfinishes.com

Bartley gel stain:
Bartley Classic Reproductions, Ltd.
800-787-2800
www.bartleycollection.com

**From "Altering the Colors of Dyes and
Stains," pp. 87–89**
Water-based dyes:
W. D. Lockwood & Co., Inc.
866-293-8913
www.wdlockwood.com

Bartley's gel stains and Solar-Lux NGR stains:
Woodworker's Supply
800-645-9292
www.woodworker.com

Minwax stains:
Available at most home centers and
hardware stores
www.minwax.com

**From "A Traditional French Polish,"
pp. 102–109**
Slow and fast gold size:
Easy Leaf Products
800-569-5323
www.easyleaf.com

Black pigment:
Homestead Finishing Products
216-631-5309
www.homesteadfinishingproducts.com

Johnson Paste Wax
Available at most home centers and hardware
stores

**From "Padding Lacquer: An Alternative to
French Polish" pp. 110–113**
Behlen's Qualasole™ and Pore-O-Pac:
Garrett Wade
800-221-2942
www.garretwade.com

Woodworker's Supply
800-645-9292
www.woodworker.com

Behlen's Qualasole and Constantine's Pad-Lac:
Constantine's Wood Center
800-443-9667
www.constantines.com

#77 Lubricite:
Industrial Finishing Products
718-277-3333
www.industrialfinishings.com

From "Brushing on a Finish," pp. 120–127
Purdy brushes:
Purdy
800-547-0780
www.purdycorp.com

Specialized natural- or synthetic-bristle brushes:
Fine Paints of Europe
800-332-1556
www.finepaintsofeurope.com

Homestead Finishing Products
216-631-5309
www.homesteadfinishingproducts.com

From "A Foolproof Finish," pp. 170–175
Zinsser SealCoat, gel finishes by Bartley and
General Finishes, and colored waxes by Briwax,
J. E. Moser, Liberon, and Fiddes:
Woodworker's Supply
800-645-9292
www.woodworker.com

Zinsser SealCoat, gel finishes by Petri and
Bartley, and Sheradale brown wax:
Highland Woodworking
800-241-6748
www.highlandwoodworking.com

Antiquax brown wax:
Antiquax
www.antiquax.com

From "An Oil-and-Wax Finish," pp. 176–180
Boiled Linseed Oil and abrasive pads:
Woodcraft
800-225-1153
www.woodcraft.com

Liberon steel wool and wax:
Rockler
800-279-4441
www.rockler.com

Kingdom Restorations, Ltd.
252-955-0156
www.kingdomrestorations.com

From "Finishing Mahogany," pp. 195–200
J. E. Moser's powdered dyes, Wizard Tints liquid
dyes and rottenstone:
Woodworker's Supply
800-645-9292
www.woodworker.com

TransTint liquid dyes and rottenstone:
Woodcraft
800-225-1153
www.woodcraft.com

From "Finishing Walnut," pp. 218–223
Artist's oil colors:
Blick Art Materials
800-828-4548
www.dickblick.com

Dye stains, gel varnish, abrasives:
Homestead Finishing Products
216-631-5309
www.homesteadfinishingproducts.com

Credits

The articles in this book appeared in the following issues of Fine Woodworking:

Photos: p. i: by Kelly J. Dunton, © The Taunton Press, Inc.; p. iii: by Mark Schofield, © The Taunton Press, Inc.; p. iv.: by Andy Engel, © The Taunton Press, Inc.; p. 1: (top) by Michael Pekovich, © The Taunton Press, Inc.; (bottom) by Erika Marks, © The Taunton Press, Inc.

p. 4: Choosing Sandpaper by Scott Gibson, issue 178. Photos by Andy Engel, © The Taunton Press, Inc.; Drawings by Brian Jensen, © The Taunton Press, Inc.

p. 13: Sharpening and Using a Card Scraper by Brian Boggs, issue 172. Photos by Mark Schofield, © The Taunton Press, Inc.; Drawings by Vincent Babak, © The Taunton Press, Inc.

p. 18: The Best Brushes by Mark Schofield, issue 212. Photos by Kelly J. Dunton, © The Taunton Press, Inc.; Drawings by Kelly J. Dunton, © The Taunton Press, Inc.

p. 26: Spray Gun Choices by Mitchell Kohanek, issue 194. Photos by Mark Schofield, © The Taunton Press, Inc.; Drawings by Vincent Babak, © The Taunton Press, Inc.

p. 34: Sand, Scrape, or Plane? by Ari Tuckman, issue 180. Photos by Mark Schofield, © The Taunton Press, Inc. except the photo on p. 34 & the bottom photos on p. 37 by Kelly J. Dunton, © The Taunton Press, Inc.

p. 38: Sanding Basics by David Sorg, issue 173. Photos by Mark Schofield, © The Taunton Press, Inc. except the top left photo on p. 40 & the top left photo on p. 43 by Matthew Gardner © The Taunton Press, Inc.

p. 45: Sand between Coats for a Flawless Finish by Jeff Jewitt, issue 211. Photos by Mark Schofield, © The Taunton Press, Inc. except photos on p. 46, bottom, p. 49, bottom right, p. 51, bottom left and right, p. 50 bottom left, and p. 52, bottom left by John Tetreault, © The Taunton Press, Inc.

p. 54: When to Stop Sanding? by Ari Tuckman, issue 189. Photos by Mark Schofield, © The Taunton Press, Inc.

p. 59: Finish While You Build by Charles Neil, issue 208. Photos by Mark Schofield, © The Taunton Press, Inc.

p. 68: Dyes Can Do It All by Teri Masaschi, issue 190. Photos by Mark Schofield, © The Taunton Press, Inc.

p. 76: Combining Dyes and Stains by Paul Snyder, issue 182. Photos by Michael Pekovich, © The Taunton Press, Inc. except photo p. 76 by Mark Schofield, © The Taunton Press, Inc.; Drawings by Michael Pekovich, © The Taunton Press, Inc.

p. 81: Foolproof Recipes for Three Favorite Finishes by Peter Gedrys, issue 210. Photos by Mark Schofield, © The Taunton Press, Inc.

p. 87: Altering the Colors of Dyes and Stains by Peter Gedrys, issue 171. Photos by Kelly J. Dunton, © The Taunton Press, Inc. except photo p. 88, center © Ken Haines

p. 91: How to Match a Finish by Jeff Jewitt, issue 148. Photos by William Duckworth, © The Taunton Press, Inc.

p. 94: All about Thinning Finishes by Jeff Jewitt, issue 151. Photos by Mark Schofield, © The Taunton Press, Inc. except photo p. 94 by Scott Phillips, © The Taunton Press, Inc. and photos p. 95, top, p. 96, center, pp. 97-98 by Erika Marks, © The Taunton Press, Inc.

p. 102: A Traditional French Polish by Sean Clarke, issue 155. Photos by Mark Schofield, © The Taunton Press, Inc.

p. 110: Padding Lacquer by Mario Rodriguez, issue 118. Photos by Vincent Laurence, © The Taunton Press, Inc.

p. 114: Wiped on Varnish by Tom Wisshack, issue 132. Photos by Jefferson Kolle, © The Taunton Press, Inc.

p. 120: Choosing and Using Brushes by David Sorg, issue 156. Photos by Mark Schofield, © The Taunton Press, Inc. except photos p. 121 by Kelly J. Dunton, © The Taunton Press, Inc.

p. 128: High Gloss Finish Made Simple by Sean Clarke, issue 206. Photos by Mark Schofield, © The Taunton Press, Inc.

p. 135: All about Wax by Peter Gedrys, issue 191. Photos by Mark Schofield, © The Taunton Press, Inc. except photo p. 135 and p. 139, bottom left by Michael Pekovich, © The Taunton Press, Inc. and photo p. 136 left and photos top right, and p. 137 top by John Tetreault, © The Taunton Press, Inc.

p. 142: Spraying Basics by Jeff Jewitt, issue 169. Photos by Mark Schofield, © The Taunton Press, Inc. except photos p. 146, top by Kelly J. Dunton, © The Taunton Press, Inc; Drawings by Vincent Babak, © The Taunton Press, Inc.

p. 154: How to Troubleshoot a Spray Gun by Jeff Jewitt, issue 213. Photos by Mark Schofield, © The Taunton Press, Inc.

p. 161: 10 Best Fixes for Finishing Mistakes by Teri Masaschi, issue 201. Photos by David Heim, © The Taunton Press, Inc. except photos p. 162 top left, p. 166 top left, p. 167 bottom left and right center by Kelly J. Dunton, © The Taunton Press, Inc.

p. 170: One Editor's Favorite Finish by Mark Schofield, issue 196. Photos by Michael Pekovich, © The Taunton Press, Inc.

p. 176: An Oil-and-Wax Finish by Charles Shackleton, issue 175. Photos by Mark Schofield, © The Taunton Press, Inc.

p. 181: Hot-Rod Your Varnish by Roland Johnson, issue 198. Photos by Mark Schofield, © The Taunton Press, Inc. except photo p. 181 © Roland Johnson

p. 186: One Fast Finish by Jeff Jewitt, issue 186. Photos by Tom Goffe, © The Taunton Press, Inc. except photo p. 186 by Michael Pekovich, © The Taunton Press, Inc.

p. 190: An Easy Durable Finish by Lon Schleining, issue 154. Photos by Mark Schofield, © The Taunton Press, Inc.

p. 195: Finishing Mahogany by Jeff Jewitt, issue 164. Photos by William Duckworth, © The Taunton Press, Inc.

p. 201: Best Finish for Pine by Peter Wisshack, issue 198. Photos by David Heim, © The Taunton Press, Inc.

p. 207: Blotch-free Cherry by Mark Schofield, issue 200. Photos by Mark Schofield, © The Taunton Press, Inc.; Drawing by John Tetreault, © The Taunton Press, Inc.

p. 213: An Antique Finish for Tiger Maple by Lonnie Bird, issue 180. Photos by Mark Schofield, © The Taunton Press, Inc.

p. 219: Finishing Walnut by Jeff Jewitt, issue 176. Photos by Mark Schofield, © The Taunton Press, Inc.

p. 224: Finishes for Foodware by Mike Mahoney, issue 201. Photos courtesy of Fine Woodworking, © The Taunton Press, Inc.

Index